THE OTHER JERSEY BOYS

Lifeguards, laughter, lifestyle, larrikins, lovin' and libations

DAVID KNIGHT

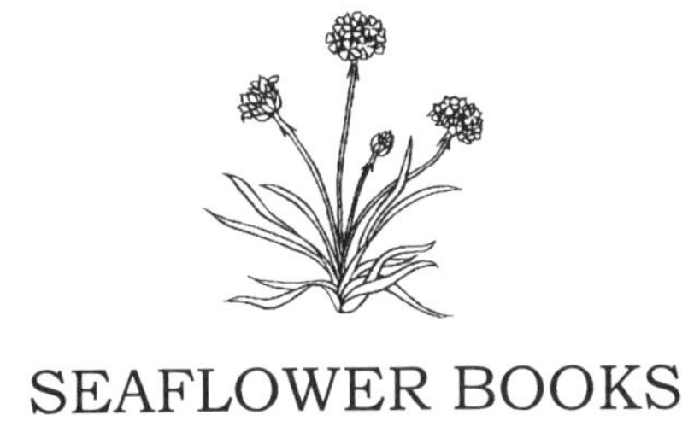

SEAFLOWER BOOKS

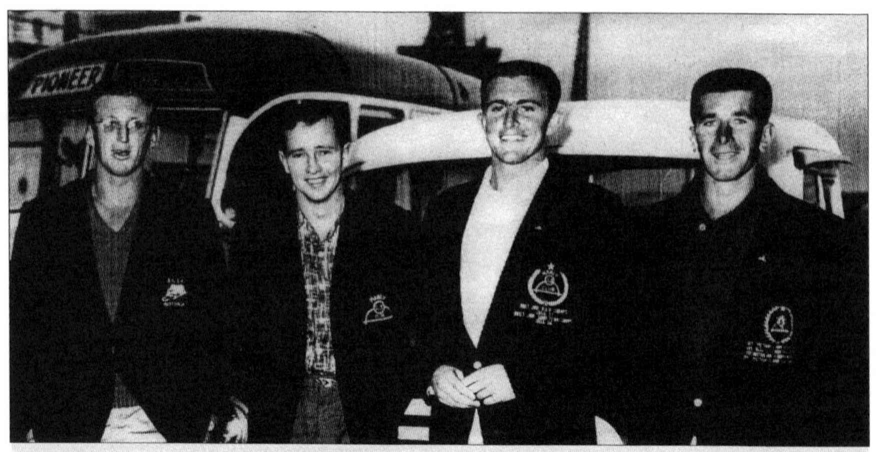

*To the men and woman who worked in Jersey as beach guards
and lifeguards between the years 1958 to 2010, in particular
the 1958 pioneers – Jim Wilson, John Booth,
Neil Beachley and Mick Hall
(pictured above)*

Published in 2018
by Seaflower Books
www.ex-librisbooks.co.uk

Origination by Seaflower Books

Printed by CPI Anthony Rowe
Chippenham, Wiltshire

ISBN 978-1-912020-56-0

Contents

About the author

Born in Newcastle, Australia, after completing university David Knight joined the Royal Australian Navy in 1972. Following a career spanning 24 years he retired with the rank of Commander and entered the world of consulting, working in Australia and Asia.

In 2009 David returned to Newcastle to enjoy the more laidback lifestyle. Soon after, David, an avid reader, began writing. Two fiction books followed, namely *The Stalking Horse* and its sequel *Skin for Skin*. *The Other Jersey Boys* is David's first non-fiction work.

David is married, with four children and two grandchildren. When he is not writing, David enjoys cooking, loves a glass of red wine and allows the very active family dog to take him for a daily walk.

Further details can be found at www.davidknightnovels.com or look for David Knight Novels on Facebook.

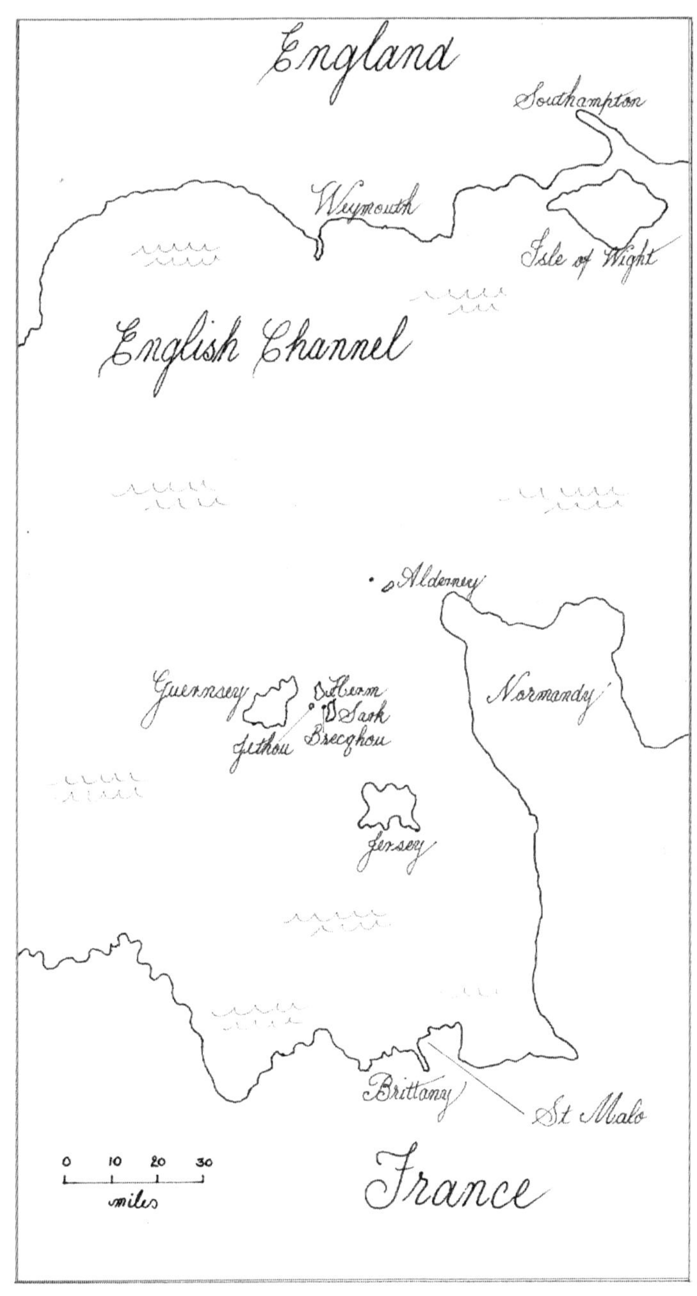

The Channel Islands

0 ½ 1 mile
Plémont Bay
Grève De Lecq
Bonne Nuit
Bouley Bay
Rozel Bay
La Saline
Kempt Tower
Jersey
St Ouen's Bay
Jersey Airport
Jersey Rugby Club
La Rocco Tower
El Tico
Lifeguard Tower
Gorey Harbour
Grouville
St Helier Harbour
Corbière Lighthouse
St Brelade's Bay
St Aubin's Bay
Portelet Bay
Green Island
La Rocque Harbour

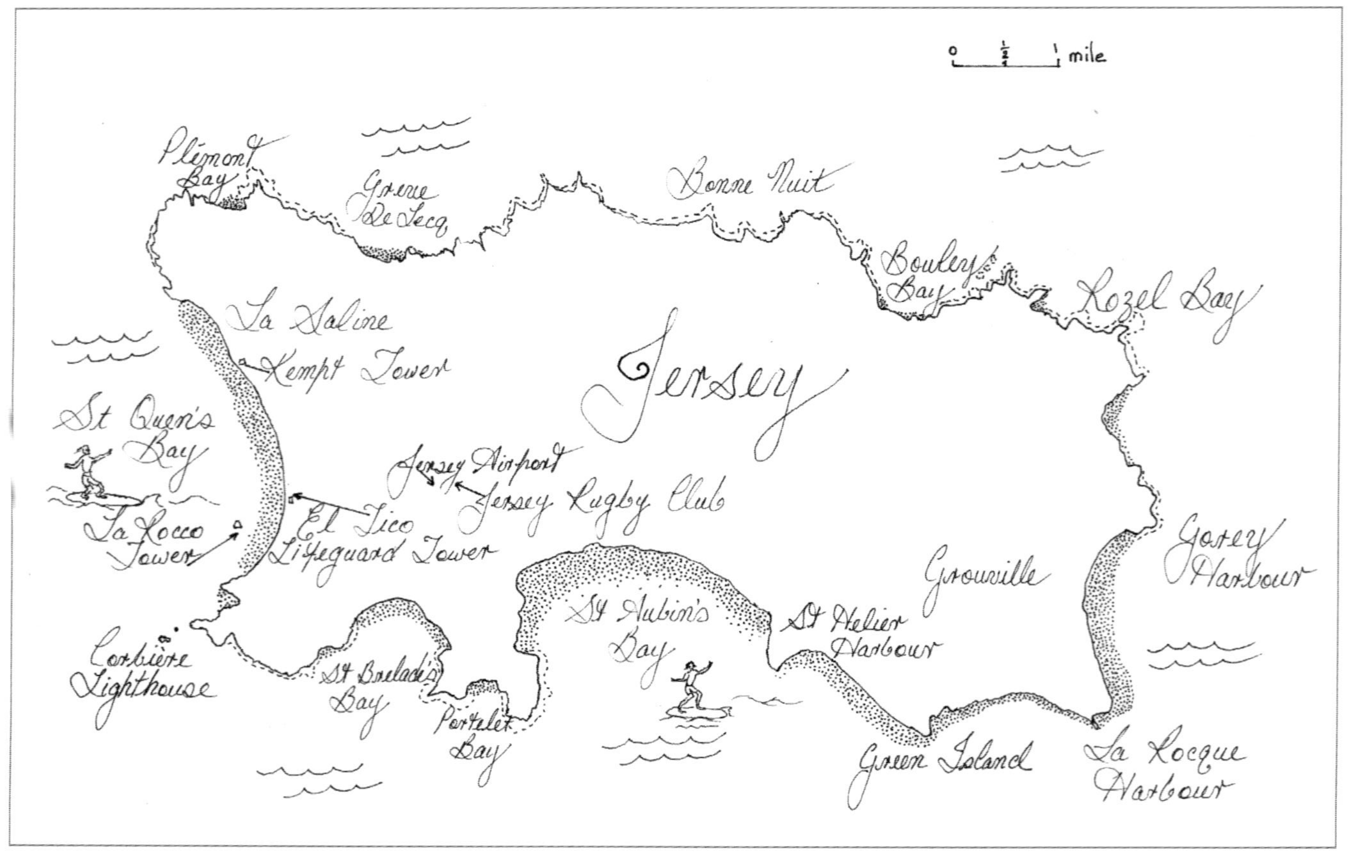

Jersey

Author's Note

I was first introduced to the surf lifesaving scene in 1964 when I and five of my mates (one of them named Steve Porter, latterly known as the 'Duke of Normandy') joined Cook's Hill surf club in Newcastle as a 15-year-old. After gaining the surf Bronze medallion I began competing in surf carnivals, firstly as a swimmer (unsuccessfully), then as a boat rower (more successfully). Many patrols followed, along with eventually the position of Patrol Captain and belt swimmer. This role could be dangerous, as several of the rescues depicted in this book attest.

In my late teens I became the club's Chief Instructor, training younger men in the skills required to attain the Bronze qualification and patrol the beach. I also became a Committee member in the august position of gear steward.

I loved the beach lifestyle: the surf, the sun, the girls, and the camaraderie. But for me, the chance to be the first in my family to attain tertiary qualifications at university, marriage with children, then a career in the Royal Australian Navy, got in the way of the beach.

In the long, hot (well, the Poms thought so) summer of 1976 whilst undergoing training with the Royal Navy in Cornwall, I was invited by Steve Porter to holiday in Jersey, where he and a group of young Aussies were enjoying an idyllic lifestyle as beach guards.

I landed at Jersey airport to be met by a small group including Steve, Kim 'Harpo' Flower, and Stuart 'Cocka' Bear. The car they were driving had no starter motor, so we had to push it (thankfully downhill) to get it started. They took me to the Doghouse at 30 St Saviour's Road in St Helier and there the fun started.

I went with them to the lifeguard tower at St Ouen's daily for two weeks. The mornings were spent recovering from the night before, then a swim, a ski paddle, a run, occasionally out to La Rocco tower in St Ouen's bay to jump off its battlements. After that it was back to the Doghouse for a hearty meal and a few 'Harry Heinekens'. Afterwards, the boys dressed for work on the doors of the pubs and nightclubs, and off we went. After they finished, someone would know where a party was, or we would congregate at one of the watering holes or even go back to a party at the Doghouse. Home sometime after midnight, bed beckoning. Then we would get up the next morning and do it all again.

One night the boys told me we were going to the movies. I breathed a sigh of relief because my liver was rebelling from too much drink. That relief was short lived because the movie theatre had a bar, so we drank. The movie started, and I naively asked why we weren't going to watch it. In reply the barmaid opened some curtains and there was the movie. I can't recall much of the second half of that film.

The boys gave me only one rule – never, ever, drink with Bill Lavarack. When I interviewed Wayne 'John Wayne' Bridges I found out why – his initiation on the drink with Bill is hilarious.

The two weeks' holiday passed quickly and before I knew it I was on a plane heading back to mainland Britain. As I sat mulling over my amazing holiday I realised that, if it wasn't for the different path I had chosen in life, I would have been there with them!

In 2015, after reading about an Australian surf club member who decided to travel to Greece to help rescue the refugees risking their lives on dodgy boats out of Africa, I thought of my mates and their adventures saving lives in Jersey. Hence this story.

Over the past few years a wide range of people have helped me in the research needed to tell this story properly. Many thanks to the 40 or so ex beach guards and lifeguards, their friends in Australia and in Jersey, and the wives, that I interviewed. Thanks also to the *Jersey Evening Post*, particularly to Corinne Wiseman, for the information gleaned from their archives. The same thanks to Roland Quintaine and the team from Jersey Archives. Also, to Marie Ramsland for her amazing copy editing.

I was privileged to visit Jersey in September 2017 as part of my research for the book. Many thanks go to Tony Hurford and David Blake for squiring me around, and to Wendy Hurford for writing the Foreword to this book. I will always treasure my meeting with Ida Lavarack, Bill's wife, to hear her story. That was one of the highlights of the visit.

Finally, a big vote of thanks to my 'committee of taste': Guy Littler, Brian Jones, Jim Reeves, Mike Gray, Ken Holloway and Barry Cardiff. They provided invaluable help and advice in guiding me through the ins and outs of the Jersey scene and who to interview. I would like to think they have gotten as much out of this as I have.

I salute the men and woman who call themselves Jersey lifeguards.

David Knight
June 2018

Foreword

by Wendy Hurford MBE

As a Jersey girl growing up in the days when the sun shone all summer and the waves were always perfect, an essential accessory was the wooden belly board to catch waves. That of course led to us noticing the bronzed bodies and the large surf boards belonging to another important feature at St Ouen's Bay – the beach guards.

The appearance of these specimens of fit manhood on the beach announced that summer had started. The annual rugby game of the beach guards versus the Jersey Rugby Club heralded the end of sun and sand and the beginning of mud and rain. These were timely reminders of the passing of the seasons in Jersey.

Included in the pages of this book, *The Other Jersey Boys*, are the many deeds and misdemeanours of this body perfect. These deeds often resulted in the female population of the Island diminishing as they moved down under to swell the land of milk and honey – Australia. Of course, the converse also occurred when Jersey girls enticed the boys to stay awhile on the Island!

Throughout the sixties, seventies and even into the eighties, the beach guards coming to the 'The Rock' was not just a seasonal visit, but rather part of a longer 'Grand Tour' over consecutive years, to take in the cultural elements of Europe, where the 'Munich Beer Festival' was heavily featured as well as the Café life of France and the social whirl of Earls Court in London.

Money, of course, needed to be earned by the Beach Guards to finance further travels and so wintering in Jersey and becoming part of the Jersey Rugby Football Club was an essential element of their lifestyle. Many a Jersey night club would see an Aussie featuring on the door to supplement their meagre income.

This was an era where the Beach Guards returned season after season and so became embedded in the fabric of life on the Island. But as travel became easier and flights cheaper, so the traditions changed, and the beach guard culture took on a different perspective. Jersey became the poorer for their loss and the stories certainly less colourful.

Many of us look back with much affection to this time …but as with all things 'Tempus Fugit' (time flies).

We are delighted that the adventures and trials of this august body of men have been recorded for future generations, even if it is to learn from their mistakes.

I and my husband, both long-time friends of many of the beach guards who worked in Jersey, commend this book to you, the reader. It is a very entertaining and enjoyable tale.

Jersey 2018

Prologue

Nineteen-year-old Australian Neil Beachley paused on the large sea wall at St Ouen's beach in Jersey in the Channel Islands and stared at the water, or rather, the lack of it. The tide was out – way out – on that mild, partly cloudy summer's day in 1958. The sun shining on small pools of seawater made the beach glisten prettily. A small crowd of beach goers walked on the wide stretch of flat sand that ended in a five-metre-high sea wall or frolicked in the cool waters of the English Channel three to four hundred yards seaward. It was a picture of idyllic bliss – or was it?

Neil and the three young Aussies with him could immediately see the problem – the forty-foot (twelve metre) tide would come in soon, and fast, 'the speed of a cantering horse' was how Neil described it. Neil could see that there weren't many ramps cut into the sea wall or steps up from the sand for people to move off the beach quickly. The German engineers who had designed the wall built by slave labour had done a good job in their efforts to stop any Allied landings during World War II. However, the lack of egress from the beach meant that more inexperienced and poorer swimmers might be in danger. That danger would come as the fast-paced incoming tide generated waves breaking against the base of the sea wall. People could, and did, get trapped. Injury or worse, death, could and did result.

Jersey, the largest of the Channel Islands, is located about twelve nautical miles off the Cotentin Peninsula of Normandy, France. It is a beautiful little island, roughly oblong shaped with the longer axis facing east-west, less than forty-five square miles (one hundred and eighteen square kilometres) in size. Like all the Channel Islands and indeed most of the English Channel, Jersey is subject to a massive twice daily tidal inflow and outflow.

But what were these Aussies doing there, so far away from their own country?

The answer was simple. They had volunteered to travel to Jersey to demonstrate Australian surf lifesaving techniques that could save swimmers in difficulty. Tourism was starting to show signs of booming in Jersey as the savagery and the austerity of World War II faded into history. Construction of new short stay accommodation and repairs to existing guesthouses and hotels were gathering pace. This, combined with Jersey's beautiful scenery and sandy beaches, its quaint architecture and its tax-free status, all contributed to this economic uplift.

But the tourists from Britain and the Continent weren't at all experienced in managing the fickleness of the ocean; they had little idea of how to handle the surf or the occasional rips that formed, let alone the huge tidal range. Most were poor swimmers, once they got in over their heads their inexperience often led to panic, and with panic anything could happen. For the bourgeoning tourist business this was a less than desirable, so something had to be done.

That's where the pioneering four Australian surf lifesavers came in. John Booth, Neil Beachley, Mick Hall and Jim Wilson hailed from the northern Sydney beaches. John, Neil and Mick were members of Manly Surf Lifesaving Club and Jim from North Steyne Surf Club. All were strong swimmers, and all had gained the prerequisite surf Bronze Medallion that allowed them to undertake voluntary patrols and to compete in surf carnivals on Australian beaches. Jim Wilson had been the Senior Instructor at North Steyne, responsible for training young men in the techniques to enable them to qualify for the surf Bronze Medallion. The four were ideally placed to show Jersey the Australian way of surf lifesaving, even if the only equipment available to them was an old and not particularly well-maintained surf reel, line and belt.

Surf lifesaving in Australia had been in existence since 1907. Similar movements had been started in other countries including South Africa, which had formed a surf lifesaving association in 1911 and New Zealand, where the first surf clubs formed in around 1910. As far as Jersey was concerned, the main factor in the quest to bring safety to its beaches was the formation of the Surf Lifesaving Association of Britain in 1955. Significantly, the founder of that movement was an Australian named Allan Kennedy.

Because of the interaction between the recently formed Surf Lifesaving Association of Great Britain, the Surf Lifesaving Association of Australia and a newly formed volunteer organisation called the Jersey Lifeguard Club, the latter successfully lobbied the States of Jersey government for permission to conduct a six-week trial of so-called 'professional beach guards' in Jersey in 1958. The impetus for this came from several key players: Allan Kennedy, Judge Adrian Curlewis, then President of the Surf Lifesaving Association of Australia, and a Jersey Lifeguard Club member named Pat McGarry. More on them later.

The Jersey Lifeguard Club, which had formed in 1953 and had affiliated with the Surf Lifesaving Association of Australia in 1956, had started to provide some volunteer patrols on weekends on two Jersey beaches, St Ouen's and St Brelade's. However, the club's swimmers lacked the skills and experience of Australian surf lifesavers. When they arrived in July 1958, the four young Australians were welcomed with open arms.

As the four Aussie surf lifesavers patrolled the Jersey beaches in the summer of 1958 they had no idea that their ground-breaking presence would spawn an association lasting between Jersey and around two hundred and eighty surf lifesavers, mostly from Australia, but also from South Africa, England, New Zealand

and Jersey. That association would last just over fifty years, continuing until the end of the 2010 summer when a new arrangement was put in place.

Their experiences and interactions with the locals and the tourists have given rise to the title of this book, *The Other Jersey Boys*. Actually, there was one woman, and what a woman; her tale is part of this book.

But let's not let the truth get in the way of a catchy title!

This is their story.

Part 1: ORIGINS

Late 1950s – Early to Mid-1960s

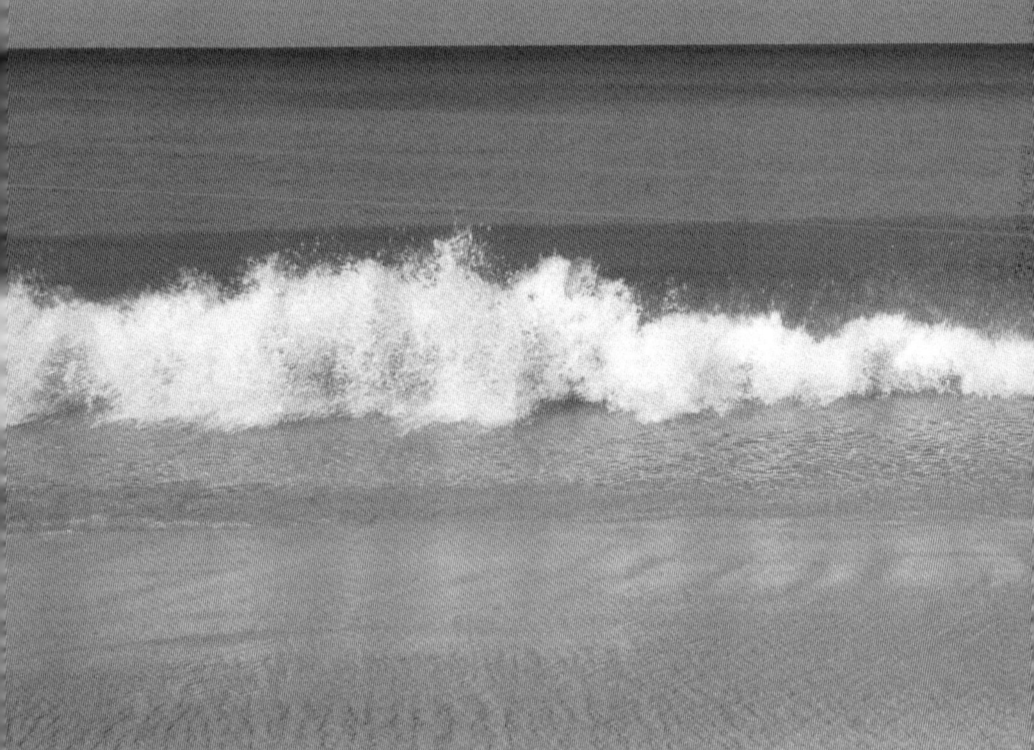

1   The Lead up to 1958

To explain how the initiative to bring the four young Australians to Jersey in 1958 came into being, it is necessary to go back just over a decade, to 1944 and 1945, the last years of World War II. Australian servicemen serving in Britain, never ones to let a war get in the way of a bit of fun, had organised several surf carnivals on a beach near Newquay, Cornwall, in the far south-western region of Britain. They were actually tasked with finding a good spot for Aussie servicemen to enjoy a bit of leave but, being surf lifesavers, they also took the opportunity to find some good beaches and waves.

Cornwall was a place where holidaymakers went for the summer holidays to get away from the daily grind. Sleepy and quiet in winter, it came alive in the summer months as holidaymakers flocked to the yellow sand beaches on the north coast of Cornwall, to towns like St Ives, Newquay, and Bude. The beaches along north Cornwall, Newquay included, were very much like Australian beaches – yellow sand and good waves – although the water temperature was a damn sight colder – around sixty degrees Fahrenheit (fifteen to sixteen degrees Celsius). Still, that didn't matter too much to the young men, they had much stiffer challenges to face from Hitler.

The first surf carnival was held at Torcarne beach near Newquay on Sunday September 3, 1944. Among the competitors were two Australian and New South Wales surf champions, Bob Newbiggin and Arthur Beard. Bob hailed from Newcastle, north of Sydney, and was a member of the Cooks Hill Lifesaving and Surf Club. He had won numerous surf and surf belt titles before enlisting in the Royal Australian Air Force in 1942 and becoming a pilot flying heavy bombers over Europe with the Royal Air Force. Arthur was a member of Dee Why Surf Lifesaving Club. Arthur also made an appearance at the second carnival in July 1945.

It was Arthur Beard who was instrumental in getting a young Australian named Allan Kennedy interested in Cornwall as a potential centre for a British-based surf lifesaving movement. Arthur fell in love with the surf at a beach called Crooklets at the Cornish village of Bude, some thirty miles (fifty kilometres) up the coast from Newquay. He described Crooklets as being the best body surfing beach in Britain.

Allan Kennedy was a well-qualified surf lifesaver, having gained his surf Bronze, an Instructors Certificate and an Examiner's Certificate which permitted him to assess squads attempting their Bronze Medallion and to pass successful candidates.

Born and raised in Byron Bay on the NSW north coast, Kennedy joined the Australian Public Service in 1937 at the age of thirty. This meant a move to Brisbane in Queensland where he resumed his association with surf lifesaving, quickly moving up the organisational ladder of the Surf Lifesaving Association of Queensland to become Superintendent, second only to the President, in 1941.

Kennedy made a name for himself with the Americans based in southern Queensland under the command of the American General Douglas McArthur. Appalled by the large number of drownings occurring amongst US servicemen on the Gold Coast (a beach mecca just north of the Queensland – NSW border), Kennedy talked the US Army into allowing him to train US soldiers in Australian surf lifesaving techniques. This initiative was spectacularly successful, and many US lives were saved.

Kennedy also railed against the Sydney-centric nature of the Australian surf lifesaving movement. The Sydney based NSW branch dominated the rest of Australia, and Kennedy wanted a national body independent of Sydney to be formed. But the inertia proved very difficult to overcome.

Meanwhile, Kennedy was transferred to Victoria with the public service and immediately set about fostering surf lifesaving in that state. He helped to form the Surf Lifesaving Association of Victoria and became its first Superintendent. However, his surf lifesaving career hit a road block when he was transferred back to Queensland in the late 1940s. He felt stymied and started to look for a new challenge.

In 1951 he found it. His application to be transferred to the United Kingdom in his public service work was successful. Kennedy began to plot a bold new plan – the introduction of surf lifesaving to Britain. He was aware that the Royal Life Saving Society dominated over there, but he knew that swimming in the surf was a very different proposition than still water swimming.

Kennedy was under no misapprehension that his vision would be difficult to bring into being. Although South Africa, New Zealand and Hawaii (not yet part of the USA) used Australian surf lifesaving techniques, the framework adopted by those countries was to employ paid professional lifeguards rather than using the Aussie volunteer model. This was a challenge of grand proportions, but he reckoned he was the man to do it.

In 1951, just before Allan Kennedy left Australia to take up a position in Australia House in London, he had a chat with Arthur Beard who was still active in competing for Dee Why Surf Club despite receiving a serious bullet wound during the war. Neil Beachley, one of the first four young Australian to go to Jersey in 1958 and who had met Arthur in Sydney, describes Beard as 'A Clark Gable look alike [who] was popular with the ladies and had all the lifesaving skills as well'. Arthur told Kennedy about Bude and Allan Kennedy decided that Bude would be the ideal location to be the centre of Britain's surf lifesaving movement if he could get it up and running.

Well versed in the Australian surf lifesaving bureaucracy by then, Kennedy spoke to two key figures about his idea. They were Judge Adrian Curlewis, the National President, and National Secretary Ken Watson, who was also secretary for the Manly surf club. Their discussion left Kennedy with little doubt that, while the two high officials vowed support which included surf lifesaving handbooks and equipment such as surf reels, the heavy lifting would rest with him. This didn't deter him in the least. So off he went to Britain, full of enthusiasm.

His new job in Australia House in London as a dairy produce inspector kept him busy. However, he quickly found several supporters in the beautiful old triangular shaped stone building located on the corner of the Strand and Aldwych Streets. Among them was Sir Thomas White, the Australian High Commissioner, who had been a central figure in the Australian arm of the Royal Life Saving Society. Kennedy quickly won Sir Thomas over. This gave him a powerful ally to use in any political battles to come. Kennedy was keen to bring the sport to Britain and met with Judge Adrian Curlewis, the President of the Surf Lifesaving Association of Australia.

Significantly Kennedy visited the island of Jersey for four days over Easter in April 1952. He was impressed by the surfing conditions, particularly at St Ouen's, and reported this by mail to Ken Watson, secretary of the Australian Surf Lifesaving Association. Allan Kennedy, however, had Bude on his mind and finally managed to get there at the beginning of May 1952.

After catching some good body waves Kennedy was sold on Bude, although the chill of the water and the lack of people on the beach, so unlike Australia, surprised him. However, what he was not surprised about was the state of the surf lifesaving equipment available. What little there was, was ancient and in poor condition. Static lines or lifebuoys were the norm and the line used was heavy and usually didn't float. Kennedy could see that to use this equipment created as much danger to the rescuer as the rescued. As he did a tour of the Cornish beaches, Kennedy was told by locally employed lifeguards that they were extremely keen to get access to the new Ross Safety Belt with its vital quick release pin mechanism. This had recently been introduced to Australian surf lifesaving.

Prior to the introduction of the quick release pin, surf lifesavers used surf belts that provided no way of being discarded in an emergency. Originally made of cork for flotation, the surf belt in the early 1950s was made of a wide strip of canvas that went around the waist of the swimmer. Attached at the front was a narrow canvas strip that went over the head and rested on the back of the neck. The belt was around nine inches (twenty-three centimetres) wide at the front and narrower at the back.

A D-ring was attached to both ends of the belt and the end of surf line threaded through one D-ring and securely attached to the other. The other end of the 200 odd yards of line was wound around a wooden drum on a surf reel. The belt was laid out flat on the beach with a loop of line which the beltman jumped into whilst scooping up the belt and throwing the strap over his head. As he ran into the water the line tightened behind him, securing the belt in place on his body around the waist.

Australian surf clubs had for a long time been using hand signals to permit the first linesman (the closest one of three to the water) to control the pace of the line being paid out and subsequently retrieved once the beltman had gotten the 'patient' under control. This was necessary because if the line was pulled in too fast the beltman and 'patient' could be dragged under. This could also occur if the beltman and 'patient' were pulled through a breaking wave where the downward force of the wave would increase the danger of being pulled under.

Unfortunately, this technique didn't help when the line became tangled in sea weed or caught under hidden obstacles such as submerged rocks. If the line suddenly pulled tight, dragging the beltman under, he might not be able to free himself from the belt in sufficient time before he was drowned. This had already happened on numerous occasions in Australia. It had also occurred in Cornwall where over enthusiastic and uneducated bystanders had been known to inadvertently cause drownings though pulling the line in too fast.

The Ross Safety Belt, invented by a New Zealander named Alec Ross, was an ingenious but simple solution to this problem. The belt itself was made in two pieces. Several stainless-steel eyelets were securely sewn into two ends of the belt and an elongated U-shaped stainless-steel pin with a narrow gap between the two prongs was inserted through the eyelets, fastening the belt into one piece. The pin was attached to the belt by a cord. One prong of the pin had a series of sharp curves to prevent the pin from accidentally coming out of the eyelets. When the pin was pulled firmly the belt fell apart and the beltman was free.

Whilst rescuing someone in trouble in the surf was one thing, resuscitating them was another. Through most of the first half of the 20th century the accepted method for resuscitating a patient was the Shafer or 'prone pressure' method, whereby the patient was placed face down to allow vomit or sea water to escape from the mouth or nose. Compression was applied to the middle of the back to expel air from the lungs. When the pressure was released in theory air would return to the patient's lungs.

In the 1940s and early 1950s a system call the Eve's Rocker was also used as a surf lifesaving technique used to attempt to resuscitate someone who didn't appear to be breathing. Named after Dr Frank Eve, the procedure used a stretcher placed on a tripod so that it could rock up and down like a see saw. In theory the sea water would drain out of the victim who was placed face down on the stretcher. But it was eventually found that occasionally water in the victim's stomach could find its way into the lungs, causing death by drowning.

This technique was replaced in the early 1950s by the Swedish Holger-Nielsen technique. In this system the victim was laid on their stomach with the elbows bent and the hands placed under the forehead. The rescuer knelt near the victim's head and brought pressure to bear on the shoulder blades to expedite expiration. By subsequently lifting the elbows air was drawn back into the lungs. The weakness of this method was it didn't help the victim who had a blockage in their throat. This occasionally was the situation if the victim had vomited in trying to force the water out of their lungs. This method was still in force in Australian surf lifesaving in the mid-1950s and would have been used by the Cornish lifeguards as well.

Kennedy promised those Cornish lifeguards to do what he could about the quick-release belt before returning to London. There he wrote yet another memo to Secretary Ken Watson asking for a surf reel, line and belt, a spare belt and some instructional handbooks. He later requested a surf ski with paddle. After a delay of more than six months the reel, line and belt finally arrived.

In the spring of 1953 Kennedy returned to Bude ready to put the first part of his plan into action. He enlisted the help of a local named Fred Lester who ran a guest house. Kennedy figured correctly that someone like Lester would see this as a means of furthering Bude's tourism potential. Lester agreed and tried to drum up support for forming a surf club but could gain little interest from the townspeople.

Kennedy returned in late June, this time with a surf ski, and in desperation presented an ultimatum – either Bude agreed to form a surf club or Kennedy would use the publicity resources available through Australia House to throw open the offer to any locality in Britain that had a decent surf beach. This obviously had the desired effect because an Australia House press release dated late June 1953 announced the imminent formation of Britain's first surf lifesaving club based on Australian principles at Bude. Kennedy had gotten his way.

Allan Kennedy, assisted by three other Australians, one of them most likely being a man named Col Hendy, trained several squads who were awarded Bronze medallions in August 1953. By this time Col, a fellow Australia House worker and a long-standing member of North Bondi surf club, had become Allan Kennedy's right-hand man in his quest.

Success begets success, and in July 1954 in the southern English county of East Sussex the Brighton surf club was formed, even though the waves were invariably small along that stretch of coastline. However, Brighton was a popular holiday destination in the summer months. The beach itself was quite long and pebbly but the latter didn't stop the holidaymakers flocking to the water, the sunshine and the famous pier. Brighton surf club continued until the late 1970s when a lack of members forced its closure. It reformed in 2011.

Another Cornish town, St Agnes, expressed an interest in this new development after the tragic death by drowning of a male visitor to the town in August 1954. Despite the heroic efforts by two swimmers, a male and a female, using a lifebelt attached to a heavy hemp rope, the man was dead before they could pull him out of the water. Kennedy, sensing an opportunity, organised a surf carnival in St Agnes later that same month. Some four and a half million British people watched a live BBC telecast of the carnival. Kennedy's publicity contacts came good and British surf lifesaving was well and truly on the map. A surf club at St Agnes sprang into being at the beginning of 1955 and in May of that year a reel, line and belt arrived from Australia, a donation from the North Bondi surf club. It was presented at Australia House to members of the St Agnes surf club by Sir Thomas White.

Allan Kennedy returned to Australia in September 1954, a happy man. He became even happier in February 1955 when Col Hendy gave him the news that the Surf Lifesaving Association of Great Britain had been formed, with Col as its first president. The Australian High Commissioner Sir Thomas White agreed to be the association's patron. In under three years Kennedy had achieved something that was widely believed in Australian surf lifesaving circles to be impossible.

The surge in British surf lifesaving was not only evident in Cornwall and East Sussex. In 1953 the Jersey Lifeguard Club was formed, with an affiliation with the Royal Life Saving Society. Although not a surf club on the Aussie model, it nevertheless had similar aims – the saving of life off the Jersey beaches and the education of the public about the dangers of swimming in the surf.

For Jersey surf lifesaving a major event was to take place in 1955 – a visit by members of the Bude Surf Lifesaving Club and a demonstration of an Australian surf line and reel. It was an outstanding success as people flocked to St Ouen's beach to watch the exhibition. This led to Jersey Lifeguard Club officials deciding in 1956 to affiliate with the Surf Lifesaving Association of Australia. The States of Jersey government gave the club a grant of one thousand pounds to purchase Australian surf lines, reels and belts. Officials from the Jersey Lifeguard Club then began to have regular correspondence with Manly surf club, presumably with Manly's Ken Watson, who was still the secretary.

At Allan Kennedy's urging Col Hendy took a trip to Jersey in 1957. There he put on his hat as Examiner and put a Jersey Lifeguard Club Bronze squad through its paces before passing them. He also set up a board of examiners and then canvassed something which would have met with outrage back in Australia. He had the temerity to propose that women be allowed to become surf lifesavers. This radical suggestion was certainly ahead of its time – it wasn't until 1980 that women in Australia were permitted to join surf clubs.

A woman named Constance Brown was a founding member of the Jersey Lifeguard Club. Constance, a spinster in her late forties when the Jersey Lifeguard Club came into being, had long been involved in rescuing people at St Brelade's beach, with her first rescue in 1926 and her last in 1958. Between those years she was believed to have rescued at least thirty people. Constance was awarded a Qualifying Certificate by the Surf Lifesaving Association of Australia but not the Bronze Medallion, presumably because she was female and there was no precedence in the Australian surf lifesaving bureaucracy.

Constance Brown, originally born in England, settled in Jersey with her family in 1919. Her father died in 1926 and subsequently Constance and her mother built and operated Brown's Café in St Brelade's Bay. From there she was able to keep an eye on the beach and to be able to complete the rescues she made. As the volunteers of the Jersey Lifeguard Club only patrolled at weekends, Constance was a strong advocate for professional lifeguards to operate on the beaches of Jersey.

For her services to surf lifesaving Constance Brown was made a Member of the British Empire (MBE) in 1967. She died in Jersey in 1984, aged eighty.

As tourism in Jersey began to gather pace and more people began to avail themselves of the lovely beaches on the island, the Jersey Lifeguard Club found itself under pressure to provide the necessary expertise to cope with the increased risk of drowning. Their membership was low, and they only patrolled at weekends or after work – they were volunteers after all. Some of the wiser heads including Constance Brown and a chap named Pat McGarry, started to think outside the box – paid lifeguards were needed to patrol the beaches during the week. For this to happen money would have to be found. They approached the States of Jersey government for funding.

At the same time a request was sent to Australia, to Ken Watson, asking whether the Surf Lifesaving Association of Australia could provide some surf lifesavers to work on the beaches in Jersey for a period during the summer. Ken, after conferring with Judge Adrian Curlewis and getting his agreement, got to work. He called for expressions of interest and four young men, three from Manly surf club and one from North Steyne surf club, were selected.

Ken had also been corresponding with Bude's Fred Lester, and a trip to Bude was included in the overseas itinerary. Adrian Curlewis wanted to take them to France and Germany as well, so those destinations were added to the list. Of course, the young men selected had to pay their own way.

2   The Pioneers

'This idea of going overseas was initiated by the Surf Life Saving Association of Australia through the then Secretary Ken Watson and with Fred Lester in Bude, Cornwall. This was encouraged by Judge Adrian Curlewis, then President of the Surf Lifesaving Association of Australia.'

Extract from an interview with Neil Beachley, one of the first four Australian surf lifesavers to work on the island of Jersey as lifeguards.

By 1958 the Australian surf lifesaving movement had become very well organised regarding surf lifesaving qualifications. The entry point was the surf Bronze medallion, possession of which allowed the holder to patrol the beach as a volunteer member of a surf patrol. Training, or drilling as it was referred to in those days, for the Bronze was a mixture of practical and theory. The latter included information on resuscitation techniques, basic first aid, and hand signals between the rescuer and the team on the beach. The former was designed to put the theory into practice and included swimming in a surf belt, the use of a surf reel and line, how to subdue a panicking patient in the surf, and resuscitation techniques.

This rigorous and thorough training was designed with one set of outcomes in mind – the rescue of a swimmer in trouble in the surf with minimal danger to the swimmer and the rescuer, and the saving of that person's life through resuscitation if necessary.

Of course, there were other lifesaving aids available on Australian beaches in addition to the ubiquitous surf reel, line and belt method. Surf boats could be used, but that required an experienced crew of rowers and a capable sweep, and it took time for the boat to be launched and to reach the person in trouble. There was the growing presence of surf boards on the beaches although they were on average fifteen-foot-long and not so easy to control for the uninitiated. There was also the problem that they were easily washed away from the rider in the surf (leg ropes weren't invented until much later).

Surf skis, which had been around since the 1930s, were also an option, again with the limitation that they required an experienced paddler. However, most rescues were made by someone who was a good swimmer going out into the surf single handed and pulling the person in trouble back to the beach. This was fine unless it was a long swim through a good-sized surf or a decent rip, in which case the danger increased markedly for both swimmer and patient.

An alternative used with good effect were rubber surf mats, also called surf-o-planes, extremely popular on Australian beaches in the 1930s. The 'surf-o' remained the preferred means of catching waves amongst the younger beach goers, with a resurgence in the 1960s when a longer version came onto the market. In the 1930s members of Manly surf club reportedly completed around 260 rescues in the 1938-39 season using the 'surf-o'.

But the tried and tested means of getting someone in trouble out of danger remained the reel and belt. With trained lifesavers on the reel and line, playing the line out behind the beltman and then pulling the beltman and patient back in, the danger, although lessened, was still present. Things could do, and did, go wrong. The nylon line, designed to float but in practice didn't always, occasionally got snagged on a rock or some underwater obstacle, which put the beltman and the patient in danger of drowning. That's where the quick release pin came in.

Neil Beachley, one of the four chosen by Ken Watson, was born in the NSW mid-north coast town of Taree in February 1939. He learnt to body surf at Black Head beach just north of Foster. His early schooling was at Taree until 1952, then he moved with his parents to Manly. Neil left school in 1953 at the age of fourteen and in the same year joined Manly Surf Lifesaving Club as a cadet (under fifteen) in 1953. He gained his Bronze Medallion in 1955 and an Instructor's Certificate in the 1957 - 58 season.

Neil was a very good swimmer and was a member of the team that won the Australian Junior Surf Teams event at Torquay, Victoria in 1956 and the Australian Junior Rescue and Resuscitation (R&R) competition at Bondi in 1957.

If the name Beachley rings a bell, it is probably because of Neil's daughter Layne Beachley, the seven-time World Woman's Surfboard Champion. Six of those titles were won consecutively (1998 to 2003) and the last in 2006. Layne's story is a fascinating one and has been vividly described in a book titled *Beneath the Waves* written by journalist Michael Gordon.

Two of Neil's traveling companions, John Booth and Mick Hall, were both Manly boys and the three were firm friends, something that still stands today. Jim Wilson, a few years older than Neil, hailed from neighbouring North Steyne and Neil knew him well. Jim travelled separately from his three companions on the trip from Australia and met them in London.

Neil recalls: 'The purpose of going to England and to Jersey was to get involved with the newly emerging surf lifesaving movement there and, once we knew we could do it, we looked at the whole thing as a bit of fun'.

John Booth, Mick Hall and Neil Beachley travelled to Britain on RMS *Orion*, a twenty-three-thousand-ton passenger liner which had accommodation for around eleven hundred passengers. The *Orion* left Sydney in early 1958 and called in at Hobart, Melbourne, Perth, Colombo, Port Said, Port Suez, Naples, and Gibraltar, finally arriving in Southampton after a six-week voyage.

Neil has fond memories of the sea voyage. He recalls: 'It was a lot of fun. Although the booze was duty free we couldn't afford to drink that much although we did end up broke by the time we got to London. The food was okay, but it wasn't first class dining. We were four to a cabin which was located down in the bottom of the ship. Dancing with the girls was our main form of exercise apart from a bit of horizontal folk dancing with the odd friendly girl'.

The *Orion*, launched in late 1934, had a small swimming pool more suited to splashing around in than engaging in swimming training, which would account for Neil's remarks about the lack of the usual types of exercise.

Jim Wilson didn't travel with the other three because he was given a special job to do – to transport a surf reel donated by a man named Edmund Lennon, a Sydney supporter of the surf lifesaving movement, to be used in the demonstrations by the four surf lifesavers. The ship on which he travelled, the twenty thousand-ton S.S. *Southern Cross*, was much newer and more luxurious than the *Orion*, having air conditioning in all cabins, hot and cold running water and three swimming pools, one of which was indoor. Jim left Sydney several months before the other three Australians.

The *Southern Cross* journeyed from Sydney to Cape Town in South Africa. It is not known whether Jim was able to demonstrate the use of the surf reel in South Africa because Jim is deceased and there are no known records of his trip available. From there the ship travelled to Southampton.

Neil and his two companions arrived in London broke, and met up with Jim Wilson. Adrian Curlewis, on a world tour organised by the Surf Lifesaving Association of Australia, was already in London and arranged for the lifesavers to meet a couple of very important people – Prince Phillip, the Duke of Edinburgh, and the German born naturalised Briton Dr Kurt Hahn. Dr Hahn was the founder of an organisation called Outward Bound which was gaining worldwide prominence. Its focus was on outdoor education for the young people through exposing them to challenging open air activities to build resilience and confidence.

Kurt Hahn was also the Headmaster of the famous Gordonstoun School in northern Scotland. Prince Phillip had been one of his first pupils after it opened in 1934 and had allegedly loved the experience. He was also a keen supporter of Hahn's philosophy, from which the Duke of Edinburgh's Award scheme was founded in 1956.

The meeting was to occur at Buckingham Palace but unfortunately the breakdown of a borrowed car meant the young Australians were unable to attend. Curlewis didn't disclose his feelings about the four young Australians missing the meeting, although he did suggest afterwards to the quartet that they might like to get involved with the Outward Bound movement. The four politely declined. They were there for adventure and they weren't really interested in being involved in the scheme; surf lifesaving was their game.

Adrian Curlewis made another suggestion. Perhaps they might be interested in travelling to Accra, the capital of Ghana in Africa, to do there what they were about to do in Britain and on the Continent. At their expense, of course. Stewart Jamieson, the Australian High Commissioner in Ghana had earlier contacted Curlewis about the possibility of establishing Australian lifesaving methods on the beaches in and around Accra. Adrian Curlewis had discussed this option with his nephew Phillip Bell, a fellow Palm Beach surf club member who was to come to London later. Bell and the young men considered that this proposal had some merit, but a quick check revealed that there wasn't a ship going to Ghana. So that proposal never got off the ground.

Neil Beachley's impression of Judge Adrian Curlewis reflects the large gap in status between the two. Curlewis had founded the Palm Beach surf club in 1928 and had been President of the Surf Life Saving Association of Australia between 1934 and 1941 and then since 1945. He had also been Chairman of the New South Wales Fitness Association since 1949. Curlewis was a lawyer by trade and had enlisted in the Army in 1939. Captured after the fall of Singapore, he was a survivor of the notorious Changi prisoner-of-war camp as well as the infamous Burma Railway and the Japanese atrocities.

By the time he met Neil Beachley he was in his fifties and a polished, well connected senior member of the Australian legal fraternity. Beachley was a young moderately educated Sydneysider experiencing his first visit overseas and describes Curlewis thus: 'He was a bit pompous when you first met him but once you got to know him he was okay. After all he was a judge and [former] president of Palm Beach surf club which was a pretty rich club in those days. He could be a little bit hard to get along with sometimes'.

After a few days staying in Earl's Court they took the train down to Cornwall, destination Bude. In Bude they worked as lifeguards as well as in the local pub to earn some extra money, no doubt organised by Fred Lester. They spent a good amount of time on the beach training young Britons for their Bronze medallion despite the generally rainy weather experienced that year.

While the young Australians were in Cornwall, at the invitation of Dr Kurt Hahn, Adrian Curlewis travelled to the towns of Salem in southern Germany and Baad in Austria in July 1958 to talk to youth groups and screen a few movies about the surf lifesaving movement in Australia. Dr Hahn had been the headmaster of the Salem School in the early 1930s before Hitler's rise compelled him to leave Germany.

On return to England Curlewis was looking forward to attending the Lifesaving Championships of Great Britain, to be held on 28 July at the Cornish seaside town of Perranporth, several miles up the coast from St Agnes. The four Australians were scheduled to compete in the championships. A deal of surf lifesaving equipment had arrived from Australia especially for the contest and nearly twenty other Aussie surf lifesavers currently in Britain had been invited to attend.

On the day the weather gods decided to intervene, and rain showers and gusty winds whipped up the surf. The waves became choppy and the Australians were surprised when, in the R&R event, several English beltmen were unable to reach the buoys and 'rescue' their patients. In fact, Neil had to rescue one of the 'rescuers'. There was obviously a big gap between the surf swimming expertise of the Australians and the British.

A decision to cancel most events was reluctantly taken. However, all was not lost as a social function was quickly organised and Judge Curlewis showed the films *Guardians of the Surf* and, ironically, *Surf in the Sun*, both of which went down well.

After several months' stay in Bude the four young Australian travelled up to Weymouth on the English south coast and caught a small mail and tourist boat to St Helier, the capital of Jersey.

Jersey is the largest and most southern of the Channel Islands, a strategically placed archipelago that includes a slightly smaller island called Guernsey, and the tiny islands of Alderney, Sark, Herm, Jethou and Brecqhou.

The history of control of the Channel Islands reflects the jockeying for position and power by the countries in the region over many centuries. Jersey was originally known as *Angia* until the Vikings arrived in the 9th century. The Vikings, Scandinavian Norsemen from Denmark, Norway and Sweden, were pagans and had been involved in ongoing battles with Christians including the inhabitants of West Francia (the early name for what is now called France). In 911 the Vikings conquered Normandy and a deal was struck between Rollo, leader of the Vikings, and King Charles III, also known as King Charles the Simple (meaning straightforward), of West Francia.

King Charles gave Rollo the title of Duke and granted him, and his supporters, possession of Normandy, which included the Channel Islands. In return, Rollo swore allegiance to Charles, converted to Christianity, and pledged to defend Normandy against the incursions of other Viking groups.

After being ruled briefly by the Norman King Richard II (the first Duke of Normandy and a descendent of Rollo), successive English kings (technically all descendants of Norman rulers after the Norman William the Conqueror ruled England from 1066) held it until the early 1200s. Then King Phillip II, the first king of France, won it in battle but agreed in the 1259 Treaty of Paris to give the Channel Islands back to England. The Channel Islands became a Crown Dependency of the United Kingdom, and although the islands are self-governing the UK has assumed responsibility for defence and international relations.

Geographically, Jersey is a reasonably low-lying island, with the highest point only four hundred and seventy feet (one hundred and forty-three metres) above sea level. This high point is part of a plateau guarded by rugged cliffs in the north, sloping southwards down to sandy bays flanked by low cliffs. In the east the rugged cliffs in the north gradually give way to a long stretch of sandy beach at Gorey, and to the west the sandy beaches of St Ouen's Bay dominate the coastline.

The climate is mild with average maximum temperatures in the summer months in the high sixties Fahrenheit (low twenties Celsius). The water temperature generally reaches the low sixties Fahrenheit (about sixteen degrees Celsius) in the summer months. Heavier rainfall occurs mainly in the late autumn and the first few months of winter. English, French and a local patois called Jerriais, derived from its Normandy roots, are spoken.

The economy of Jersey reflects its unique geo-political position. Value Added Tax (VAT) was not included on goods and services until 2008 (introduced as a Goods and Services Tax or GST) and the lack of taxes substantially helped Jersey's tourism industry. Many holidaymakers were looking for a relatively cheap holiday, with the same currency and language, more sun than at home and nice sandy beaches. Jersey was a perfect match. Products such as jewellery, cosmetics and perfumery, electrical goods, and especially alcoholic drinks and tobacco goods were all cheap and plentiful. Alongside the 'luxury' market, an increasing number of 'gift' shops began to open in St Helier, selling cheap plastic goods and souvenirs. Hire cars were also inexpensive, and petrol prices markedly lower than the UK.

The real growth industries, which in turn were closely related with population trends, were tourism and later financial services, as Jersey became a major international offshore financial centre and tax haven. The period from 1950 to 1990 was the second period of rapid population increase for Jersey after a period in the early and mid-1800s. Between 1951 and 1991 the population rose from 57,310 to

84,082, an increase of almost fifty percent. This increase was most rapid in the 1950s and 1960s.

The period after the war was a time when hoteliers borrowed money and expanded their properties, while at the other end of the scale the smaller town dwellings, still with four or five rooms for sleepers, were converted into guest houses. Holiday villages and holiday camps also came to Jersey, catering for the same market as their parent groups in the UK.

The politico-legal system is a curious mix of Norman, English and modern French. Legislation governing Jersey is controlled by the Assembly of the States of Jersey. By way of overview the twelve Parishes of Jersey each elected a Senator, a Deputy and a Connétable (Constable). Six out of the twelve Senators were elected every three years for a term of six years. Connétables and Deputies were elected at irregular intervals for a term of three years.

In contrast to the rank of Senator, the office of Connétable was an ancient one and historically it has related to upholding the law. Prior service as a policeman was a common means of ascending to this position. The Connétable was the highest office of the Honorary Police in any Parish. The progression starts at being appointed a Constable's Officer, thence to the offices of Vingtenier (community policing), Centenier (responsible for charging or bailing offenders), Chef de Police, and ultimately Connétable. The relevance of these terms will be become apparent later.

As mentioned previously the tidal range has a huge impact in Jersey and indeed the English Channel. Imagine the English Channel as a rectangular tank, 300 nautical miles in length and having a uniform depth of 36 fathoms (216 feet) pivoted at its mid-length. If inclined in either direction the water flows towards the lower end, thus giving the effect of high and low water at opposite ends. At the point of pivot, however, the level remains constant.

Of course, the English Channel does not tip, but external forces created by the position of the moon and sun relative to the earth create the same effect, originating from the Atlantic Pulse which keeps the English Channel alternating between high and low water with the time of high water at one end coinciding approximately with the time of low water at the other. This effect is called an oscillation and occurs twice daily in the English Channel. A huge anticlockwise gyre (a roughly circular movement of water) is the result and the tidal range in the Channel Islands of up to forty feet (twelve metres) is amongst the largest in the English Channel.

Now to the Jersey beaches, of which there are many. Those in the south include Beauport, Havre des Pas, Ouaisne (pronounced Way-Nay) Bay, Portelet Bay, St Aubin's Bay, St Brelade's Bay and Green Island. In the west is St Ouen's Bay. To the north, nestled amongst the rugged cliffs, are Bonne Nuit, Bouley Bay, Grève de

Lecq, and Plémont. On the east coast are Archirondel, Grouville Bay, and La Rocque Harbour.

The most popular beaches are located on the southern and western sides of the island. The largest, St Ouen's on the west coast, extends in a gentle arc for about five miles (eight kilometres) from south to north, and is marked at the southern end by the famous La Corbière lighthouse, sited because the treacherous nature of the rocks and tides there make it dangerous for navigation. St Ouen's can be a dangerous beach because of its exposure to occasional powerful swells generated in the English Channel, as well as rips on the outgoing tide. Running the entire length of the beach is a ten foot (three metre) high sea wall. About two miles (three and a half kilometres) north of La Corbière lighthouse on the southern part of St Ouen's beach is a beach café called El Tico which opened in 1948. It is near there that the Jersey Lifeguard Club was located and where the Australians were to have their major base of operations.

Just to the south of El Tico and about eight hundred yards (five hundred metres) from the high water mark out into St Ouen's Bay is La Rocco Tower. This tower is commonly mistaken for a Martello Tower, many of which were built as coastal forts during the early nineteenth century by the British during the Napoleonic War. It is in fact a Conway Tower, so called because it was one of twenty-three built in Jersey by Field Marshall Henry Conway, Governor of Jersey, in the late 1770s. They predate the Martello Towers although they were built for the same purpose – defence of the island. La Rocco Tower is a round tower with a gun emplacement at its base and is a popular spot for the adventurous as it is easily accessible at low tide.

St Brelade's Bay, commonly known as Brelade's, is a horseshoe shaped sheltered inlet on the south coast about three miles (five kilometres) west of St Helier. It is the most popular beach in Jersey and its soft sand, generally safe swimming, beach activities and seaside cafes makes it a favourite for locals and holidaymakers alike. Towards the eastern end of the beach and situated slightly inland is a Martello Tower. The Australians were to make their other base of operations on the sea wall near the tower and next to a ramp running onto the beach.

It was these two most popular beaches that the four young Australians were to patrol.

❁

The Aussie quartet arrived at the end of July 1958. However, the Jersey Lifeguard Club had been successful in obtaining only enough money to fund two positions, so a compromise was reached. Two Aussies would work six days a week on the beaches in the mornings and the other two would work on the wharves during that time. Then they would switch over. That way they could make enough money to live on, barely, as the wharf jobs were dependent on the tide. If the tide was out, no ships could enter the harbour to be loaded or unloaded. That meant no work and no pay.

A title for the four was also agreed – they would be called beach guards.

Some locals who were interested in the beach guard work supplied the four with accommodation in several no-frills guest houses on a hill above St Brelade's beach in the south-west of the island. If they were lucky, they occasionally got breakfast thrown in. The beach guards walked to work for a brief period, but not long after they arrived they were provided with an old utility van for transport and it was used to cart their gear to and from their accommodation to St Ouen's and St Brelade's beaches. The lifesaving equipment they had on the beach was basic – a reel, line and a belt, one for each of the two beaches.

Neil Beachley describes the situation they faced with the beachgoers: 'Holiday makers would get out to St Ouen's Beach where the tide comes in fast, like the speed of a cantering horse. All those clowns would go out into the water and think that they were safe. The next thing you know they were in trouble and trying to get back to shore as the water rose above waist deep and we had to go and get them. The Germans built a seawall at St Ouen's beach and other beaches during the Second World War and the holidaymakers sometimes got trapped against that in the incoming tide.'

Neil paints a neat picture of the capital St Helier and the tourists: 'St Helier in those days was full of people trying to escape from the taxman in Britain, given that Jersey was a tax haven. There was also a lot of construction going on post Second World War, even in the late 1950s. It was quite a pleasant little town – it wasn't a city as it is today. There were many tourists, mainly British people on holiday, and they're the ones that usually got into strife in the water.'

Partying wasn't really on the minds of the young Australians. Neil says: 'We didn't play up too much as we were pretty serious about lifesaving and didn't really have too much money to be able to go out too often. But the girls were very friendly, some locals and some tourists – they preferred to be called holidaymakers rather than tourists. It was a bit like a Billy Butlin's holiday camp – they all came to have a good time.'

There was another, unofficial, international surf lifesaving presence on the island that also commenced in 1958. A Jersey businessman named Harry Swanson, who owned a live entertainment venue on St Ouen's Beach called the Watersplash Inn, hired three young South African lifeguards to patrol the beach near his establishment and to do odd jobs for him. The Watersplash was about 550 yards (500 metres) north of where the Aussies were located.

These three young men, Shorty Bronkhurst, Bobby Burdon and Cliff Honeysett, had been in London during the previous winter and had decided to immigrate to Australia. Then they went to the movies and saw a short film made by Jersey Tourism that would change their immediate futures. It showed some nice-looking waves at St Ouen's beach, so they decided to go and check it out. After landing menial jobs at Parkins Holiday Camp on the Jersey north coast, they quickly constructed three fourteen foot (four metre) long wooden surf boards and tried them out, first at Plémont beach then at St Ouen's. Harry Swanson spotted them and signed them up. These three young South Africans had the distinction of playing a major role in introducing stand up surfing, surf board riding, to Jersey. But that's another story.

All too soon the beach guards' 1958 stay in Jersey came to an end and the four Aussies prepared to leave. Jim Wilson was thinking about returning the following year, but the others were not so enthusiastic. Perhaps a tragedy that occurred on the beach the day after they left helped to convince Jim. Neil Beachley recalls: 'Two or three people were taken out in a rip with nobody on the beach at St Brelade's and they died. Had we had been there it might have been a different story. Unfortunately, there was nobody on the beach to take over from us because we just set the whole thing up and they weren't trained up yet'. This was yet another reminder of the danger that the ocean presented, even at the normally placid St Brelade's.

Adrian Curlewis, along with his wife who was travelling with him, had arranged to meet the four Australians at a seaside resort town called Weissenhaus on the Baltic Sea near Kiel, Germany, on the weekend of 23-24 August 1958. The Australians took a ferry south from St Helier to St Malo on the French Brittany coast, then hitchhiked to Weissenhaus after a brief stopover in Hamburg. It was here that they met Phillip Bell, the nephew of Adrian Curlewis, who accompanied them to the Baltic coast. The surf reel that Jim Wilson had brought from Australia also found its way to Weissenhaus.

The sea temperature in the Baltic in August was like that in Jersey, so the young men would not have noticed too much difference when they plunged into the water, although Neil recalls that it was 'bloody cold'. They gave several demonstrations of surf lifesaving techniques to what is described as a good and enthusiastic crowd which included representatives from the German Life Boat Organisation, the German Sea Rescue Brigade, the German Red Cross, and the DLRG which is short for *Deutsche Lebens-Rettungs-Gesellschaft* - the German organisation responsible for swimming and lifesaving education. Also in attendance were some of the members of the Outward Bound movement. Phillip Bell, who spoke fluent German and French, acted as interpreter.

After the demonstration Judge Curlewis presented the donated reel to the Outward Bound College at Weissenhaus.

From the Baltic coast Judge and Mrs Curlewis travelled to the French resort city of Biarritz on the southern part of the Bay of Biscay, only about twenty miles (thirty-five kilometres) from the Spanish border. It was a beautiful spot and the beaches were picturesque, with rolling breakers as well as dramatic headlands and rocky outcrops. The four surf lifesavers used their normal means of travel, hitchhiking, to get to Biarritz in time to meet the Curlewis imposed deadline of 9 September 1958.

The Australians Allan Kennedy and Col Hendy had visited Biarritz several years before. Kennedy noted that two beaches were ideal for body surfing although the lifeguards there at the time couldn't surf the waves. Kennedy thus thought that the Australian way of surf lifesaving would be a winner. Thus, Biarritz had become part of the 1958 agenda, originally the most important part according to Curlewis who was driving the internationalisation of Australian surf lifesaving know-how.

The team of four arrived before the due date but some unexpected problems, possibly red tape, forced a delay to the timetable. Adrian Curlewis had to enlist the aid of the Australian High Commissioner to France, Alfred Stirling, who managed to sort things out. On Sunday 7 September the four Aussies gave several demonstrations of the Australian techniques to the locals, followed by discussions and once again the screening of the two Australian surf lifesaving films. According to Neil Beachley, a large crowd was in attendance, 'resembling those on Bondi beach on a hot summer's day'.

Their commitments completed, the four young Australians elected to return to London. But before they did, they decided to have a surf in Biarritz. It was then that they fell afoul of the law and ended up in jail.

Neil Beachley takes up the story: 'There was a little policeman with a funny hat and a whistle on the beach at Biarritz and we were out surfing because the waves were good. One of us was riding a surfboard and the rest of us body surfing. The policeman went berserk about us being out in the surf. When we came in he grabbed us. We didn't realise the beach was closed and because he was so excited about us not taking any notice of him, the cops put us in the paddy wagon and took us away. Somebody came along and vouched for us and told the policeman we knew what we were doing but we didn't know the beach was closed because none of us spoke French'. Thankfully the lads were released from the lockup and were free to leave, which they did without delay.

The inability to speak the local language was to get other Australian beach guards into a spot of bother in various European countries over the forthcoming years.

Back in London Neil Beachley and John Booth got jobs as brickies' labourers. Mick Hall worked in London for a month or so before deciding to return to Australia. He booked passage on the *Orion*, the same ship as had transported him, John Booth and Neil Beachley to England. Jim Wilson got a job working for a newspaper or magazine, Neil can't remember which.

Neil and John Booth lived in Earl's Court and did all the usual things that Australians did. Neil had an interesting brush with a famous Australian (or perhaps more accurately a now infamous one). He says with a touch of humour: 'I remember doing singalongs [in a pub] with Rolf Harris, but I came out of it okay'.

In the first half of 1959 John and Neil left London and travelled to Canada when they worked in the city of Toronto for about eight months. It was there that they met some other Australian surf lifesavers from Manly, North Bondi, Bilgola and Queensland. The group decided to travel to Mexico.

While they were in Mexico they did a bit of teaching of lifesaving methods in Acapulco because there were a lot of people drowning along that part of the coast. Neil recounts: 'There's a beach near Acapulco called *Revolcadero* which means 'revolving surf' and it could be dangerous. We spent about a month there and had a lot of fun. That would have been in about the end of 1959'.

After brief stopovers in Los Angeles and Vancouver, Neil Beachley boarded a ship in Vancouver and sailed to Fiji where he worked another year. John Booth came straight home to Sydney. Neil finally got back to Sydney around the end of 1960. He soon got a job in Sydney, but he was asked by his employer to go to Papua New Guinea to fix a couple of things up there. He ended up spending the next eighteen months in PNG.

Neil Beachley finally got back to surfing at Manly around about the end of 1962, where he has remained until this day. But although for Neil, Jim Booth and Mick Hall that was the end of their relationship with Jersey and beach guards, it wasn't the case for Jim Wilson, who deserves the credit for setting up the formal Australian lifeguard relationship with Jersey that was to last another 50 years.

Jim Wilson stayed in London for a year and went back to Jersey for the 1959 summer. After an incident where one of the Jersey Lifeguard Club's enthusiastic but amateur members lost his life trying to rescue three holidaymakers, the States of Jersey government once again provided the funding for two beach guards. The Jersey Lifeguard Club through Secretary Pat McGarry was given responsibility for administering the payments. Jim teamed up with an Englishman living in Jersey named Bill Turton to patrol the beaches of St Ouen's and St Brelade's, assisted by the volunteer surf lifesavers on the weekends.

As well, the South Africans were back at the Watersplash. One of them was a strapping young man named Bill Lavarack who, as well as being a good rugby player, was a champion surf swimmer, having represented South Africa as a surf belt swimmer in the 1950s. As a former member of the Pirates Surf Club in Durban and a professional lifeguard on the beaches around Durban, Bill was a larger than life character who was fearless in the water. Described by Ida, his Jersey-born (called a Jersey 'Bean') partner and later wife, as a shy man, although those that associated with him on the beach, at work or on the rugby field would never have thought that. Bill found that alcohol helped overcome his innate shyness, so he drank, and when he did, mayhem often ensued.

Bill arrived in Jersey via London after he had crewed on a yacht named the *Lady Diana* on passage from South Africa to Britain. How he came to be onboard the yacht was typical of Bill's approach to life. Working as a lifeguard on the beach in a town called Amanzimtoti, just south of Durban, Bill got fired because of an incident in a hotel one evening. The hotel was a sort of wild west replica, according to Ida, complete with winding staircase and chandelier. After a few too many drinks Bill decided to slide down the balustrade of the staircase and then leaped up and began to swing on the chandelier. Unfortunately, he pulled it out of the ceiling and it, and Bill, crashed to the floor. Out of a job and deciding to chance his luck elsewhere, Bill hitched a ride on the *Lady Diana* to Cape Town and on to England.

Bill worked at the Watersplash for a couple of seasons and started courting Ida, whom he had met through Ida's brother. A carpenter by trade, Bill was gifted with his hands and soon got work. He also started playing rugby with the Jersey Rugby Club and was a regular on the beach at St Ouen's and knew all the Aussies. He, and occasionally Ida, would drink with the beach guards in the various watering holes in Jersey.

Back to the beach. Pat McGarry by now had established a firm connection with the Surf Lifesaving Association of Australia and corresponded regularly with that body. Pat was also active in involving the Jersey Lifeguard Club in events away from Jersey. A team, headed by Jim Wilson, attended the 1959 British Surf Lifesaving Championships in Cornwall and ten of the Club's members took part in an event held in Biarritz, France in the same year. Whether Jim Wilson went with them is not known.

On 30 August that year an international surf carnival was held on St Brelade's between teams from Australia, Jersey and South Africa. The last team would undoubtedly have been drawn from the ranks of the South African Watersplash employees whilst the Australian team might have had some 'ring ins' (Jersey 'beans') although other Australian lifesavers from mainland Britain may have been co-opted. In any event a huge crowd watched the carnival held in calm seas.

The scene was set for a much bigger Australian presence in Jersey in 1960. The pioneers had done their job, particularly Jim Wilson, and the Jersey beach guard service was up and running.

3 1960 - The Sacking

'So, we got an official letter addressed to me as the senior lifeguard, signed by Pat McGarry, the Secretary of the Jersey Lifeguard Club, advising us that we were dismissed.'

Duncan Page, Senior Beach guard in 1960,
describing the sacking of the beach guards in August 1960

In **1960 the Expired** Air Resuscitation (EAR) technique, also known as mouth-to-mouth or mouth-to-nose resuscitation, became standard in surf lifesaving. This method was adopted to overcome the weaknesses in previous techniques. The victim was placed prone on their back and the head tilted back (maximum head tilt), the mouth and throat checked for obstructions and then the resuscitator commenced breathing air into the victim's mouth or nose. A plastic S-shaped tube, if available, could be inserted down the victim's throat if required to ensure any obstruction was by-passed. In addition, cardiopulmonary resuscitation (chest compressions) was introduced to pump blood throughout the body.

1960 also saw some other significant events occur on planet Earth. Technological advances were at the forefront. The American Garry Powers in his U-2 spy plane was shot down over the Soviet Union, creating a massive political storm and heightening Cold War tensions between the USSR and the West. Earlier that year, France became the fourth member of the nuclear club by successfully testing its first Atomic bomb in the Sahara Desert.

On a lighter note, *The Flintstones*, that modern Stone Age family animated comedy TV show, made its debut on American TV.

In Jersey, another comedy, this one a comedy of errors (although it didn't appear that way to six Jersey beach guards), was about to occur.

With the success of 1958 and 1959 fresh in his mind and an increasing groundswell of public opinion behind the beach guard concept, Pat McGarry from the Jersey Lifeguard Club had a significant victory. He had managed to convince the States of Jersey government to substantially increase their funding commitment to employ professional beach guards. As a result, there was enough money to pay for six positions, three times the number of 1959. The Jersey Lifeguard Club set about advertising worldwide for beach guards. In Australia Jim Wilson, who for unknown reasons had elected not to return to Jersey for the forthcoming summer, had the job of selecting the candidates.

Two young men from North Cronulla surf club on the southern beaches of Sydney, twenty-year-old Ken Woods and twenty-five-year-old Duncan Page, saw an advertisement in the *Daily Telegraph*, a Sydney newspaper, and decided to apply. They both held Instructor's Certificates and felt they were well qualified for the job. They were aware of the Expired Air Resuscitation method but weren't yet trained in it.

Ken recalls: 'Duncan had a golf driving range at Beverley Park [a suburb of Sydney] at the time and we were surfing mates, members of North Cronulla surf club. I was a wool classer and we decided that Jersey wouldn't be a bad place to go. Duncan's dad was an Englishman and he thought it would be good for Duncan to go over there too. We wrote a letter to the Jersey lifeguards and we received a reply asking us to go and see a guy called Jim Wilson at Manly. We were interviewed by Jim and we got the job'.

Two other twenty-one-year-old surf lifesavers, John Yabsley and Bob Harris, members of the Cronulla surf club, applied as well and were selected by Jim Wilson. John and Bob knew Ken and Duncan slightly, but they weren't close mates. The four made their preparations to travel to Jersey. Both Ken and Duncan owned surf boards, the new craze on the beach. Ken's description of them reflects the trend towards shorter boards at the beginning of the 1960s. 'I had a foam board about ten-foot long. Duncan's board was made of balsa with no stringers.' Both boards went with them to Jersey.

Ken Woods and the slightly older Duncan Page had broadly similar backgrounds as teenagers. Both loved the bush, and both worked in the outback. And both had had their share of adventure during that period.

Duncan Page was always interested in horses. He attended Hurlstone Agricultural School in south-west Sydney as a kid and, like many others, left school in 1948 at the age of fourteen. He describes himself as a little fat kid back then. That was to change markedly. He got a job in Sydney working as a saddler for Davidson & Smith Saddlery.

But the lure of the bush called, and he decided to go and work in the NSW country. He got a job at an isolated place named Terry Hie Hie as a jackaroo at a sheep and cattle station called Myall Plains. The station was south of Moree in north-west NSW, about three hundred and seventy-five miles (six hundred kilometres) from Sydney. 'The old boss started the station years before', recollects Duncan, 'he was the first white man in the district. He got up there by Cobb and Co coach'.

Duncan was a keen shooter, one who was determined to go to great lengths to get the rifle he wanted. Duncan says, 'I had gone to America on a Dutch ship called the *Oranje* working as a bell boy [the equivalent of a bell hop] just to buy a rifle. I was fifteen at the time. You couldn't get new firearms in Australia until about 1950 and I wanted a particular rifle which was a .22 Marlin 39A starling rifle. But when I got to America they were the most expensive rifle you could buy so I finished up buying a Mossberg repeater which I still have. I've always been a rider and a shooter – I've been riding horses since the age of about ten. Blakehurst [a southern suburb of Sydney] where I lived in those days was semi-rural when I was a kid'.

Being a jackaroo didn't pay much. He got two pounds ten shillings a week in wages, but he loved the job. Things were a lot different in those days; people in the country were firm believers in the old ways and they didn't mind travelling long distances.

Duncan remembers going up to a station near Nyngan (two hundred and eighty miles or four hundred and fifty kilometres from Moree) to pick up a horse. The station owner politely asked Duncan 'Would you like to stay for dinner?' Duncan accepted eagerly. It was the middle of summer and Duncan recalls, 'It was stinking hot ….. and I went to dinner wearing a pair of shorts, thongs and a tee shirt. The owners of the property were sitting there in the dining room in collars and ties. They always dressed for dinner'.

Ken Woods almost didn't make it to the bush, let alone Jersey. At the age of fifteen, a month after he left high school in Bexley, a southern suburb of Sydney, he went with his family on a holiday to the NSW central coast town of Long Jetty. It was there a terrible thing happened. Ken, a slightly pained expression on his face, recalls the incident. 'I was doing somersaults off a jetty, lairising, and I landed on my head in shallow water and I broke my neck quite severely'.

Ken was rushed to St George Hospital in Sydney and he was tested to see whether his spinal cord was damaged. He describes it as a terrifying experience. The medical staff took a lot of care to get him onto the bed at the hospital. Following accepted practice, they put a brace around his neck and placed a fifteen-pound headband on his forehead. However, this didn't work, so they shaved Ken's hair off and they drilled several holes into his skull, then put a calliper over the top of his head onto a pulley. A forty-two-pound weight was attached to the calliper to pull his head back and to align his spine. He says his feet were tied to the bottom of the bed.

Although the doctors determined that he had no paralysis, Ken was forced to lay still for three months as a precaution to stabilise his spine. He describes it as, not surprisingly, 'extremely uncomfortable'.

Despite his seemingly dire situation Ken was determined not to let it get him down or to become dependent on others. 'During the first week I was there', he says, 'a nurse would feed me'. Ken then came up with an ingenious way to help himself. 'A bit later, when I had been cleared of being paralysed, I rigged up a way to see to feed myself. Because my head was so far back I got a glass reading screen on the pole over my head and put a mirror on the screen. I could focus onto my dinner using the mirror and I could feed myself'.

For a young person of his age Ken's stoicism was astounding. His head was flat on the bed and he had lead pillows around his head to keep it from moving. Ken remembers that the nurses could not turn him over at all but amazingly he didn't suffer from pressure sores. He says, 'I think they must have wiped under my back every now and then'.

After three months of lying still Ken was allowed to move but the hospital staff put a plaster cast on his torso as a precaution. It started just below his face and finished down over his hips. He was let out of hospital then, very pleased to be able to walk.

After two months the neck to hip plaster was removed, to be replaced by a felt collar around his neck for another two months. Then that was finally removed, and Ken was back to normal, mostly. 'Even now occasionally if I turn my head it becomes uncomfortable', states Ken. He was sixteen and ready for the next challenge.

It was then that Ken made his choice of career. 'I had an affinity with the bush and thought wool classing would be good.' He got a job with a company called Bridgeland and Brown in Sydney while he completed a technical education course of study. Ken went to tech at night for two years and then six months full time to complete his training. Then he went bush in late 1955.

Ken recalls, 'I had a good run of sheds [where the sheep were shorn] from around Nyngan out to the Darling River [in western NSW] and some in south west Queensland around [a town called] Surat. Then I also had a run in Tasmania; I went there three years in a row in the Fingal Valley south-east of Launceston near [the towns of] St Mary's and Avoca. The wool classer works with the shearing team to help with the picking up and the wool pressing. The fleece is thrown onto a table, someone takes the dags [dried faeces] off the wool and the wool classer goes around and then grades the wool according to its style and size. Then it's pressed and goes to the silo'.

Wool classers earned pretty good money in those days. When Ken was working out west of Nyngan (western NSW) in 1957–58 he was earning thirty-six pounds a week after tax and board and lodging were taken out. He was also paid travel expenses from Sydney to whatever shed he was working in. There were other perks as well. When he journeyed the couple of hundred miles from Nyngan out to the Darling River he got to sit in the front of the truck whilst the others had to sit in the back. He claims he had the best bed, too. Like Duncan Page he experienced the old school formality, particularly in some places in Tasmania. 'I'd wear a collar and tie to sit down for dinner every night', he laughs.

In between sheds back at home he spent a lot of time surfing at Cronulla beach. Ken says: 'I had enough money to go to England by the time I was eighteen'. However, that wasn't to happen for a few more years.

The 1960 quartet of Aussies left Sydney on 18 April, the day before Ken's twenty first birthday. They boarded the Italian owned T.S.S. (short for Turbine Steamship) *Fairsky* and settled into their four-berth 'A' deck cabin for which they each had paid the substantial amount of six hundred pounds (the equivalent of nearly seventeen thousand dollars today). The *Fairsky* was one of several ships used on the England – Australia migrant passenger route. The ship was a twelve thousand ton converted World War II aircraft carrier which had been extensively remodelled and modernised for its passenger role. It had air conditioning, as well as a large area for entertainment called the Lido. Deck games were the norm and a swimming pool provided relief from the heat. Dinner dances and variety shows abounded. Despite the distractions Ken Woods and Duncan Page trained hard. They tied their legs together with some tubing and swam laps in the swimming pool for about half an hour at a time to maintain their swimming fitness levels.

Unsurprisingly, the Aussie surf lifesavers had a good time during the slightly over five-week voyage which took them from Sydney north to Brisbane, then Singapore, Ceylon (now Sri Lanka), through the Suez Canal to Aden, Naples, and finally Southampton. Ken and Duncan didn't really socialise too much with the Cronulla surf club boys onboard, there were too many other distractions. Ken says: 'There were about two thousand people on board the ship with about eight girls to every guy. The girls bought us drinks. Duncan didn't drink, but I did. We were traveling with some guys who were going to England to play rugby league and some were also going to Wimbledon to play tennis'. The pair made friends with them.

Most times the pair went ashore they escorted female passengers. Ken recounts: 'The girls would say "You look after us when we go ashore, and we will buy the drinks". The girls were quite wealthy. No-one travelled by plane in those days because of the cost. Not much romance was involved on the trip – just great girls'. Maybe the last statement was true, maybe not. Ken had a grin on his face when he said this.

In Egypt the group went to see the Pyramids and had a run in with authority which almost proved disastrous. 'We almost got shot on the Sphinx by a guard because we climbed up on it without permission', Ken says.

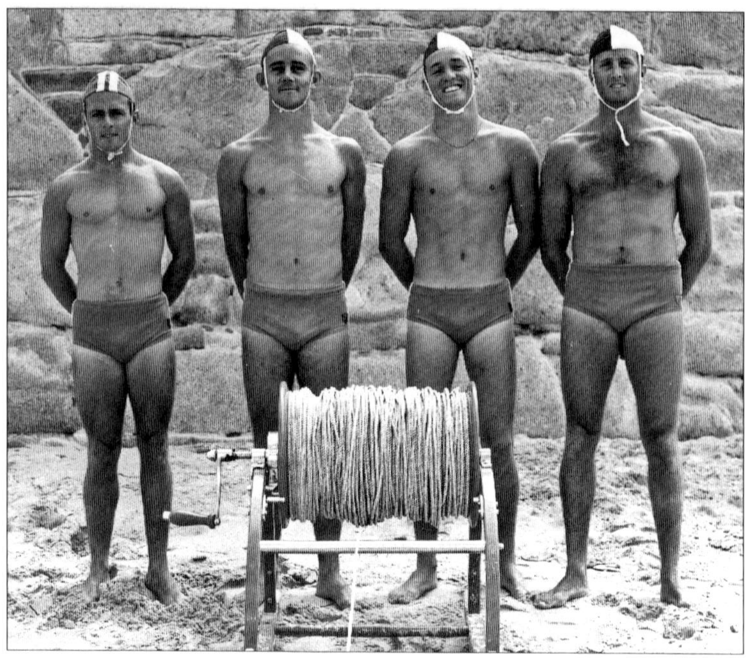

Full-time professional beach guards introduced by the States of Jersey in 1960. Of the six, four were from Australia.
From left to right: Ken Woods, Bob Harris, John Yabsley, Duncan Page.

Photo courtesy of the Jersey Evening Post

Duncan Page recalls another scary incident. 'Bob Harris almost didn't make it to Jersey. He was standing on the rail of the ship at the stern one night after having a few to drink. I grabbed him and pulled him back on board. If he would have fallen over, we would never have found him.' Undoubtedly true. Although ships had an emergency procedure involving a manoeuvre designed to bring the ship back to the point where the person went overboard, the exercise was made more difficult at night because of reduced visibility. Even though Bob was a good swimmer, the amount of alcohol he had consumed may have diminished this advantage and indeed he might have drowned.

The *Fairsky* berthed in Southampton in late May 1960 and the group of lifesavers and rugby league and tennis players travelled by train to Wimbledon outside London. They were all struck by how green and lush the countryside was, particularly Duncan and Ken who were used to the dry conditions back home in the bush. Says Ken: 'We understood what green was as compared to the Australian outback'.

The Aussie tennis players had arranged some accommodation in Wimbledon because they were aiming to enter the pre-Wimbledon tournament in an attempt to qualify for the big one. However, they arrived two weeks after the first tournament finished and thus missed it. Bad planning on their part! Despite this, they generously offered to share the accommodation with the lifesavers for a few days until they left for Jersey. After a bit of sightseeing and a scratch touch footie game in Hyde Park with their new mates the four lifesavers took a train back to Southampton and then a ferry to Jersey.

As the ferry passed La Corbière lighthouse on the south-west tip of Jersey the young Australians gazed at the green countryside and the brown Jersey cows grazing in the fields. They began to feel excited about their impending responsibilities of ensuring the safety of the beachgoers on the island.

When they disembarked on the wharf at St Helier the four were greeted warmly by Pat McGarry and another member of the Jersey Lifeguard Club called Dennis Langton who was one of two assigned to administer the beach guards. McGarry and Langton took them to their lodgings, the Pembroke Hotel in the village of Grouville, just over three miles (five kilometres) east of St Helier. The hotel was located on the south-east coast of Jersey, well away from the beaches they were to patrol, next to the Royal Jersey golf links. Why this rather out of the way place was chosen is not known. Ken remembers that the weekly tariff was six pounds which included breakfast and an evening meal, an amount totalling almost half of their weekly pay.

The hotel featured in a rather salacious incident a few months after the Aussies arrived. Duncan says: 'There was an attempted murder at the Pembroke Hotel one night. It was about the time that [Australians] Kel Nagle had won the British Open [golf championship – in early July 1960] and Jack Brabham [who was to become the World Motor Racing Champion] was doing well. I had gone into the lounge room which was alongside the kitchen. There were big batwing swinging doors from the kitchen into the dining area. I went in there to watch the TV. Suddenly I heard this unholy commotion in the kitchen – there was shouting and screaming going on. So, I walked over to the doors and looked through the port holes into the kitchen. There was a guy with a carving knife and the barmaid was up against the wall trying to fend him off with a bar stool. He was trying to stab her with it and she was swinging the bar stool at him. I walked in and said, "What's going on?" With that the fellow dropped the knife and ran out the back of the kitchen and disappeared onto the golf course'.

Duncan recalls that the hotel owner phoned the police and four or five policemen came out to the hotel. They looked everywhere on the golf course for the fellow – this was about nine o'clock at night, but it was still light as it was summer. However, they couldn't find him.

Everything then quietened down, and Duncan decided to retire for the night. 'Out the back of the hotel', he says, 'there were a series of small cabins. I had a cabin and the barmaid had the cabin next door. So, I went to bed. About two o'clock in the morning and there was a commotion in the cabin next door – the fellow had come back and was banging with his fist on the door. However, what he didn't realise was that the police were still there having a drink with the owner. So, the cops just opened the door of the hotel, walked out and arrested the guy and that was the end of that. I can't recall whether he was an employee at the hotel or the boyfriend of the barmaid'.

Ken adds: 'The pub was a den of iniquity. The wife of the owner was having an affair with somebody and he [the owner] was having an affair with somebody else. The guy the police arrested may have even been the cook'. So much for the quiet life in the 'burbs of Jersey!

The four Australians were to be joined on patrol at St Ouen's and St Brelade's by two other beach guards. One of them was the Englishman Bill Turton, now the Chief Instructor of the Jersey Lifeguard Club. Jim Wilson had told the Aussies that, based on his experience with him in 1959, Bill Turton was a good guy, and that proved to be the case. The other beach guard was a South African, not from the Watersplash but from Durban, noted for its sub-tropical climate and good surf beaches. Twenty-eight-year-old Charles 'Chucky' Salzman was well known to some of the Watersplash guys, Cliff Honeysett in particular.

On St Ouen's beach, with Chucky Salzman not yet in Jersey, the others were issued with woollen costumes, patrol caps (identical to those used on patrol on Australian beaches) and tracksuits. They were also given the use of two old Robson surf skis weighing about 60 pounds (27 kilograms) that had come from Australia which Ken Woods describes as 'leaky'. After that a sub-committee of the Jersey Lifeguard Club which had been given responsibility for the day-to-day dealings with the beach guards, tasked them to do a trial swim at St Ouen's beach using a reel and belt provided by the club.

When one of the five beach guards picked up the belt and tried to pull the quick release pin out he found it was very rusty and hard to shift. It obviously hadn't been maintained during the winter months. Ken Woods asserts that none of the lifesaving gear was well maintained. For the trial they paid out about two hundred yards of line and tied a ribbon round the line at that point. The line was rewound onto the reel then each of them swam in the belt out into the water until the ribbon was revealed. Each in turn pulled the pin and swam back in and the next one in line did the swim. That constituted their proficiency test.

Duncan recalls: 'When you put your head in the water at that time of year it was so cold your face ached something fierce. The water temperature was about sixteen degrees Centigrade'. Curiously, the sub-committee members didn't ask the beach guards to demonstrate their proficiency in resuscitation. Says Duncan, 'We used the old Holger Nielsen resuscitation techniques back in 1960. We weren't examined in our resuscitation techniques during our proficiency, but we did have Instructor Certificates, so we knew what we were doing'.

Presumably Charles Salzman did his proficiency test when he arrived in Jersey soon after.

Their arrival had aroused interest from the press, and a reporter named Mike Rumfitt from the *Jersey Evening Post* went to St Ouen's the day after the proficiency test to interview the Australian beach guards. The *Jersey Evening Post* was first published in 1890 and was the acknowledged source of local news on the island. Mike Rumfitt's newspaper article gave a comprehensive account of each beach guard's experience and qualifications and details of where they would patrol.

Mike Rumfitt must have had access to Charles Salzman's application to the Jersey Lifeguard Club because he stated Salzman 'has nine years' experience as a professional beach guard with the Durban Corporation. He has been commended for bravery and has knowledge which covers beach organisation and crowd control. He holds the bronzed medallion of the R.L.S.S. [the Royal Life Saving Society] and a St John Ambulance certificate. His practical experience of various resuscitation methods includes the revolutionary mouth-to-mouth system'.

Ken says that Charles Salzman was a quiet sort of bloke of average height who was very fit. 'He could swim all day', recalls Ken, 'but he wasn't all that fast in the water. He was a smoker, but so were a lot of other people then'. Notably, surfing and surf lifesaving contests were sponsored by major tobacco companies throughout the 1960s and into the 1970s.

Notwithstanding Salzman's age and qualifications, Duncan Page was appointed senior beach guard, most likely for two reasons. Duncan held an Instructor's Certificate and he was also a renowned international athlete. More on this later.

Once the Australians got to know Chucky Salzman, they probed him on some of the incidents that he had experienced in Durban as a lifeguard. They were stunned to hear that he had taken part in over nine hundred rescues on the beaches in and around Durban. Chucky also told them a few stories, one of which is somewhat reminiscent of the 2015 brush with death that the Australian surfer Mick Fanning, three times world surfing champion, had in Jeffries Bay, South Africa. Salzman was involved in a training exercise with a few lifeguards on one of the beaches along the Durban coast in the mid to late 1950s. One of his colleagues swam about two hundred yards out into the surf to act as patient and Chucky was to rescue him using the belt. Just as Chucky got to the patient a Great White shark emerged out of nowhere and took the man before vanishing beneath the waves, leaving Chucky unscathed. Salzman's reaction to this was not recorded. It certainly didn't deter him from continuing as a lifeguard.

One rescue effected by Salzman stuck in the minds of the Australians. He was working at one of the beaches in Durban which had an exposed reef about two hundred and fifty yards off the shore. On this particular day a yacht that was sailing by somehow struck the reef. The yacht, which had two men onboard, was being battered by the waves crashing onto the reef so Chucky donned the belt and swam out to rescue them. He got the first man without any problem and as they were being towed back in to the beach the guy said to Chucky, 'You'll never have to work again, I'll look after you – you are magnificent, saving my life'.

Chucky went out and got the second guy who said much the same thing on the way in. However, once the pair were on solid ground they just took off and Chucky never heard from them again. He never did get 'looked after' and in 1960 he found himself in Jersey. Such is life.

The *Jersey Evening Post* article also reported that the States government had voted the previous year (1959) to appropriate to the Jersey Lifeguard Club almost three thousand pounds. The club was to administer the weekly payment of eleven pounds ten shillings (the average wage in Great Britain at the time) to each of the beach guards who were to be employed for sixteen weeks (June to September). That amounts to just over eleven hundred pounds, so the Club had left over around eighteen hundred pounds from which the purchase of equipment and the payment of the initial advertising had to be deducted. This would have left quite a substantial amount of money that year for use by the Jersey Lifeguard Club itself. That money was to come in handy later in 1960.

During the day the beach guards had access to an old ex-Army jeep which belonged to the Jersey Lifeguard Club. It was equipped with a radio that connected to a three-way radio in the hut used by club members, just near the El Tico cafe. The jeep was used to provide transport up and down the beach or to other beaches in the case of an emergency. In an interview for the *Jersey Evening Post* Duncan Page commented: 'The radio scheme is the most modern I've come across. It will be of terrific benefit in a bay [St Ouen's] of this size'. Duncan went on to say: 'In Australia a bay of similar size would have three or four lifesaving clubs operating on it'. Like those before them, the beach guards of 1960 obviously thought St Ouen's was going to present a challenge.

Soon after they arrived in Jersey the Australians bought a little blue Ford Thames panel van from the Ford dealer in St Helier. This became their means of transport between the two beaches, their accommodation and for after work excursions.

Surf lifesaving and beach guards were really a novelty in Jersey in those early days. Many people were curious about the beach guards and wanted to quiz them about life in Australia and how they went about rescuing people. The lads became friendly with quite a few locals as a result. In those days the shops closed in Jersey on Thursday afternoons and Sundays, so people would come and pick the Aussies up and take them out on excursions after they had finished work on the beach.

Ken Woods remembers one of them, a guy called Charlie Mayne who had a jeweller's shop in St Helier and who owned a Lotus Elite sports car. Other fellows had Aston Martins and similarly nice cars. Ken recalls: 'They were very friendly towards us – we had a very good relationship with all the local fellows. One of the guys used to take us to Le Moulin de Lecq Hotel in the parish of St Ouen. The hotel had the cog wheels of a [twenty-one-foot diameter, eighteen ton] water wheel in the bar and was built in about the 14th century [parts of it were built in the 12th century]. It was a great spot for a drink. That guy was a great friend of many of the Manchester United football team who got killed in the plane crash in Munich in 1958. He used to take them to that hotel'.

Four of the six beach guards worked the weekdays at St Ouen's with the other two at St Brelade's. That was the official working roster – unofficially they were on the beach just about all the weekend as well, apart from some time off for meeting the locals. The volunteers from the Jersey Lifeguard Club patrolled at weekends but, recalls Ken Woods, as far as rescues went on the weekends it was the first one to the person in distress; no one had priority.

The beach guards were not provided with any means of shelter at either beach. The club had a little wooden hut alongside El Tico but the beach guards based there were ordered to stand patrol on the sea wall. At St Brelade's the other two beach guards were based in an open area below what was termed the Sabrina steps, named after the Sabrina Hotel that stood on the promenade inland from the sea wall.

On each of the beaches there was a patrolled area with the red and yellow flags as one would see on any beach in Australia. There were also signs saying *Bathe Between the Flags* but because the holidaymakers weren't used to the beach and the surf many took no notice. Most of the patrol work on the beach was preventative, getting the uneducated to stay between the flags and out of trouble. At the height of the summer season there were usually several hundred tourists on the beach at St Ouen's and slightly more at St Brelade's.

But the holidaymakers weren't the only source of problems for the beach guards. Belly board (plywood planks five or so feet long and slightly turned up at the nose) riding had long been popular in Jersey, particularly at St Ouen's, the best surfing beach. In addition, surfboard riding was starting to catch on; the Jersey Surfboard Club had been formed in 1959. The surf boards were monsters in those days, weighing fifty to sixty pounds (twenty-three to twenty-seven kilos) and hollow, therefore susceptible to filling with water. Leg ropes weren't yet invented so when the board rider fell off, a regular occurrence, the board would be pushed into shore sideways by the waves and collect anything and anyone in its path.

With uneducated holidaymakers plunging into the water anywhere they felt like it, and belly boards as well as surfboards dotted haphazardly through the waves, injuries were bound to happen. Consequently, the States of Jersey government introduced laws limiting surfing areas. Despite this, the beach guards still faced the problem of the odd errant surfboard scything its way through the surf area between the flags.

The surfboards owned by the beach guards were also a handy means of rescuing people. The skis were old and too heavy to easily carry into the water. Similarly, unless the surf belt, line and reel needed to be used because of multiple rescues, the surfboard was preferred.

The beach guards would often go out for a wave after work if the surf was good. Ken says: 'If we were out having a surf the locals would call out to us "Come in, come in, you'll drown". We quite often surfed until ten o'clock at night if the surf was good. It was still light until then. The locals would come and stand on the sea wall and watch us'.

The Cronulla boys John Yabsley and Bob Harris liked to have a good time socially and were more the party animals than Ken Woods and the teetotaller Duncan Page. The latter two had a few casual girlfriends in Jersey and they'd go to their place for dinner or go out with them occasionally. None of them were very happy that the Pembroke Hotel was so far away from the action, which made them feel rather isolated (despite having transport).

Ken and Duncan were keen on exercise. They regularly ran around the Royal Jersey golf course near the Pembroke Hotel, or played touch football there and also on the beach at St Ouen's. The limited bathing facilities at the Pembroke Hotel were an issue. Duncan says, 'There was only one bath tub and there was only enough hot water for one bath. So, the first fella that got in got the hot water'.

The pair also got on very well with the South Africans at the Watersplash. Duncan recollects: 'When it was quiet on the beach we would go for a walk up to the Watersplash and talk to the lifeguards up there or just sit around and play cards. It was only about five hundred yards from the lifeguard hut to the Watersplash. Because we had a lot in common with the South African lifeguards up there we chatted about lifesaving. We even had an international meet with them, a surf meet, on a very small scale – South Africa vs Australia. Something like a surf race and a beach sprint'.

The beach guards became aware that a few cracks were starting to appear in the relationship with the Jersey Lifeguard Club hierarchy, particularly with the Club Captain Dennis Langton. According to senior beach guard Duncan Page, Dennis was a bit of a stickler for the rules. 'He wanted us to stand on the sea wall with our hands behind our backs and look out at the water with patrol caps on all the time', states Duncan. He also took issue with the headwear the beach guards were wearing instead of their patrol caps. Says Duncan, 'We wore straw hats to keep the sun off our faces and heads. Chucky Salzman always wore a Foreign Legion cap to protect his neck'. Not surprising, with no shelter available to the beach guards.

Several other incidents occurred during the period leading up to the end of July 1960. One involved a plane testing its engines. The Jersey airport was located just over a mile (two kilometres) to the east of St Ouen's beach. On a regular basis planes would take off and fly up and down the beach to test their engines. They would fly up the beach on one motor then turn around and fly back on the other motor. When they got just about got over El Tico the pilots would start both motors up and land the plane at the airport.

Duncan Page recalls that one day an official from the Jersey Lifeguard Club came running up to him. Overhead was a plane flying on one engine. The official ordered Duncan to 'get in the jeep'. He obeyed, and the man jumped in the other side. The official said, 'Follow that plane, it's in trouble'. Duncan replied, 'No, they're just testing the engines', but the official was adamant. Duncan drove the jeep up to the northern end of the beach, following the plane which continued to fly on. With typical Aussie humour Duncan, when they got to the end of the beach, said sarcastically, 'Do you want me to pull back on the wheel of the jeep and take off?' There was no answer. By this time the plane had disappeared out of sight. The pair drove back to El Tico in silence.

Strange as it may seem, there may have been a reason for this seemingly bizarre behaviour by the official. There is a record of correspondence in the late 1950s between the Jersey Lifeguard Club, the States of Jersey Harbours and Airport Committee and others regarding procedures to be followed in the event of an aircraft crashing in St Ouen's Bay. However, as Duncan recalls, there was no evidence that the aircraft in question was showing any signs of being in trouble.

A second incident sometime later appeared equally bizarre. There was a big sea running onto the Jersey western coast and St Ouen's beach was getting pounded. At the northern end of the beach off the area known as L'Etacq, a small freighter about two hundred feet long was trying to forge past the headland and was making heavy weather of it.

Duncan Page was again ordered by the same official to 'drive out to the point'. Duncan with the official drove north in the jeep which had a surf reel in the back. Duncan says the official gave him an order, 'Take a line out to the freighter'. Duncan, naturally taken aback at this bizarre request, queried, 'What?' The official repeated his statement to Duncan, 'Take a line out'. By this time Duncan had had enough and says his retort was scathing: 'I know what you want. You want me to take the line out and hook it onto the freighter and put the line in my teeth and swim back to the beach'. Duncan says the official didn't respond.

Then there was an incident at St Brelade's where Duncan Page was on duty on his own. He can't remember why the other rostered beach guard wasn't there. It was late in the afternoon and a lady friend came down to the beach to pick him up at about 5:45 p.m. The daughter of a senior officer in the British Army, the lady friend ranked high in the island's social strata. It was a dull, overcast afternoon and she urged Duncan to finish early, saying, 'Let's go'. He replied, 'No, I have to wait until six o'clock'. Duncan resolutely maintains that at the proper time he and his lady friend packed up the lifesaving gear and put it into the storage areas in the nearby Martello Tower. They left the beach at about five minutes after six and drove to the Pembroke Hotel.

After they left St Brelade's Dennis Langton, who must have turned up soon after, was involved in a rescue of a swimmer in difficulty. Dennis subsequently asserted that the rescue had been made at 5:45 p.m. and that the beach guards weren't patrolling the beach. In response, Duncan says he told Langton that he had a witness of impeccable reputation who would refute Langton's allegation. Duncan thought the matter had been laid to rest. But these strange behaviours and erroneous claims were nothing compared to what was to happen next.

On Saturday 30 July 1960, whilst patrolling on St Ouen's beach Duncan Page was handed a letter typed under the official Jersey Lifeguard Club letterhead, the first sentence of which stated:

> 'I am directed by the Management Committee of the Jersey Lifeguard Club to inform you that as you are no doubt aware, there has been increasing concern for the manner in which the Professional Life Guards Scheme has been operated'.

The letter cited a lack of cooperation, failure to carry out instructions, lateness and refusal to patrol as contributing factors behind the need for the letter to be written. Then it dropped a bombshell by stating:

> 'In view of this [the reasons], and the fact that the Management Committee

consider it imperative that beach safety be maintained at the highest levels, it has now been decided that there is no alternative but to terminate your service …'

The letter was signed by the Jersey Lifeguard Club Secretary Pat McGarry. The management committee referred to in the letter was headed by the honorary life President Senator George Troy and included President E.R. Holmes, and Vice Presidents E.H. Le Brocq and Deputy B. Smale. Senator George Troy and Deputy B (Bobby) Smale were both elected members of the States of Jersey government.

Ken Woods and Duncan Page assert that the letter was written after the Jersey Lifeguard Club made a complaint about the beach guards to a senior political figure in the States government, but they didn't know which one. However, one doesn't have to look much further than Senator Troy and Deputy Smale, either of them would have had the political clout to authorise the sackings. Ken and Duncan also assert that prior to the letter was delivered the Jersey Lifeguard Club had provided no warning about any problems that had occurred.

The beach guards were gobsmacked. The six would be out of a job on completion of seven days' notice commencing Sunday 31 July. The Jersey Lifeguard Club's own Bill Turton immediately resigned his position of Chief Instructor in protest. Although devastated, to a man the beach guards were determined not to let the matter rest.

Says Duncan Page, 'It was all about the rather rigid form of discipline that they expected us to maintain on the beach. In comparison, back in those days any surf lifesaving club in Australia would allow people to wear zinc on their nose and protective clothing against the elements'. There was obviously a complete disconnect between the use of common sense and the slavish adherence to robotic 'he-man' behaviour expected by the club's hierarchy.

But what of the allegations of failure to carry out instructions, lateness and refusal to patrol? Was there any truth in these?

Duncan Page says that part of the complaint was about where they were patrolling at St Ouen's. The length of the beach meant there was a very large area to patrol for four beach guards, notwithstanding the Watersplash lifeguards, who weren't employed by the government. The beach guards couldn't just stand on the sea wall in one spot and look out to sea as Dennis Langton naively expected. The beach guards had to be checking everywhere up and down the beach where people might be swimming. Duncan notes, 'There were no complaints about the fact that we were saving people'.

Another part of the grievance was the allegation that they hadn't been patrolling for the entire allotted hours, or they hadn't turned up at all. Duncan Page feels that this related to the claim that the beach guards had left St Brelade's beach early on the day of the rescue. He was incredulous – he had someone with an unimpeachable background to verify his story, but this had been ignored by the Jersey Lifeguard Club.

There was a third factor which came to light after the beach guards expressed their astonishment at their sacking. A few weeks before, the ex-Army jeep had been left on St Ouen's beach overnight. The incoming tide had submerged the jeep and had caused extensive water damage. The beach guards were blamed by the Jersey Lifeguard Club but Ken Woods and Duncan Page state unequivocally that the person who left the jeep on the beach was Dennis Langford.

The situation was essentially a 'I say – you say' standoff, except that the beach guards were the little guys in the fight. The Jersey Lifeguard Club had backing from on high and the beach guards didn't. Things were not looking good.

News of the sacking travelled quickly. Michael Rumfitt of the *Jersey Evening Post* soon got to hear about it and ran a story on 2 August which generated a storm of public protest. The *Sun* newspaper, a well-known British tabloid carried the news, as did the *News Chronicle*, another British daily. Australian and South African newspapers picked up the story and sought information from their London agencies and correspondents.

The beach guards had gained fame worldwide, but for all the wrong reasons.

Desperate to salvage something out of the mess, the six beach guards tried to press the Jersey Lifeguard Club to pay them for the balance of their contract, about eight weeks in wages. They were informed that, under the rules pertaining to payment of lump sums, the amount for each of them was under the limit and therefore ineligible to claim through the courts. Ken Woods and Duncan Page went to see a solicitor who confirmed this. The lawyer added that if the beach guards' individual claims were aggregated the total amount of money sought was above the limit. Consequently, Ken and Duncan advised the Jersey Lifeguard Club that the beach guards were intending to take legal action as a collective body. This was publicised on the front page of the *Jersey Evening Post* on 3 August.

The Management Committee of the Jersey Lifeguard Club, realising that perhaps they weren't on ground as firm as they had previously believed, then launched a public attack on the beach guards by writing a letter to the *Jersey Evening Post* which was published on 4 August. The letter, penned by the Vice Presidents E.H. Le Brocq and Deputy B. Smale, made a startling claim designed to refute the assertion that the beach guards were not consulted prior to the sacking. The letter stated that Bill Turton had 'sat on the Management committee and had an opportunity to put forward arguments from the professionals [the beach guards]'.

Michael Rumfitt sought a comment from Bill Turton and his response was published in the newspaper the next day. Bill stated: 'I couldn't help laughing when

I read that…..Whenever I told them how the professionals were feeling they got annoyed and asked me to leave the room while they discussed the matter privately'.

The snowball of public opinion in favour of the beach guards gathered size and momentum as the facts started to emerge. One source of support for the beach guards came from a most unexpected direction – the rank and file of the Jersey Lifeguard Club. The headline in the 5 August edition of the *Jersey Evening Post* said it all:

**'LIFE GUARD CLUB MEMBERS ORGANISE PETITION
AGAINST SACKING PROFESSIONALS'**

They were among two hundred local people around St Ouen's Bay who signed the petition. More were expected to sign when the petition was circulated at St Brelade's Bay. This was a serious indictment on the hierarchy of the Jersey Lifeguard Club from the rank and file members and had the immediate effect of bolstering the sagging morale of the beach guards. The *Jersey Evening Post* quoted one of the beach guards as saying: 'It [the petition] has done a lot to cheer us up to know that club members and many of the ordinary residents of the island are right behind us – even if the club officials are not'.

John Le Fondre, the proprietor of the El Tico café, was quoted in the paper as saying: 'The whole thing is very unfortunate. It is obvious to all that these boys know their job. There have been no fatalities'.

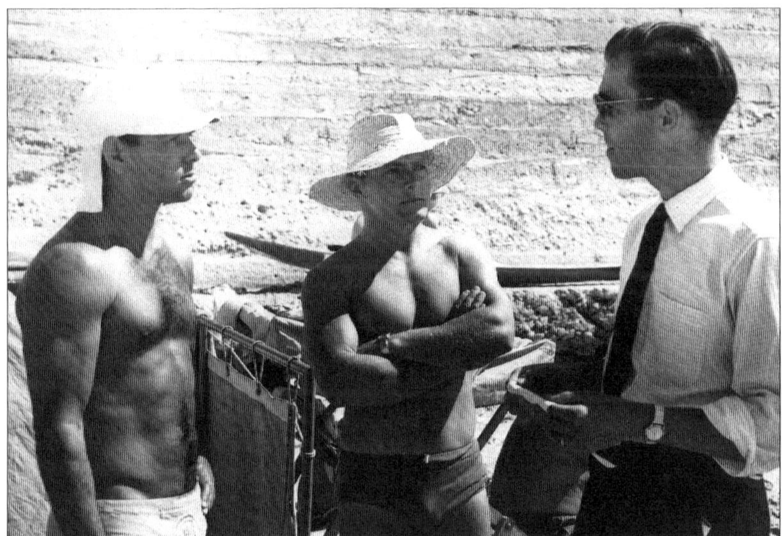

Charles Salzman (South Africa) and Ken Woods (Australia) with Mike Rumfitt (*Jersey Evening Post*). *(Photo courtesy of the* Jersey Evening Post)

Another business owner, Mr L.S. Grouvel of St Ouen village, made a telling comment to the paper: 'The club has done nothing to tell the public its real reasons for the dismissal. Until they tell us my support is with the professionals'.

In the same edition of the *Jersey Evening Post* were four Letters to the Editor, one from a man named R.P.J. Gately who gave his address as c/o Overseas Visitors' Club, London. All were in support of the beach guards.

The *Jersey Evening Post* reported that the completed petition would be presented to Senator Krichefski, president of the States of Jersey government's Harbours and Airport Committee. He would be asked to consider calling for a government enquiry to be held into the reasons behind the dismissals.

The Management Committee of the Jersey Lifeguard Club seemed determined to hold the line. They met to discuss finding replacements for the beach guards after several lifeguards on the British mainland, who had heard about the sackings via the press, had contacted them to offer their services.

Amid the furore the beach guards continued to patrol the beaches. The four working at St Ouen's, together with the South Africans working at the Watersplash, were involved in the rescue of five people, one of whom was hospitalised. It was their busiest day of the season. Their success in saving lives added fuel to the fierce debate.

The public outcry seemed to be influencing the management committee of the Jersey Life Guard Club because on 8 August they issued a statement via the *Jersey Evening Post* that an independent inquiry, by a person named Harry Potts who had the full confidence of both the club and the former beach guards, was being held into the sackings and a report would be provided to the management committee.

Presumably after the delivery of the report, on or just before Thursday 11 August Ken Woods and Duncan Page were finally invited to meet with Jersey Lifeguard Club Vice Presidents E.H. Le Brocq and Deputy B. Smale. Ken and Duncan were elated. At last those high up on the totem pole were willing to hear their side of the story. During the meeting Duncan told about his witness who would attest to him being on St Brelade's beach until after knock off time, and about who he believed was responsible for the jeep being left on the beach overnight.

According to the *Jersey Evening Post* report on Saturday 13 August, the Jersey Lifeguard Club Committee met on 11 August and voted in favour of a motion to reverse the earlier decision and to reinstate the beach guards to their positions. The beach guards were ecstatic and felt vindicated in their strong defence of their reputations and professionalism.

This must have been a most embarrassing back down for the Jersey Lifeguard Club Management Committee, and it was to have further consequences for the club. However, equally embarrassing was the fact that the Management Committee in the meantime had gone ahead and hired another team of six beach guards from the mainland applicants. This decision was to cost them financially, as they now had to pay for two sets of beach guards for another eight weeks!

The new beach guards duly arrived and the original six took them down to St Ouen's beach where there was a reasonably big surf running. What happened next is truly the stuff of comedy. Ken says: 'Well, the English guys took one look at the waves and said: "We're not going out there"'. They were still water lifeguards and had never been in the surf. Ken magnanimously adds: 'We held no animosity towards them, by the way'.

To add insult to injury, from about that day on it started to rain, and it rained, and it rained, and it just kept raining for the next month. Ken laughs: 'So everyone, we six lifeguards and the six British lifeguards all sat in the hut in El Tico. There was no one on the beach'. And no lifesaving work for any of the twelve to do.

Thus, the saga of the sackings ended as it had begun, farcically. But, most importantly, the beach guards were back working on the beaches of Jersey.

At the end of the season the six beach guards said their farewells. Ken Woods and Bill Turton stayed on in Jersey, Bill because he lived there. Duncan Page went to Rome to watch the 1960 Olympics and then went on to other adventures which will be described later. Charles Salzman went back to South Africa and Bob Harris and John Yabsley left also. The only one to return as a beach guard was Bob Harris, but that wouldn't be until 1962.

Ken Woods moved from the Pembroke hotel to a quaint twenty-seven room guesthouse called *Les Vineries* in the village of Maufant in the middle of the island. He worked for the couple who owned it and they treated him like a son. In the mornings he would collect vegetables from the garden for the meals. Amongst other odd jobs he waited on the tables for the guests. After doing the washing up he was free for the day. He would go down to St Ouen's beach for a surf or do his own thing. In the night time he took the guests out in a bus to party nights around the various pubs and clubs.

Ken stayed in Jersey over the winter of 1960-61 and into the following summer. He didn't associate with the 1961 beach guards at all. Instead he spent most of his free time with the South African lifeguards from the Watersplash. They used to do some work at the Watersplash holiday camp near St Ouen's beach, owned by Harry Swanson.

Ken says they used to dress up as clowns and do crazy diving to entertain the guests at the holiday camp. Obviously, Ken had forgotten about his earlier neck injury. Cliff Honeysett (one of the South African lifeguards) and Ken did the lights on the stage. Ken recalls: 'Frank Ifield the singer was there in those days doing the crooning. I remember one night this girl who was a very voluptuous singer and she wore a low-cut dress and we had to lower the microphone so that she could sing. We would try to drop the microphone down the front of her dress'.

Ken had a female friend who worked at the Watersplash. He described her as 'A showgirl, much taller than me. She went over to Paris after that and she said to me before she left, "Come with me" and I said "No". I had no money'. So that was the end of that relationship.

By the end of summer 1961 Ken decided it was time to go home. Before he left he gave his surfboard to a Jersey Surfboard Club member named Gordon Burgis. Gordon was to go on to become the British Surfing Champion in 1962 and represent Great Britain in the World Surfing Championships at Manly, Sydney, in 1963.

Although Ken wanted to go home, he was broke. But he found a solution. 'My father paid my fare home to Australia on the second trip of the *Oriana* [a forty-two-thousand-ton passenger ship]', he says, 'and I got off the ship with four and a half pence to my name. I came home steerage class'. This was a far cry from his voyage over to Britain on 'A' deck.

4 Consolidation

'Everyone was going overseas to experience our British heritage and to have a good time, to travel around and do some sightseeing.'

Extract from an interview with Mike Gray,
Australian beach guard during the 1960s

Pat McGarry, the Secretary of the Jersey Lifeguard Club, had seemingly positioned himself among the 'villains' by signing the dismissal letter at the end of July 1960. His personal view on the matter is not known, but what became apparent was that Pat was committed to the concept of professional lifeguards. Undaunted by the debacle of the sackings and the embarrassment of the reinstatement, not to mention the cost of employing double the number of beach guards, half of whom were incapable of rescuing anyone in trouble in the surf, Pat pressed on. He managed to convince the States of Jersey Tourist Department that the initiative needed to continue into 1961 and beyond. Pat wanted the best available, and he knew they had to come from Australia.

But because of the rancour between the Jersey Lifeguard Club Management Committee and the beach guards, Pat pushed for the administration of the professional lifeguards to be taken out of the hands of the club. He suggested that they be overseen directly by the Tourism Department. This idea was accepted.

Given the green light to proceed, Pat McGarry set about engaging with a man who from personal experience he knew to be reliable and trustworthy. That man was Jim Wilson, the surf lifesaver from North Steyne who had been on the Jersey beaches in 1958 and 1959. Jim would assume the title of Chief Beach Guard and receive a slightly higher salary than the other beach guards. Jim was tasked with assembling a team of six in addition to himself.

Jim Wilson picked five surf lifesavers – Michael Abbott from Manly, Bruce Douglas from North Bondi, and Ken Fawkner, David O'Brien and Michael Rodger, all from North Steyne. Jim recruited a sixth, but that person dropped out at the last minute. It was too late to find a replacement before the lifesavers left for London, so they sailed without a full complement.

As luck would have it Mike Abbott met a mate in a London pub. His name was Mike Gray, a member of the North Bondi surf club and a member of that club's senior R&R team. Gray, recently arrived in Britain with only twenty-five quid in his pocket, had been working as a lifeguard in a heated pool in the London suburb of Acton for a short period but wasn't too fussed about the job. Abbott told Gray about what he was going to do and where he was going to do it. He also mentioned that they were a man short. Mike Gray, up for adventure, was interested so he went to meet Jim Wilson at another pub. After a brief conversation Jim hired Mike Gray on the spot. This was the start of a three-year involvement with Jersey for Mike Gray and a series of friendships lasting a lifetime.

Mike Gray was born in 1939 and went to school at Scots College in Sydney. He left school in 1955 and got a job with the Ampol Petroleum Company as a trainee. Ampol in those days was the ninth biggest company in Australia. The company exposed him to the administrative side of the business, in accounts, credit and sales.

In 1961, when Mike was twenty-one, Australia suffered a credit squeeze. This came about because Harold Holt, the then Federal Government Treasurer (later as Prime Minister to mysteriously disappear in the surf in Victoria) decided to end controls on imports as a measure to curb inflation. Australia was riding high on the sheep's back and the economy was booming. Consequently, imports soared and so, perversely, did inflation. The economy stalled. This forced Holt to introduce a mini budget in late 1960 that, amongst other things, reduced tax deductions on borrowings by business and restricted bank credit. Ampol was among many companies that were impacted, and staff layoffs resulted.

Whilst Mike wasn't dismissed, two of his mates were. Coincidently, the three were contemplating travelling overseas. So that prompted Mike to resign as well. In his words: 'I thought well if they can just dismiss people as result of the credit squeeze then I won't have any loyalty to them. Up until then I felt extremely loyal'.

In March 1961 the trio travelled to England on the *Fairsky*, a five-week voyage. It cost Mike one hundred and sixty-eight pounds, a lot less than that paid by Ken Woods and his mates the year before. Mike and his friends obviously weren't accommodated on 'A' deck. Mike says: 'We were the back cargo for all the Poms looking to immigrate to Australia. There were a lot of young Australians on board'. During the cruise Mike met another two Aussies from Melbourne. One of them was a guy named Roger Kennedy who Mike was to meet again in Jersey in a few months. Mike recalls: 'Everyone was going overseas to experience our British heritage and to have a good time, to travel around and do some sightseeing'.

Jim Wilson's band of beach guard recruits started in Jersey in the first week of June 1961. However, after only six weeks Michael Rodger decided that the beach guard life in Jersey wasn't for him, so he quit. Jim asked the other beach guards if they knew anyone who could replace the departing Australian. Mike Gray remembered meeting Roger Kennedy on the *Fairsky*. Roger was a member of the Lorne (Victoria) surf club and Mike knew he was a good swimmer. Roger at the time was working for a stockbroker in London. When Jim offered him the job in Jersey Roger chucked his job in straight away and arrived in July. Roger was to stay on for five years.

The roster was similar to that used in 1960. Four beach guards worked at St Ouen's, two at St Brelade's and the other one was rostered off duty. Working hours were between ten in the morning and six in the evening. As head beach guard, Jim Wilson was provided with a green Hillman by the States of Jersey. He used to alternate between beaches. The ex-Army jeep had been repaired and painted yellow and red, the surf lifesaving colours. The beach guards used the jeep to get to the beaches each day. At the beginning of the 1962 season the beach guards got a brand new Landrover to use for transport.

When the 1961 beach guards first arrived in Jersey they lived in accommodation up on the hill above St Helier. However, after what Mike Gray describes as 'a fairly heavy night on the Guinness' they were unceremoniously evicted. For a short period, they stayed in a variety of places, some wholly unsuitable, like camping in Martello Towers, others slightly better such as sleeping on people's floors. Then Jim Wilson managed to line up a fellow called Bill Duquemin who had a house for rent in Duhamel Street, St Helier. This was to become what was affectionately known as the first Doghouse. Many more Doghouses were to follow.

The Doghouse was to gain a reputation for being something between a party house and a den of iniquity. It also served as a somewhere to crash for visiting friends. Mike has fond memories of the Duhamel Street Doghouse: 'There were always people, mates calling in to see us and staying temporarily in the Doghouse. There was one older guy who came and stayed with us for a while. He had lost his wife and was just traveling around the world'.

Bill Duquemin also owned a fish and chip shop which was located only a couple of doors away in Duhamel Street. The boys, who never bothered to cook at the Doghouse, used to eat dinner at Bill's fish and chip shop or at a café called the Della Rosa which was down near the Adelphi Hotel (a favourite watering hole), just over five hundred yards away. Fish and chips cost about two bob in those days, a pint of beer cost ten pence. Everything was tax free and cheap.

Their wage was the same as in 1960; eleven and a half quid a week which Mike describes as 'quite good money'. Jim Wilson as head beach guard was getting fourteen pounds ten shillings. Mike says: 'England [and Jersey] in the 1960s was still recovering from after the war. I couldn't believe how impoverished the place was. I was trying to save money – I managed to save a couple of quid a week because I arrived with virtually nothing and I had a winter to get through'. Mike intended to stay on after the season finished.

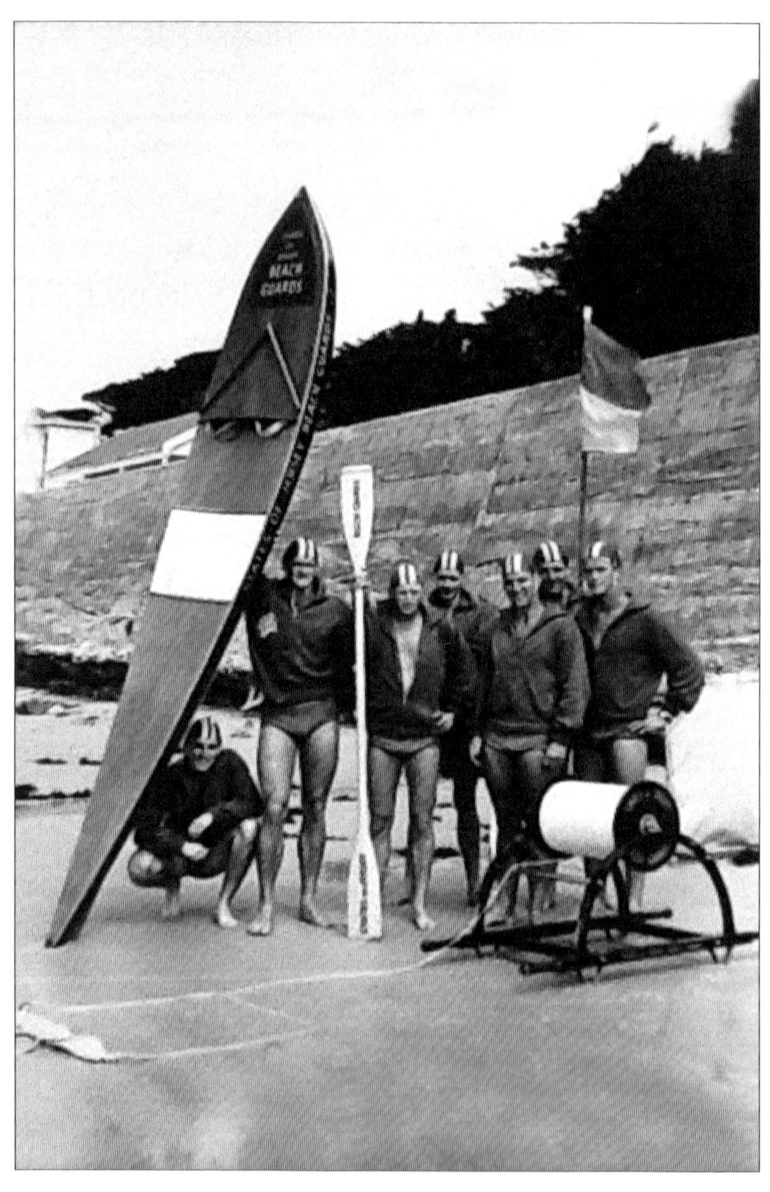

The Australian Beach Guards at St Brelade's in 1961
Left to Right: Mike Rodger, Bruce Douglas, Jim Wilson, Mike Gray, Dave O'Brien, Mike Abbott, Ken Fawkner   (*Photo courtesy of the* Jersey Evening Post)

The beach guards didn't particularly enjoy patrolling at St Brelade's beach because, Mike Gray says, 'It was too calm and boring'. However, on occasion it did get a little dangerous on an incoming tide when a bit of a rip formed. He can't recall whether they did a two- or a four-week rotation between there and St Ouen's. St Brelade's was a much more popular beach for the bathing public, and much safer. The calm conditions allowed speed boats to zoom around in the bay waters. Deck chairs abounded as well as kiosks and cafes. Mike has fond memories of a couple who owned a little cafe-kiosk near to where they patrolled. Their names were Mike and June Cotter. Mike recalls: 'They were a terrific young couple, very friendly. He was English, and she was a very pretty girl. We had a coffee with them every now and then'.

The beach guards were provided with a wooden hut near El Tico which served as their base at St Ouen's. Mike describes it as, 'A demountable – we'd put it up at the beginning of the season and take it down at the end and we had that the whole time I was there'. The Jersey Lifeguard Club was still functioning after the drama of the previous year, but members rarely did patrols. The fallout amongst the rank and file members had been substantial. The beach guards were running St Ouen's beach seven days a week.

As they spent a lot of time on the beach, things could get a little boring, particularly if the conditions were benign or the weather wasn't good. St Ouen's was no different. To relieve the boredom, the boys would go for a swim or take a surfboard out for a wave, or just sit and talk or play cards. Every now and then one or two of them would take the jeep or Landrover for a drive run up or down the beach. Just in case of emergencies, they had positioned what is called a box line in the back of the vehicles. A box line is a length of nylon line wound onto a rotatable drum with a surf belt attached. It was to come in handy many times during rescues.

Boredom went with the beach guard territory. St Ouen's was lightly populated during the week days with a larger crowd on the weekend so, Mike says, 'to be honest about seventy to eighty percent of the time we'd just be sitting around doing very little. If there were people swimming you went down and sat on the beach to watch them'.

The Watersplash wasn't very far away and a chat with the South Africans was an option to overcome the tedium. Cliff Honeysett, in his third year in Jersey, oversaw the Splash and his entourage included Bill Lavarack. As well as the usual banter, most of the interaction concerned the growing number of surfboard riders. The beach guards and the Watersplash guys managed to mostly contain the surfboards which were constantly being washed into the flag area. The beach guards put the flags out just about in front of El Tico and tried to keep the boardriders well away, but occasionally they'd have to act to stop them riding too close to the swimmers.

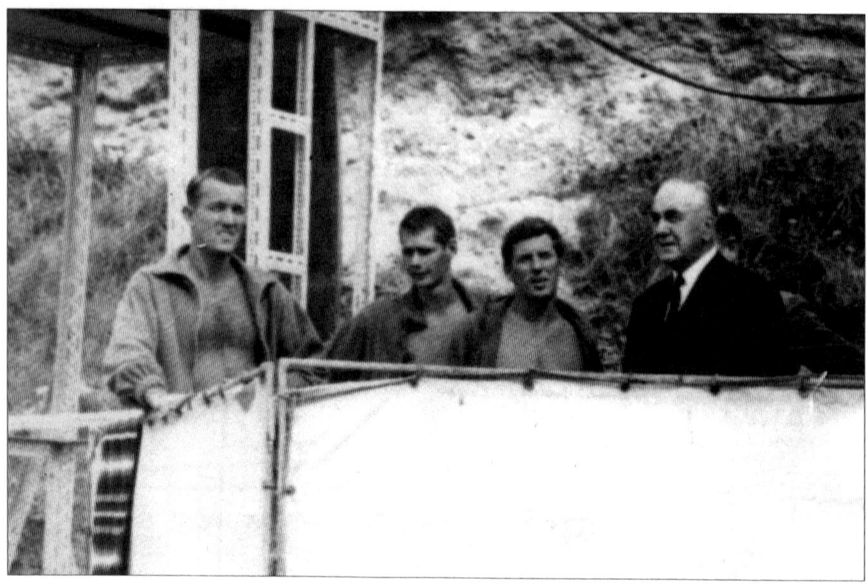

Visiting dignitary at the Beach Guard hut El Tico, 1961
Left to right: Dave O'Brien, Mike Gray, Roger Kennedy and Sir Eric Harrison (Australian High Commissioner to Great Britain) *(Photo courtesy of Mike Gray)*

Mike Gray got to know Jim Wilson quite well during the 1961 season. Mike describes him as a 'Damon Runyon sort of guy [humorous, colourful and interesting]. He wasn't that good a swimmer, but he was good at drilling – he was in the demonstration team for North Steyne [surf club]. He was a very funny man, a very good talker and a little bit of a con man'.

Mike recalls that Jim was good at smooth talking the Tourism Department officials. As a result, the bureaucrats left the management and the operation of the beach guards with him. Jim would go into the Department once a week to pick up the pay packets. Mike says: 'I don't even know if he filled in timesheets. When I took over as chief beach guard I also had very little contact with the Department. I'd just go in once a week as a formality to pick up the pay packets'. It seems that the Tourist Department had adopted a hands-off approach to the beach guards, which was fine with the Aussies.

Mike was also quite impressed by one of the beach guards, Bruce Douglas. Mike recalls enviously: 'He was a giant of a guy – the closest I've ever seen to Superman. He was about six foot four and built like a brick shithouse. He was probably the finest looking specimen of a man I've ever seen. He was a great guy to have on the beach in Jersey because he was a counterpoint to some of the big South African guys [from the Watersplash]. Some of them had a superior attitude. Well Bruce was as big as any of them and stronger than all of them, so they respected him'.

As the 1961 season drew to a close Mike Gray learned that he had been chosen by Jim Wilson to take over the reins as Chief Beach Guard for 1962. Jim Wilson and Mike Gray also managed to convince the Tourism Department of the need for an extra man in the team because the guys were working seven days a week and needed a day off. The total number of beach guards was to rise to eight. The beach guards said their farewells and left Jersey. Another year had passed with no lives lost on the beaches.

Mike Gray and Roger Kennedy went back to London. Mike had a letter of introduction from a friend to an official in Australia House. A Federal election had been called in Australia. Polling day was in early December 1961. In the lead up to the election the requirement arose for Australians living in, or passing through, Britain to be able to obtain details about the election and how they could vote. After an interview Mike not only got a job but was asked if he knew of any other Aussies who might be available. Did he ever!

As Mike recalls: 'I was living in a flat with about twenty of them in Ealing in west London. So, I said "How many do you want?"' Six of them got jobs for six weeks. Mike says: 'We were based in Australia House in The Strand and every day we went to work in the one suit we might have owned'. As so often happens, knowing someone is half the battle when looking for work.

Mike flatted with a group of people at Ealing and that house over the next four years became the place where lots of people would stay temporarily. It became a drop-in point whenever Mike was in London. Amongst those guys was Ken's mate Dave Thompson. Dave had travelled with Mike to England on the *Fairsky* after being sacked by Ampol, even though his uncle was the Chairman of the company. Dave had also found work in Jersey at the airport during the summer.

After the work in Australia House had finished Roger Kennedy, whose father was the CEO of Electrolux in Australia, organised for Mike, Dave Thompson and him to become dishwashers in Switzerland at a ski resort over the winter of 1961-62. Mike says with some pride, 'They normally employed Italians, so we were the first non-Italians to work in this ski resort'.

That job was to last for three and a half months, '113 days to be precise', recalls Mike with feeling. They were paid very poorly, the equivalent of five pounds a week. Mike says with disgust, 'I got about seven days off in that time but did a lot of skiing even though they didn't want me to because I might break my leg and then they wouldn't have a dishwasher'.

They managed to do a little bit of traveling around on the pittance they managed to save from the dishwashing jobs. Mike and Dave left Switzerland in March 1962 and travelled down to Spain, almost broke. There they ran into a Tasmanian named Brian Hill who was a surf lifesaver and who was interested in working in Jersey.

Mike travelled back to Jersey in May 1962 to organise the coming season.

5 Extra-Curricular Activities

'We'd drive out to the L'Etacq Hotel like the Untouchables. During work in the pub the boys weren't allowed to drink'.

Extract from an interview with Mike Gray,
Australian beach guard in the 1960s

The 1962 team was a mixture of old and new faces. Roger Kennedy and Dave O'Brien returned, as well as Bob Harris after missing the 1961 season. The new faces were Ken Fawkner and Bill Burke from North Steyne, Bob Armstrong from Whale Beach (just south of Palm Beach in Sydney) and the man Mike had met in Spain, Brian Hill from Devonport on the north coast of Tasmania. Brian must have felt right at home in his new job – the sea temperature in Devonport in summer was approximately the same as in Jersey.

They lived in the Duhamel Street Doghouse which had room enough for all of them. Their pay was the same, except now Mike was earning three pounds extra per week as chief beach guard. The beach guards quickly settled into the familiar routine, although there was no rotation between St Ouen's and St Brelade's. This was because Bob Armstrong and Roger Kennedy got jobs teaching swimming at the upmarket L'Horizon Hotel on the waterfront at St Brelade's after the completion of patrol hours. They were at St Brelade's full-time apart from the occasional day off. The extra beach guard also allowed two people to have a day off together. To make this work Mike Gray became one of the five on the beach at St Ouen's.

The new Land Rover which was provided by the States of Jersey was equipped with a portable two-way radio to communicate with the beach guard hut. It had a surf reel in the back and roof racks for the old Robson surf ski.

There was another significant change in 1962. The beach guards got to know a fellow named Chris who ran the L'Etacq Hotel down near the St Ouen's waterfront where they regularly went for a beer after work. After a bit of smooth talking the boys managed to get employed seven nights a week as drink waiters. With tourism on the rise in Jersey, busloads of holidaymakers would descend on the L'Etacq to party. As Mike says: 'They wanted to do their "knees up mother brown" and have a few grogs'. Usually there would be six of the beach guards rostered on as drink waiters.

Each night the buses would arrive, and tourists would come in a flood. Having worked up a thirst during the day of course they'd all want their drinks at once. For the first thirty minutes it was pretty busy. 'That's when you had to make your tips' says Mike, 'because after that everything slowed down'. The pub would stay open until about half past eleven in the evening. At eleven the buses would come to pick up the tourists, load them on and off they would go. Then the beach guards would make their way home to the Doghouse.

The eight young men pooled their money and bought an ancient and quite large black car. Mike can't remember the make although he thinks it was about a 1936 model. With a big smile on his face he recalls: 'We'd drive out to the L'Etacq Hotel like the *Untouchables* [a movie about the 1930s American gangster and illegal grog supplier Al Capone]. During work in the pub the boys weren't allowed to drink. Chris the owner wasn't overly impressed with the boys' performance, but he wasn't able to get anybody else, so he was stuck with them. Mike admits, 'We were actually quite bad at the job'. Unsurprisingly, the beach guards weren't re-employed the next year.

Recalls Mike, 'We got paid ten bob a night but with tips you would finish up with about two quid each a night. We pooled our tips. That year [1962] I was making an average of thirty quid a week tax free'. Good money indeed. The first beach guards would have been quite envious.

By the end of the 1962 season Mike had saved enough money to spend a couple of months on the continent and pay his share in the VW Combi that Dave Thompson purchased while they were in Switzerland the previous winter. Dave fitted it out while they were on the island to sleep four. At the end of the season they took off for Europe, literally – a helicopter carrier flew the Combi and its passengers over to St. Malo in France, about 20 miles from Jersey. It was the cheapest way to get there by far.

By then they had also organised jobs in Denmark for the 1962-63 winter. Brian Hill had worked with, or had some contacts with, a company called the Hudson Bay Fur Company. It was a huge company in Canada, and through that contact he'd organised five jobs working in a mink factory in Copenhagen. Mike, Brian, Ken Fawkner, Dave Thompson and Jimmy Platt, a Cockney fella they'd met in Jersey, worked in the Danish capital for three months until the middle of February 1963.

Mike recalls: 'We were supposed to be mink sorters but really we were just labourers who were paid very good money for what we did; forty quid a week with overtime. We all lived in a hotel in Copenhagen. The work was pretty basic but long hours. All we had to do was roll out stands with rows of different mink furs on them. Our boss would sort them and show them to buyers. We learnt a bit about what to look for in a mink fur during our time there, but we weren't sorting them. Even though we were paid overtime, we had so much spare time that I remember reading the book *Mila18* by Leon Uris in a day at work. It's about a thousand pages long. But most of the time we just sat around talking, or we'd get into a big packing case and have a sleep'.

In 1963 a young man from Maroubra named Chris O'Connor came over to Jersey with a guy named Ron Siddons who had been a professional beach inspector at Maroubra. Chris wasn't to become a beach guard until 1964 but he lived at the Doghouse and Mike Gray got him a job as the lifeguard at St Aubin's pool which at that time wasn't part of the beach guard responsibilities. Mike employed Ron Siddons, who had been a Maroubra beach inspector, as he had been recommended by another beach inspector from Maroubra whom Mike knew. Ron only stayed six or eight weeks as he found the beach work too boring. He was in his early thirties, but he was the fittest man they had ever had on the beach and would often run four lengths of St Ouen's (over eighteen miles) if there was nothing else to do. Ron Morton, who was also very fit, often ran with him. After Ron left, an Aussie named Geoff Meyer took over his job.

By 1963 there were at least ten Australians living permanently in the Duhamel Street Doghouse, including non-beach guards. This didn't include casual visitors from London or elsewhere, who might swell the numbers to nearly double that. The enterprising Bob Morris, as well as cooking up breakfasts for a small charge, also made dinners for two shillings and ten pence, usually steak or sausages with salad or vegetables, all 'salvaged' from the hotel fridge where he and Ron Morton worked the nightshift. They were both entrepreneurs from the start. Interestingly, Bob Morris ended up owning three fish restaurants and one of them, at Fairy Bower, was among the best in Sydney. Mike Gray says: 'I always liked Bob, but he could be a bit fiery. We are still in touch when he is in Australia'.

Mike says that the boys didn't drink at the Adelphi Hotel all that much in 1962 but the following year it became their pub. In the earlier years they drank at various spots and sometimes, mainly on a Saturday night, at a place Mike thinks was called the Bird Cage. The name gives a clue as to why it was popular.

As the number of beachgoers at St Ouen's started to increase in 1963, Mike found that five beach guards were not enough on busy weekends. Mike states: 'I made the case to the Tourism Committee, which they ultimately accepted, that we had more areas to patrol, including L'Etacq, about three miles north from our hut at El Tico, and later at Grève de Lecq, further north in the next bay. Because I liked St. Ouen's and it was more demanding if things got busy, I spent more time there than Jim Wilson had done'.

The locals and tourists were normally friendly and liked to talk to the lifeguards.

Mike supposes they saw the lifeguards as something exotic – bronzed Aussie lifesavers and all that. And at that time the lifeguard concept was still all very new. But there were also a lot of casual workers from England working in hotels, restaurants and the like, including some attractive young females. Mike recalls: 'Quite a lot [of girls] married beach guards, and just about all of those that I know of are still married today. But if I tell people that I once worked as a professional lifesaver in Jersey, their eyes often light up and they seem to assume that we were all either lying about on the beach or else in bed with some gorgeous female. This may have been the case for some, or many, and I don't deny that we had a share of that while we were there, but in my own case I was still keen on a girl in Australia and I didn't want to get involved in another relationship. Yet it certainly was one of Jersey's attractions, and part of the lifestyle we all shared in to varying degrees. But it is not by any means what I remember most about Jersey'.

There was one particular Lothario who Mike remembers well, although Mike chooses not to reveal his identity. This guy was simultaneously involved with two very attractive young women who maintained a fairly constant demand for his attention. It got to a point where he had one of them climbing out of the back window of the Doghouse, as the other one was knocking on the front door. Mike's most lasting memory of him, however, is seeing him standing at the bar of any hotel he was in, drinking a pint of Mackeson's Stout in preparation for another round with the ladies.

The boys also formed various other friendships with the locals. Mike was very friendly with a couple from Manchester who were both musicians. His name was Bernard Wild, and his wife's name was Edith. Bernard helped the beach guards in a rescue once and got written up in the *Jersey Evening Post* as the 'bystander', so that became his nickname. Edith was a great pianist and Bernard was a drummer. Roger Kennedy was also a drummer and the two Australians often had meals with them. Bernie befriended a lot of beach guards over the years until he died in the late 1980s, Mike thinks. Edith died in 2015.

There was also a local bookie who would shout the lifesavers a meal once a year. Pat McGarry and other members of the old Jersey lifesaving fraternity were also keen to welcome the Aussies and maintain a relationship, particularly in 1961. Then there were the local surfers and the Bronze squads they had taken through who often hung around.

Mike recalls that Ken Fawkner, Mike's deputy for 1962 and 1963, was another character. Every now and then people with hire cars would drive on the beach at St Ouen's at low tide and get bogged. Ken would then walk nonchalantly over with a shovel and say: 'Looks like you're in a bit of trouble here with the tide coming in and all. And I suppose y'know there's a five hundred pound fine if you get bogged and the (hire) car goes underwater?' Then he would add, 'For ten quid you can borrow my shovel, and I might even give you a hand'. His shovel got a lot of use.

One consequence of Ken's sales pitch was that the beach guards had a keg of beer fairly regularly with the proceeds from his shovel. If business was good, it might be twice a month on a Friday night. Ken's father had been the head brewer at Resch's brewery, so Ken knew a bit about beer. He'd buy a keg of Watneys Red Barrel, then ice it and gas it. The beach guards often invited the local Jersey 'beans' around to share it with them. Mike says the locals had never drunk cold, gassed Watneys before. He says: 'And I can tell you it was much better than the warm, flat beer "Mary Ann" they were used to'.

Bob Harris was also a larrikin of the typical Aussie variety. One night, Mike, as Head Beach guard, got a phone call from the local police asking if he knew someone called Robert Harris. When he told them he did, they asked, 'Is he a beach guard?' Mike answered in the affirmative and was instructed, 'Well come down to the station and get him'. When Mike got to the police station he was told that Harris was found drunk while riding a 'borrowed' bicycle and that he'd been apprehended on his way back to the Doghouse. After the police had finished telling Mike this, Harris added with a smirk, 'Yeah, and it took three of you to catch me!' Mike says that Bob was lucky not to be thrown back into the cells for the night.

In 1963, the year after working at the L'Etacq hotel, Ken Fawkner and Mike worked occasionally as drink waiters at a different hotel in St. Helier, but Mike can't remember its name. Some of the other beach guards might also have worked there casually. The place was a lot classier than L'Etacq, and the money was better, but Mike didn't work there more than half a dozen nights as he was now on fifteen pounds a week (tax free) and could save a fair bit. The other beach guards were now on twelve quid a week, and as his 'official' deputy, Ken got one pound more. Mike had the use of the Hillman most of the time as well.

By the time the end of 1963 season came around Mike decided to go home. He says: 'My mother was sick, crippled with arthritis, and I'd had enough of winters in the Northern Hemisphere for a while. And I didn't have a job lined up for the winter. So, I decided to go back to Australia and save enough money to travel some more, but also to get a qualification of some kind as I was getting tired of travelling "last class". It was a combination of things, not any one thing in particular, but I was also torn between coming back to Jersey for another season because I'd enjoyed working with the 1963 team most of all. Yet even at that stage, I didn't have the faintest idea what I really wanted to do with my life'.

As part of his role of Chief Beach guard Mike provided a written report to the States of Jersey at the end of the 1963 season. This report states that over the summer thirteen people were rescued, thirty-five people were given first aid treatment and the beach guards answered distress calls as far away as the north coast bathing spots at Grève de Lecq and Portelet. Most importantly, no-one drowned while the beach guards were on patrol.

In the report Mike recommended the orderly replacement of the life lines on the surf reels and the box lines which were made of sisal, which was cheaper than nylon or terylene but wore out faster. He suggested ordering the better-quality lines from Australia because they had a distinctive red thread running through them which would help offset the danger of the line being stolen.

As a further aid to future rescues Mike suggested the extension of the dedicated telephone line to the south along St Ouen's beach, to a spot known as Le Braye slipway just over six hundred yards south of El Tico. The telephone line had already been extended to the north. This allowed members of the public to alert the beach guard hut at El Tico if someone was in trouble away from the immediate vicinity of the normal patrol area.

Mike took the opportunity to advise the States of Jersey Tourism Department of the imminent departure of the South African Cliff Honeysett, one of the more capable South African lifeguards based at the Watersplash and to suggest that an additional beach guard be employed for the 1964 season. That would provide for three teams of three, with the Chief Beach guard free to go wherever necessary. This suggestion was accepted. Mike also nominated Ken Fawkner as his successor as head beach guard, which was accepted.

The final suggestion Mike made was to reiterate his previous year's call for the construction of a permanent beach guard control centre to replace the demountable shed. This was made more in hope than expectation and it was to be repeated by Chris O'Connor, who succeeded Ken Fawkner as Head Beach guard in 1966. The existing hut, a wooden demountable measuring around eight feet wide by about sixteen feet long and eight feet high, sat on a piece of flattened ground carved out of the hillside below the El Tico cafe. A series of windows ran the length of the side of the hut facing the beach. The hut was surrounded by an improvised fence constructed of a series of metal frames on which canvas had been strung. Next to it was a skeletal metal frame which stood about fourteen feet high which was used to house the surf skis. A telephone line ran to the hut. The overall impression was of a makeshift arrangement that was crying out for a more permanent structure.

Mike stayed in Jersey until the end of September 1963, then went back to the flat in Ealing with Bob Harris. The couple who had lived in the flat above them in Ealing were old friends with them by now. Mike recalls: 'Greta Elkins was a famous Australian opera singer, and her husband was named Ike – a truly great bloke. Greta often sang with Joan Sutherland, and at this time, Ike and Greta were living in the basement of Joan Sutherland's home in Kensington. So, for our final few days in London, Harris and I stayed with them in Joan Sutherland's house. I'm not sure if that great lady (but a very natural and unpretentious one) ever knew that a bicycle thief (unconvicted) had slept in her house, but I doubt if she'd have really cared anyway'.

Mike and Bob Harris flew out of London early in November 1963. Mike's stepfather paid his airfare home, about four hundred pounds Australian for an economy flight with Qantas. Mike says: 'When we got on the plane, Bob said to me, "How much money have you got?" "About 25 quid", I answered. Without a blink of an eye, he said, "Well, I've got two quid. Let's share!" We did, but on the condition he didn't buy cigarettes'.

After returning home Mike got a job with Ampol. He went on to get married and he and his wife found themselves working in Aboriginal education for the next forty years.

Mike sums up his time in Jersey like this: 'Jersey was a great time in my life. I loved the island, the beaches, the pubs, the amazing scenery everywhere you looked, and I loved the lifestyle we had at that time of my life. I lived, worked with and met some terrific people, many of whom are still my closest friends today, and just as many who were, but are no longer with us. And I know that it was those three years I was overseas, and those three seasons on the beaches at Jersey, that helped set me up for life and become secure in myself. When I left there at the end of 1963, I may not have known what I was going to do with my life, but Jersey and those other overseas experiences, gave me the confidence to follow the different paths that my life took me and continues to do so'.

Part 2: SEASONS IN THE SUN

Mid-1960s – Mid- to Late 1960s

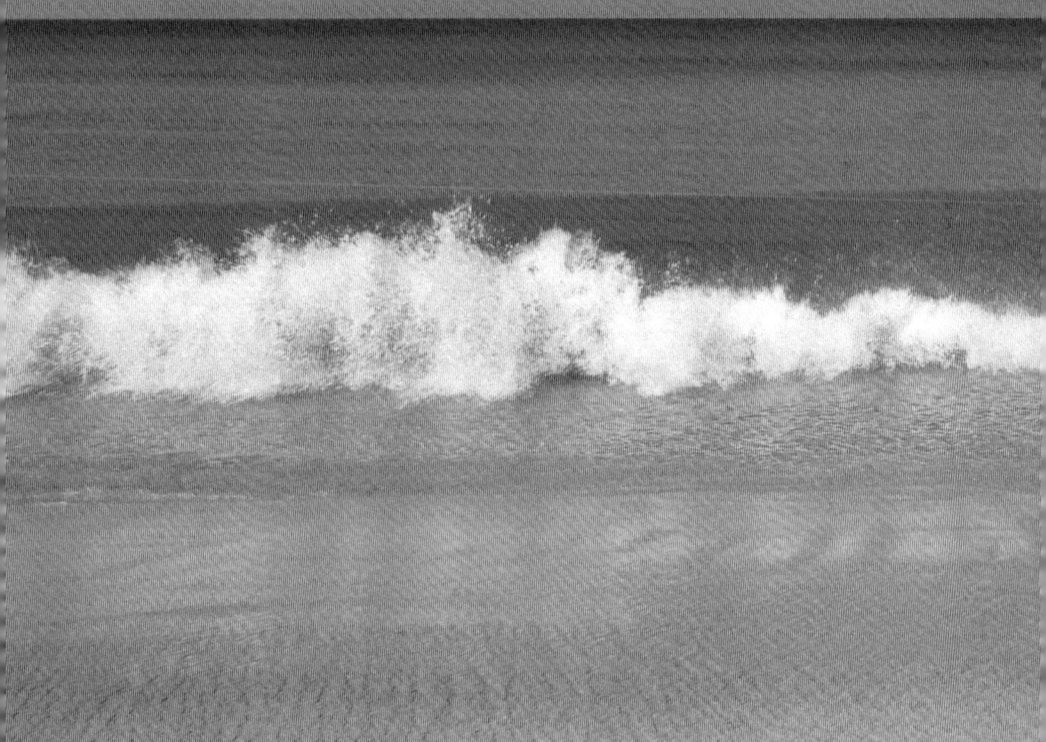

6 Boom, Boom

Jersey from the 1960s through the 1970s and 1980s experienced a boom in tourism and finance, two of the three fundamental pillars (the third being agriculture) that underpinned the local economy. With economic prosperity came population growth, fastest in the 1960s with about ten thousand additional people and slowing in the 1970s when about six thousand new residents settled.

The lack of an inheritance tax on the island, or Estate Duty as it was called in Britain at the time, gave Jersey a massive advantage for the wealthy British who wanted to avoid having their heirs paying a substantial percentage of the value of the estate they inherited. If the estate was broken up well beforehand and the money was invested through Jersey financial institutions, no taxes were payable.

Jersey's company tax laws also benefitted those who chose to register a company on the island but not live there. In that case they avoided paying any tax at all apart from a token amount of several hundred pounds. This brought in a lot of money as the profits were held in Jersey banks. As more and more banks, many of them multinationals, set up branches in Jersey the island began to transform into an international financial hub. The political stability of the island helped considerably. Schemes came into being that permitted almost any tax to be avoided, so financial planners and accountants added to the growing number of bankers and tax exiles moving to Jersey. By the end of the 1960s, Jersey's banks had deposits of almost three hundred million pounds. This was a ratio per capita of ten times that of Britain. In 1970 alone, deposits increased by forty five percent, and then kept on rising.

There was no difficulty in enticing skilled people with the right credentials – bank staff, lawyers, accountants and financial administrators – to come to Jersey to live as the personal income tax rate was only twenty percent, significantly lower than that paid in the UK. Housing prices increased as did the average wage. With the increase in money pouring into the government coffers, the States of Jersey built new schools, new hospitals, new roads, a new harbour, and a new marina. Unemployment was barely two percent.

If finance was becoming a major industry, tourism was even bigger. Increasingly affluent holidaymakers from the UK and Western Europe were taking advantage of cheap air fares or ferries to get to the island. British tourists were attracted to Jersey because whilst it was seen as an 'overseas' destination, the language and customs were largely similar to home. And they could use the same currency as back home to pay for things.

In 1969 around eight hundred thousand tourists holidayed in Jersey, up by over forty percent from eight years previously and a massive three hundred and twenty percent more than in the early 1950s. By the end of the seventh decade of the twentieth century this accounted for about a quarter of the gross value added to the local economy. It was never to reach that peak again.

Once in Jersey the tourists found plenty of new and upgraded accommodation available, ranging from holiday camps and guest houses spread across the island to five-star hotels scattered along the southern coast. Hire cars and fuel were cheap and the yellow sand of the beaches or the nearby promenades attracted those seeking to relax in the sun. Cabaret style entertainment was available for those who wanted it, nightclubs abounded, and there were hundreds of charming pubs to have a drink in. The newfangled 'bistro' type of eating was coming into vogue, but for those who preferred more formal dining there were plenty of restaurants to choose from.

For the tourist Jersey's history and historical buildings were on display, including the remains of the German occupation: the fortifications, the tunnels and the underground hospital. The internationally acclaimed Jersey Zoo was also a popular attraction with the holidaymakers. Held in early August, the annual Battle of the Flowers parade was a drawcard. A long line of floats, festooned in flowers, predominantly chrysanthemums, whose designs were a closely guarded secret right up until the parade itself, were displayed in all their glory with thousands of spectators in attendance.

With the tourists came seasonal workers to fill the positions in the construction, entertainment, catering and hospitality industries. Initially the seasonal workers were students but as the demand grew itinerant workers from Spain, Portugal, and Italy began to predominate in the hospitality sector. Young British people were also in the mix as the attraction of working in a tourist mecca that offered cheap alcohol and tobacco acted as a lure. An added incentive was any Brits who worked a season in Jersey could avoid paying tax in both the UK and Jersey.

So, how did these boom times impact on the beach guards employed by the States of Jersey? Well, the surge in tourist numbers certainly had a big impact because beach guard numbers grew steadily to cope with the influx of holidaymakers. The increasing number of tourists also helped them to find secondary sources of work to supplement their meagre incomes from the beach. That work ranged from labouring to construction to architecture (in the case of one beach guard) to employment as bouncers and doormen at pubs and clubs.

Was it the economic boom that attracted the young Aussie men to Jersey? It would appear not to be the case, for they did not make a killing financially - they were a long way down the pecking order when it came to earning power. Their wage was low for the time they put in – six days a week with a second day off every few weeks when the roster permitted. The lifestyle was certainly attractive – days spent outdoor on patrol at the beach or the pool which was great when the sun was out but not so good when it wasn't. The chance to use the skills gained in Australia as a surf club member or as a lifeguard to save someone's life would have been a buzz, certainly.

For Australia economically, the era of riding on the sheep's back was drawing to a close, but despite this there was plenty of work and prosperity was taking hold in the nation. Britain after World War II had gradually begun to distance itself from Australia economically. Ironically, it was Japan, the arch enemy in the Second World War, that took over as Australia's largest export market in the mid-1960s. Despite the increasing prosperity at home, these young men who came to Jersey chose to work and live nearly seventeen thousand kilometres away.

So, what made them decide to take on the beach guard life? Well, obviously they were young fit males (females did not feature in the Australian surf lifesaving scene until into the 1980s) with a spirit of adventure: they wanted to experience life outside Australia and were prepared to travel halfway around the world to do it. The beach guard job provided them with a meagre cushion of income which may have alleviated some of the risk of launching into the unknown. An important criterion was that they had to fit in with the other beach guards, living and working as a tight knit group for up to six months at a time. For most their surf club backgrounds and more than likely involvement in sports such as rugby union or rugby league meant they had experience in being team players.

There was arguably another factor in play. Most of the beach guards were not looking, at least at that stage, in pursuing a conventional career or way of life. That may have come later, but at that time in their lives they were living in the now. The fact that many of them had left school at fifteen or sixteen and thus had no particular aspiration to continue their education into tertiary studies (there were several exceptions) put them in a position where they could decide to take off into the wild blue yonder with hardly a second thought.

A lot of their mates back in Australia were following the orthodox way of life – taking up trade apprenticeships or electing to continue at school and on to university, having steady girlfriends and a settled, stable existence. Although the age when couples first got married started to trend upwards with the introduction of the pill in the 1960s and resultant increased lifestyle choices, society still had a firm expectation that marriage was the proper outcome of a committed relationship. It would seem that the succession of young men who made their way to Jersey were determined to buck that trend, or at least ignore it for a while.

There was one thing that the beach guards could not ignore – the increasing number of young single women living and working in Jersey in the summer season. Women outnumbered men on the island. These women seemed to be attracted to the fit, muscular, sun-tanned and friendly Australians who were always up for a chat, a joke, a drink and anything else on offer. Of course, the Aussies invariably knew where the best parties would be, and they were fun to be with. Short term romances abounded, although quite a few beach guards ended up marrying girls they met in Jersey and bringing them back to live in Australia. The accounts of some of those women, including how they coped with coming to live and raise children in a strange land, are scattered through this story.

From about the mid-1960s onwards the beach guard routines and patrol locations had been pretty much worked out. With the increasing tourist arrivals, beach guard numbers hit a high of fifteen in 1969. After that year the numbers scaled back to around a dozen throughout the 1970s and beyond. Additional patrol locations such as the West Park tidal pool had been added to their responsibilities. Because of several deaths in the water at a spot known as La Crabière, on St Ouen's beach north of El Tico, a lifeguard came to be stationed there. The lads at El Tico were in due course asked to do a regular loop in the jeep or Land Rover north from El Tico to places such as L'Étacq on the northern end of St Ouen's Bay, as well as Plémont Bay and Grève de Lecq on the north coast. By the early 1970s a lifeguard was working five days a week at Grève de Lecq. Plémont was added to the list shortly afterwards.

This period also saw more beach guards returning for successive seasons in Jersey. John Roberts from Manly did five seasons but not successively, in 1964-65 and 1968-70, then worked in Jersey until the end of 1972. Interestingly, and in contrast to the earlier years, a significant number of them came from the coastal city of Newcastle, NSW. Jerry Shannos, who hailed from Newcastle, arrived in Jersey in 1968 and did nineteen successive years as a beach guard, eighteen of those spent as Chief Beach Guard. Steve Porter, also from Newcastle, did five successive seasons from 1973. Brian Jones, another Newcastle lad, did three successive seasons from 1971 then worked on the island before coming back to the beach for a period in 1976. Wayne Bridges, yet another Novocastrian, spent five successive seasons as a beach guard from 1976. Jim Reeves from Newcastle had one season in 1976 and was to return for a further twenty-two seasons in the 1980s, 1990s and 2000s.

Jim's record was amazing enough, but it was surpassed by a beach guard named Paul Berghouse, who hailed from Sydney's eastern suburbs. Paul started in Jersey in 1977 and stayed until the beach guard service was taken over by the Royal National

Lifeboat Institution at the start of the 2011 season – thirty-four consecutive years! Paul still lives in Jersey. More on him later.

These young men were among the approximately one hundred and ten Australians who worked as beach guards in Jersey during the summer seasons between 1969 and the late 1980s. This period was arguably the halcyon years of Jersey as far as the beach guards were concerned, although those who came before and those following on would probably disagree.

Following are some of the stories of those Seasons in the Sun.

7 Growth

'Col got on the radio to the beach guard hut at St Ouen's and asked: "Have a look at these people out beyond me in the water, are they okay?"'
'The call came back: "Oh geez no, they're in the shit".'

Extract from an interview with Col Ambrosoli,
an Australian beach guard in the 1960s.

Throughout the middle of the 1960s the Australians began to firmly entrench themselves on the beaches of Jersey, contributing in no small way to the tourism boom. Over this period the States of Jersey Tourism Department accepted recommendations by successive head beach guards and slowly increased the numbers patrolling beaches of St Ouen's and St Brelade's, as well as other popular bathing areas, from ten in 1964 to twelve in 1968. Professional surf lifesaving in Jersey was indeed a growth business in those times, although the pay scales didn't quite match the additional numbers.

Although the young men were employed in a professional capacity they, with some exceptions, weren't Beach Inspectors, the term used for professional lifeguards in Australia in those days. The Aussies were all members of surf clubs, and Sydney surf clubs predominated at that time. North Steyne surf club provided a lot of the beach guards in the early 1960s, with some from North Bondi or Maroubra and, rarely, surf clubs outside Sydney such as Lorne in Victoria and North Cottesloe in Western Australia. There was even one beach guard from New Zealand, a member of Maranui surf club located near the capital Wellington.

Although the 1964 beach guard numbers remained constant at ten, that year West Park tidal pool in St Aubin's Bay, between St Brelade's Bay and St Helier, had been added to the spots patrolled by the beach guards because it had become a very popular bathing spot. Chris O'Connor took over as chief beach guard. New beach guard John 'Ant' Roberts became the first beach guard to work at West Park. Ant got his nickname from when he was a surf club cadet (under 15) in Sydney where he paddled a Billy Wallace (renowned surfboard maker) made 16-foot hollow ply 'toothpick' surfboard and his mates said he looked like a little ant on the board.

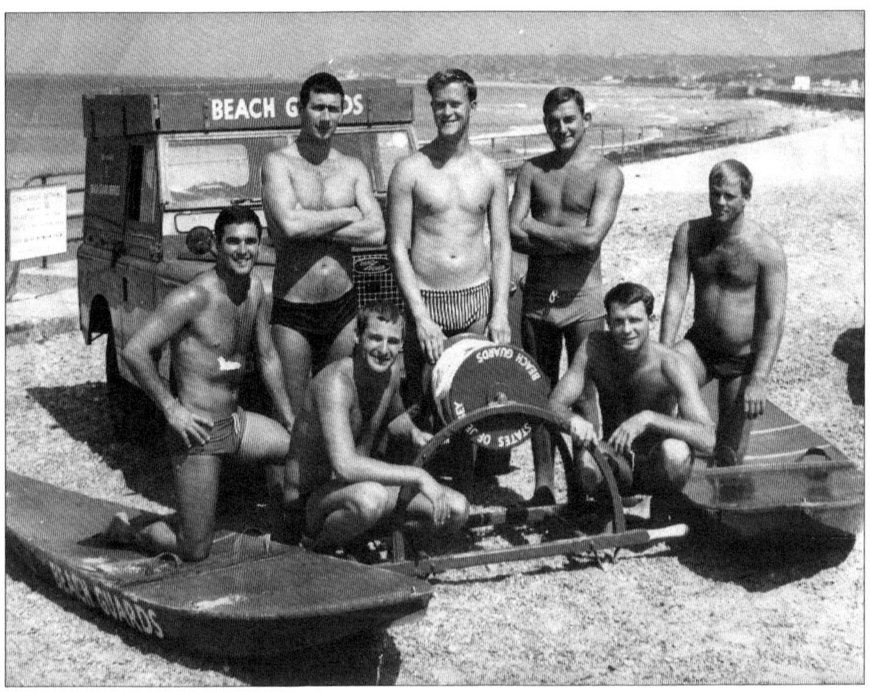

1964 Australian Beach Guards at El Tico, St Ouen's
Left to right, Rear: Ron Morton, Col Ambrosoli, Ken Fawkner, John Paton, Peter Williams
Font on Reel: Noel Bennett, Chris O'Connor   *(Photo courtesy of the Jersey Evening Post)*

Although the West Park pool was quite safe as far as swimming was concerned, Ant Roberts remembers the occasional accident with people slipping on the weed which formed around the pool. Unusually, he worked tidal hours. The pool had a semi-elliptical shape enclosed by a concrete wall. The tide would come in and submerge the pool, rendering it unusable, and so Ant would knock off work. As the tide went out the pool would catch the water and then Ant would be back on duty.

In the same year two independent lifeguards, Australians by the name of Dave Barrell and Geoff Hodgson, worked at the Watersplash, employed by its owner Harry Swanson. The South Africans were no more – the Australians ruled the island as far as lifesaving was concerned.

When Col Ambrosoli arrived in Jersey in early 1964 a lot of this expansion was still to come. A couple of North Steyne blokes who were over in Jersey had written to him in September 1963 saying that there were two beach guard positions available for 1964 and suggested that if he wanted one of them he had better let them know by return mail and a job would be his. He wrote straight back and asked them to book him in. Peter Williams from North Steyne was the fellow who got the second beach guard job. In 1964 there were nine Aussies on the beach in Jersey and Col knew nearly all of them, although he only knew Ken Fawkner, the head beach guard, slightly at that stage.

Col, tall, dark-haired with a slim, muscular build, found the Duhamel Street Doghouse to be a bit of a culture shock. It had four bedrooms - the 'pit' which was on the ground floor, the mezzanine which was halfway up the staircase, the top room which was a big room, and the 'bridal suite'. The pit had three Aussies living in it, the mezzanine two, the top room three and the bridal suite only one, so the bridal suite was a very sought-after room.

Names were drawn out of a hat for who was in which room. The draw of course was rigged by the longer serving Aussies, but everyone, particularly those allocated to the pit, took it in good spirit. New boys Peter and Col were in the pit for the first year. Col, showing an enterprising side to him, immediately went out and got a job to tide him over until the season started. He worked for about three months as a 'blockie's' labourer building a school, mixing the cement and concrete as his fellow workers were laying the concrete blocks. He describes the weather as 'bloody freezing'. Doing this sort of work also was quite a change as he'd been in retail sales previously and had never done any manual work for a living. He remembers that his hands used to bleed in the cold and were very sore until they toughened up. Col says there were a few other Aussies working in Jersey. One of them was a bloke called Ian Peacock from Western Australia. He was the South Australian junior surf belt champion and was much more capable of being a beach guard than Col was, but Col got the job and Ian was employed as a beach guard the following year.

When the 1964 season started the Jersey Lifeguard Club were struggling for numbers because they didn't have any one with an Instructor's Certificate to train Bronze squads. Col had that qualification, so he trained six Bronze squads (teams of six) that year. Most of the guys were local young blokes but there was one Australian called Phil Bernasconi (what he was doing in Jersey is unclear) who was to become a beach guard later. The graduates of the Bronze Medallion training kept the Jersey Lifeguard Club going for a few years longer. The club members operated in conjunction with the beach guards much the same as in Australia where the professional lifeguards coexist with the amateur volunteer surf lifesavers at weekends and public holidays.

Col says the wage they were getting on the beach was just over twelve pounds a week which was enough to pay for the board in Duhamel Street, feed them and allow them to go to the pub every night! He recalls it used to cost them about a quid to get legless at the pub. A pint of beer cost about a shilling. The nearby Adelphi Hotel was still the pub of choice – the staff used to put a beer called the Brewmaster on ice for the beach guards. The Aussies found the normal English beer to be 'too bloody warm'. The trouble was the only part of the Brewmaster beers that was cold was the bottom, so they had to drink quickly to get down to the cold part!

Carrying on the tradition of previous years, the boys used to put on kegs of beer up behind St Ouen's Beach after work. They would put the keg in the local butcher shop in town to get cold then they would take it to the beach and have a barbeque. Col says: 'We used to get plenty of females up there and have a bit of fun and games. We reckoned we were the first ones to do that'. Well, they certainly weren't the last.

In 1965 John 'Straw' Andrew arrived on the beach and the beach guard numbers increased to eleven. Straw's nickname came from the colour of his hair. Straw, a fitness fanatic and a top notch former rugby league player, brought a more organised training regime with him. Assisted by Col Ambrosoli, he devised what the lads called the 'torture trail' which wound its way up and down through the sand hills behind the lifeguard hut at El Tico. Straw would take the Aussies up there and run them all through the sand hills until they were all exhausted.

The beach guards also used to play touch football and cricket on the beach during quiet periods when the tide was out. The two guys from the Watersplash, who had returned for another season, often joined in.

In the middle of the 1965 season there were two drownings within a week along St Ouen's Beach near a well-known entertainment venue called Chateau Plaisir. This was located at La Crabière, about one and a half miles (two and a half kilometres) north of El Tico. This was despite a large sign which was erected on a nearby ramp saying, 'Do not bathe here - dangerous currents'. Chris O'Connor and Phil Bernasconi, who was now a beach guard, drove up there and dragged one swimmer out and gave him mouth to mouth and tried to resuscitate him but they couldn't revive him.

As a result, the States of Jersey Tourism Department approved a beach guard equipped with a two-way radio to be situated in front of Chateau Plaisir. Col recalls: 'You'd get driven up there and you'd do two hours sitting there with no one around. Anybody that went into swim there you'd run down and tell them to get out. That prevented any more drownings up there'.

The lifeguards were constantly amazed when the Poms came to the beach on their two weeks annual holidays. The ones that stood out most of all were those from the north of England. They typically worked in mostly industrial jobs, very working-class people, and when they came over on the two weeks holiday they hit the ground running. They had two weeks' worth of money and were ready to party as soon as they got off the plane.

They would come down to the beach and sit there and one of the beach guards would give them that great Aussie greeting: 'How are you going, mate? They would say: 'Eh by gum, good'. The boys would say: 'Make sure you don't get sunburnt'. They'd say: 'We came here to get tan'. The standard reply was: 'You don't need to be tan all on day one, put some cream on'. 'Oh no', they'd say, 'I want tan'.

When the lifeguards drove back into St Helier on the way home after work, they would sometimes detour by the hospital because they knew what they would find. Sure enough, there was always a queue of sunburnt Poms stretching down the road with blisters all over them seeking treatment.

None of the holidaymakers without a swimming background had a clue on the beach safety wise. According to Col, their attitude to the beach was, 'A lot of white bubbles, you're going to get knocked around by those white bubbles, so the safest place is the smooth green water away from the bubbles. But they would go out four or five steps and find themselves out of their depth, but despite the danger they loved it'. And it kept the beach guards busy.

As the day ended the Poms would go back to St Helier and party hard. Col says laughingly, 'At the end of their two-week holiday they would go up to the airport, still with two pounds fifty pence left in their pocket, drinking pints. When the announcement for their flight was made, "Flight such and such is due to leave in seven minutes", they would drink as fast as possible to spend all their money'.

The increasing number of tourists meant there were more people on the beach, and more getting into trouble in the water. In 1964 the beach guards had undertaken about a dozen rescues, but this number increased to thirty-eight in 1965, with forty-five people provided first aid. 'There was one day where we had fourteen rescues, thirteen at St Ouen's and one at St Brelade's', recalls Col. 'We were pulling them out everywhere. It was one of those days. It was late in the afternoon and the tide was coming in, the swell came up and people were getting into strife all over the place. We were trying to keep them in between the flags to no avail. Anyway, that was a big day, and no one drowned'.

In mid-season there was one quite dramatic rescue. Col Ambrosoli happened to be in the jeep doing a patrol along the beach by himself when he by chance caught a glimpse of about five or six heads popping up in the swell just about equidistant from the Watersplash and the patrolled area at El Tico. Col got on the radio to the beach guard hut and asked: 'Have a look at these people out beyond me in the water, are they okay?'

The call came back: 'Oh geez no, they're in the shit'.

Col can't remember whether he decided to swim out or the beach guard on the radio told him to go out to them whilst the others ran up to where he was. Anyway, he swam out to them.

There were three or four girls and a couple of men struggling in the water. A few of the girls were very distressed. 'They were screaming their bloody heads off', says Col.

One screamed out to Col: 'Where's the lifeguards, where's the lifeguards'.

Col, trying to calm them down, shouted: 'I'm a lifeguard. All of you come over here and gather around me, we are all going to float and there will be more lifeguards coming'.

Col could see the other beach guards running towards to where they were, but the lads were still some distance away. Col said in as quiet and calm a voice as he could manage: 'I want you all to follow me, we're going to dog paddle this way'.

One of the girls in particular was very panicky but wisely Col wasn't going to get anywhere near her in case she dragged him under in her distress. The group was at least one hundred metres off the beach when he first arrived but by the time the other beach guards got there he had them to within about fifty metres of the shore.

The other beach guards swam out and, as Col relates: 'Every one of them went straight to a girl and left the two guys on their own. You can guess where they grabbed them. Anyway, we got them into shore but there was still one more bloke not out of the water singing out "What about me" and I said to him "Mate, put your feet down and touch the bottom'. He did so, and he just said "Oh". And that was that'.

There were several other rescues of note performed by the beach guards in 1965. One went very well and the other could easily have resulted in at least one death. Both involved Ant Roberts, who had transferred to the beach from the pool that year.

In 1965 a lot of Jersey residents were asking why the local Jersey men weren't allowed to work as beach guards. This was despite the Jersey Lifeguard Club beginning to struggle again, even though Col Ambrosoli had put through a half dozen Bronze squads the previous year. The problem was that the local kids were more interested in surfing than lifesaving, a problem that was evident back in Australia as well where many surf clubs found it difficult to attract members.

Peter Williams and Ant Roberts were involved in a rescue at La Saline, the beach part of the area called L'Etacq, at the northern end of St Ouen's beach. L'Étacq was renowned for its very strong currents. A local alerted the beach guards that a woman was in trouble. Chris Fawkner, Charley Hull, Pete Williams and Ant Roberts raced up there in the Land Rover.

When they got there the beach guards found that a man was trying unsuccessfully to undertake a rescue using a box line that had been placed near one of the hotels for the summer months. While Chris Fawkner and Charlie Hull were preoccupied with getting the man back in, Peter and Ant swam out to the woman, a local Jersey 'bean', who seemed to be in a bit of trouble. She was only about one hundred metres off the beach but drifting very close to the rocks. She was a bit hysterical, so Ant grabbed her and gave her a bit of a slap in the face to calm her down. Together the pair got her in to the beach. The woman was in shock, so she was taken away in an ambulance. She spent a couple of days in hospital recovering.

A couple of Centeniers (members of the Jersey judicial system responsible for charging or bailing offenders) arrived at La Saline soon after the rescue and congratulated the beach guards. The rescue of a local resulted in good publicity in the *Jersey Evening Post*. This effectively put an end to the calls for local beach guards, although this was to resurface in the 1970s.

The following week Peter and Ant were in the Land Rover on St Brelade's beach on patrol. There was a knock on the window – it was the lady that that they rescued. She had about two pounds in cash in her hand. She said she wanted to give it to the lads, but Ant politely was about to decline. Just then he felt a tap on his knee and a quiet whisper came from Peter, 'take it'. Ant smiled and said: 'thank you' and took it. That night they went up to their local pub and had a few beers on her.

Later that season Ant was involved in a rescue between El Tico and the Watersplash where he almost drowned. A young guy got into trouble in some rough surf. Ant was the only one in the jeep, so he raced to where the guy was, jumped out and slipped on the belt attached to the box line. One of the local lads who had been doing some surf lifesaving training but didn't have his Bronze medallion happened to be there so Ant asked him to take charge of the line, hoping that some of the other beach guards would appear. Ant wasn't all that fond of the belt, particularly the pin release mechanism, and as a precaution almost every day he was on patrol had greased the safety pin to ensure it would come out easily.

Ant swam out to the man in trouble and when he had secured the patient he gave the haul in signal. Unfortunately, a group of tourists who arrived on the scene decided to help the young local pull Ant and the patient in. Having no clue about the proper procedure and the danger, of course they tried to pull the pair in as fast as they could. There were about five people on the line and they hauled Ant in so rapidly that he was pulled straight to the bottom. Ant had to let go of the patient or he would have been underwater as well.

Ant recalls the event with horror. 'I was bumping along the bottom without any air, so I had to pull the pin and thankfully the belt just came away from me. I swam my way to the surface and that first breath of air was beautiful'.

Because they were now reasonably close to shore, the patient managed to get in without any further assistance. Ant says: 'When I got to shore I didn't say too much. I mentioned to the kid to remember that you only have three on the line, but he couldn't really do much because the tourists just took over and they had no idea. That's one rescue I'll never forget'.

When the weather conditions in the English Channel were conducive a big surf, around six to ten feet (two to three metres), would roll in along St Ouen's Bay. If the swell was still big late in the afternoon the beach guards would stay at the beach and would body or board surf because for them the waves were magic. It was even better when the wind subsequently blew off shore as it would make the swell glassy (smooth).

Several plywood surf skis arrived from Australia in 1964 for use by the beach guards. Straw Andrew and Col Ambrosoli liked to use them, and they were always on the lookout for waves near a series of volcanic islands well offshore from St Ouen's beach. Straw said one day to Col: 'There's a wave breaking near a volcanic rock about a mile offshore' so out they paddled on the skis. However, to catch the waves, they had to sit out to sea behind the rock and take off at an angle across the face of the wave as it broke and try to steer into the deeper water. Unfortunately, Straw got wiped out as a wave broke and his ski got washed on top of the volcanic rock and down into a crevasse. Straw swam onto the rock to get the ski and got knocked ass over head by a wave.

Impacting on the rock caused Straw to lose a fair bit of skin but he was determined to recover the ski. Eventually, aided by Col, he got the ski, which was looking decidedly the worse for wear, back into the water. As the pair started to paddle back towards shore Straw's ski started to sink. Col relates: 'So, we tied it to my ski and both of us got on my ski. As we were paddling back we could see the jeep from the lifeguard tower roaring along towards us. We eventually got in to the beach to be met by Chris O'Connor, the Head Beach guard at the time. Well, he went off his head. Straw and I were standing there with our heads down taking it. "You stupid pair of pricks, it's taken a year to get these bloody things here. What am I going to tell the States of Jersey?" He got stuck right up us'.

As the 1960s progressed, surf board riding took off in Jersey in a big way. Inevitably conflict arose between the authority of the beach guards and the independence of the board riders who were reluctant to surf in the allocated areas, particularly when the surf was good where the public bathed. It was no different from Australia with the rivalry between the board riders on one side and the surf club members and the Beach Inspectors on the other. The period of confrontation in Jersey occurred eight or ten years later than in Australia because board riding didn't develop as early in Jersey. Of course, leg ropes weren't yet invented and when the boardriders fell off, as they invariably did, in or near the patrolled areas boards would wash in amongst bathers, at times causing injuries.

Although many of the beach guards were also board riders, they had little sympathy for the persistent offenders. What made it more frustrating was that, despite repeated pleas, the States of Jersey government officials declined to provide the beach guards with any authority to impound boards or to order surfers off the beach. The beach guards wanted the boards registered so that they could identify repeat offenders. All they could do was to warn offenders and watch powerlessly as they were ignored. A sense of frustration grew at this lack of authority.

Col Ambrosoli remembers a beach guard named Howard 'Pud' Langford and his involvement in a rescue of a board rider one day in 1965. The board rider had lost his board and was really struggling, nearly going under. Pud, a big man, had the surf belt on but he wouldn't go in the water and he wouldn't get out of the belt. Col and the other lifeguards were pleading with him to go and rescue the board rider, but Pud said, half in jest: 'Stuff him, he's only a board rider, let him drown'. Eventually Pud got in the water and rescued the unfortunate fellow.

One source of delicious, and free, food the lifeguards latched onto were the spider crabs which usually appeared for about five weeks during the summer. During this period there were thousands of these crabs in the water off the beaches of Jersey. Usually they ran in the early part of July, sometimes earlier. Spider crabs have a football shaped body – no pincers, about the same size as a blue swimmer crab but with long spindly legs. The boys would dive to get them in about ten or twelve feet of water, swim down and turn them upside down. As soon as they did that all the legs would contract to their bodies and the beach guards could surface with four crabs tucked under one arm with a fifth in the other hand.

With an eye to make a quid and to get a feed, the beach guards developed a cunning technique to collect large amounts of them. They would hook up an inflated inner tube and a bag and when the spider crabs ran they would collect a couple of sugar bags full of spider crabs and go up to the nearby Jersey airport and sell the whole lot for cash in ten minutes to the airport staff. They sold them for twenty pence a crab. That doesn't sound like very much, but twenty pence bought them a pint of Guinness in those days. They also used to cook them behind the El Tico lifeguard hut in a kerosene tin. The boys say they were beautiful eating, very tasty.

One enterprising lifeguard concocted a plan which wisely, in hindsight, was never enacted. He wanted to use a boat to collect the spider crabs and sell them to the local fishermen who would have taken everything they caught. However, it was highly illegal, and they would have ended up in jail if they had been caught in the act.

❁

A lot of the holidaymakers coming to Jersey in the summer were Scottish, many from Glasgow and their accents were impossible to comprehend. One thing the beach guards did understand was that they liked to drink, and when they drank, they liked to fight. If they couldn't have a fight with someone outside their group they'd fight amongst themselves.

If they got into too much trouble they'd be put off the island. Under the island legal system, anyone arrested by the police in Jersey and facing prosecution must be charged by a Centenier (responsible for charging offenders) who would present the case to a Magistrate. The cops would lock the offender up and the Centenier would come in a day or maybe two days later, depending when he was available. Such offenders who were charged by the Centenier might get barred from the island for twelve months or so.

Danny Brosnan, who worked as a lifeguard in Jersey between 1966 and 1969, had a run in with the Scottish holidaymakers. He was taking out a local girl and they and two other beach guards were having a drink in the Adelphi Lounge on the Parade in St Helier (about 500 metres from the Doghouse). There was a group of Scotsmen, Jocks or Jimmies, the beach guards called them, drinking in the bar.

Two reasonably attractive South African girls had attached themselves to the beach guards and the girls would turn up everywhere they went, so the boys christened them the Models. However, the novelty soon wore off and quickly the boys got sick of them hanging around. To discourage the girls, the beach guards instituted a fine of fifty pence if any of them talked to the Models.

With the Models hanging around the Australian group at the Adelphi, a Jimmy started talking to them in his incomprehensible accent. Seeing this, one of the beach guards said to the Scotsman: 'That's fifty pence, mate'.

The Scots guy said in his best Glaswegian accent: 'What are you talking about?' So, the beach guard repeated: 'It's fifty pence'. The Jock looked at the girls and asked them what this guy was on about and the beach guard said: 'That'll be another fifty pence'. Angrily, the Jock tipped a pint of beer over him and the beach guard whacked the Jock in the mouth.

The owner of the pub came out and threw the Jock out of the hotel. The Jock said angrily: 'What about him' [meaning the beach guard] and the owner said: 'You started it by tipping the beer over him'.

Half an hour later about fifty Jocks turned up and filled the pub. Danny thought he'd better get the girl out of there, so he went to leave, followed by the other Aussies. However, one of the Jocks punched Danny as he walked out. Before Danny could retaliate, he spotted a group of policemen, several with dogs, outside the pub waiting for the Jocks. As Danny didn't want to get arrested for fighting he and his group stepped outside. The Jocks went to follow and then saw the police, which stopped them in their tracks.

The group of Aussies, along with the girl, decided to walk up the road to get away from the scene. However, the Jocks had other ideas. Danny describes it as being, 'Like the Charge of the Light Brigade. The Jocks ran up to us screaming and yelling. I saw the first one coming and I grabbed onto his shirt and down we went. The rest of the Jocks played football with us all the way up and down the street until the police were able to stop it'.

The beach guards had no desire to be involved in the brawl because the way the law went in Jersey their jobs could be on the line, but they had little choice. Wading into the melee, the cops grabbed the Scotsman that Danny was wrestling with and broke up the brawl. The police asked Danny to make a statement so that the Jock could be charged, but Danny didn't want to. However, after the cops told him that if he didn't press charges they would charge Danny, he quickly changed his mind.

Danny Brosnan said: 'Well, book him then'. Then he said: 'After you do, just let me into the cell you're going to hold him in and we'll sort things out'. But the copper wouldn't play the game and replied: 'No, we can't do that'.

Of course, all the Aussies in Jersey heard about the brawl so the next night about forty Aussies all turned up, ready to take the Jocks on. Pud Langford, who was a boxing trainer, even had his hands taped up. Luckily for them, they couldn't find a Jock anywhere. Things calmed down, but Danny says he couldn't turn his neck for about two days afterwards, it hurt so much. He didn't disclose whether the girl spoke to him again.

About two weeks after the incident there was a rescue not far from the lifeguard hut at El Tico. Straw Andrew and Danny jumped into the Land Rover and raced to where two guys were floundering in the water. The Land Rover had a box reel on the back. Danny says: 'All the rescues in Jersey were pretty easy to work out. You would find a vee in the sand and that was usually where the rip was. You could follow it out, so you knew roughly where the people in trouble were'.

The two guys were being carried further out by the rip. Danny donned the belt and when he got to them they were screaming out in panic. Danny said to them (perhaps redundantly): 'Are you okay?'

One of the guys said: 'No, we're drowning'.

Danny, probably unnecessarily, asked: 'Where are you from?'

'Scotland', he said, 'yeah, yeah, we're from Scotland'.

With that Danny promptly pulled the pin on the belt and said to the Jock: 'You're going to have a lovely time in France this time of the year' as he started to backstroke away from the Scotsman. The guy started to scream louder.

Straw Andrew pulled the belt in and yelled out to Danny: 'Are they okay?'

Danny replied matter of factly: 'No, they're drowning'.

Straw screamed out: 'What's the matter with you?'

Danny said: 'They're Jocks', and Straw said: 'Oh shit'.

Then Straw put the belt back together and he said to Danny: 'You get on the line and I'll go in the water and when I put my hand up you pull in the line'.

Danny replied noncommittally: 'Well, I'll think about it'.

In Straw went, diving under waves, looking back at Danny to see if he was still there. Reluctantly Danny pulled them in.

The Aussies also learned a thing or two about the independence of the women who lived and worked in Jersey. Danny Brosnan was a bit slow off the mark, but he quickly adapted. He met a girl on the first night he was in Jersey and she agreed to go out with him the next night. He took her to the pub and he bought a couple of pints of beer. When it was time to buy the next one she said: 'I will get these'. Danny, being chivalrous, replied, 'No, no'. The girl again said: 'I'll get them' but Danny ignored her and got the two pints. When he came back to the table she said: 'If I can't buy the next round I'm leaving'.

When he got up the next morning and all the guys had gathered for breakfast in the little kitchen in the Doghouse, he told them the story and concluded: 'What a strange bird'.

Straw Andrew regarded him with astonishment and said: 'You fucking idiot, you're trying to stuff it up for all of us'.

Danny wised up quickly. After that when the girls at the beach asked them which pub we were going to that night, if the boys said, 'We're not coming out tonight because we haven't got any money', the girls would say, 'We've got money, tell us which pub you are going to'. And of course, they did.

8 Out of Season Adventures

'She had an unusual name, Wanda Bonk'

*Extract from an interview with Danny Brosnan,
an Australian lifeguard in the 1960s.*

Those that stayed on in the northern hemisphere at the end of the summer season were involved in some epic off season journeys through Europe. Some of the lads did casual work wherever they could get it, but most just lived (very frugally) on their savings until it was time to go back to Jersey.

Col Ambrosoli recollects on an adventure that almost ended in tragedy at the end of a trip around Europe. It was just before they were due to start back on the beach for the summer of 1965. One of the entourage was a fellow by the name of Frank Morton who wasn't a beach guard, just an Aussie on holidays with them. Col describes him as not a bad bloke although he did have the nickname of Boofhead. They were in Biarritz in France. With Col and Frank were Peter Williams and Col's wife to be, Margaret, whom he'd met in Jersey. Peter, Frank and Col decided to go for a body wave because the surf was good. Off they went into the water which Col describes as being 'bloody cold'. After a few waves Peter and Col decided to call it a day.

Back then there was a big sea wall at Biarritz that Col says resembled the one at Manly. Col and Peter got up on the wall to check on how Frank, 'Boofhead', was going. As they watched Frank they noticed him begin to swim in but unknowingly he swam straight into a rip. The boys began to signal to Frank to swim up the beach away from the rip, but he couldn't get out of its clutches. The pair asked some French people if there was a life belt anywhere around, but they were unable to make themselves understood.

Eventually after expending a lot of energy Frank got in to about fifteen to twenty metres from the beach but couldn't get any closer.

Col said to Peter: 'You're a better swimmer than me, you get in and get him'. Peter went into the water and Col got in up to his waist, but he was nearly pulled off his feet by the undertow. Peter got to Frank and managed to pull him towards Col and Col somehow grabbed them both. They managed to drag Frank Morton out of the water. He was in the foetal position, his face a purple colour. Thankfully he recovered.

Biarritz seemed to have a hoodoo on the Australian beach guards, noting Neil Beachley's earlier story.

❁

Danny Brosnan relates a story about his first trip which occurred at the end of 1966. He and a few others bought a Kombi van off some guys in Jersey that had been across to Europe before. The Kombi van had a tent, cookers, dinner plates, cutlery, the whole shebang. The boys had been given the name of a German woman who was a civilian secretary for the American army in Hamburg as a contact, so they went there to look her up.

When they got to Hamburg they found out she was in Berlin, so they went to Berlin and tracked her down. Danny recalls with a straight face: 'She had an unusual name, Wanda Bonk'.

Through Wanda the boys met several other female civilian secretaries who were connected to the American employment office and all of the beach guards got jobs through them. Danny had an engineering certificate and got a (slightly unusual) job as a tank mechanic. The guy he was working with was German. He couldn't speak English and Danny couldn't speak German, but they worked together for four months and, somehow, they were able to communicate. Along with the civilian secretaries and Wanda Bonk, the boys had a wonderful time in Berlin.

After that the travellers journeyed to Austria, through Yugoslavia into Greece, back to Italy, then into France. Most of the boys parted company in France, although Danny and a mate stayed together. The pair, who only had the equivalent of about four pounds ten shillings between them, decided to hitchhike up from Biarritz to Paris to meet up with several of the secretaries from Berlin who were travelling to Paris by train.

As no-one wanted to pick up two males, they decided to separate. Danny walked down the road and was picked up by a guy driving what Danny describes as 'one of those little French billy carts'. As he was talking to the driver he saw his mate go by sitting up in a big truck.

The guy who gave Danny a lift was a bit strange. He professed to have little English but understood Danny when he said: 'I'm going to Paris'. But after going through Bayonne, only a short distance from Biarritz, the guy drove his car into a forest. He said to Danny: 'Fatigue, fatigue, need to have a sleep'.

Danny was by this stage getting a bit on edge as they were a long way into the forest, way off the main road. The driver stopped the car got all scrunched up on one side of the car. Danny was thinking: What's going on here?' He picked up the map to look at it and the next minute the guy put his hand on Danny's crotch. A second later Danny had the Frenchman by the throat and was squeezing hard.

After that little misunderstanding the guy drove back onto the main road and of course he then said: 'No, no, I turn off now, you get out'. Danny recalls there was just miles of forest and he was in the middle of it. He had a small carry bag but as Danny opened the back door of the car to get his bag the guy started to drive off. The bag came out sideways and it got caught in the closing door. Danny was running alongside the car and the bag eventually came out. He slammed the door and was very pleased to hear it make a terrible noise as if he had broken it.

Luckily, straight after that a nice red Opel car came along. It stopped, and Danny cautiously got in. The driver was a Dutchman, 'as lovely a guy ever there was'. He was in the French underground during the war and got shot in the hip by the Germans. His family were diamond cutters from Amsterdam. He and his wife had a villa in Spain. Every year his wife would fly to and from the villa and because of his bad hip the Dutchman would drive down and back. Danny had a day and a half with him on the way to Paris. He said to Danny: 'This is my address. Wherever you go, can you send me a postcard, my grandson collects stamps?'

For the next ten years, wherever Danny went he sent either a card or a letter or something like that to the Dutchman. Danny put all the stamps on it he could find and stayed in touch with him that way.

Reportedly, the reunion in Paris with the secretaries was not quite as exciting as the hitchhiking to get there.

Danny Brosnan was involved in a very funny situation involving the making of a Spaghetti Western in Spain during the winter following another season on the beach. After a spell skiing in the Austrian Alps (Danny was a good skier) he and a few Aussies decided to drive down to Spain. They loved all the little fishing villages. They met a guy in a town called Sitges, on the coast near Barcelona, and he said, 'I bet I know where you're going - you're going down to Almeria (about two hundred kilometres east of Gibraltar) where they make the Spaghetti Westerns'.

The boys replied: 'Never heard of those, what are you talking about?' The guy told them they made the movies *The Good, the Bad and the Ugly, A Fist Full of Dollars* and *For a Few Dollars More* near Almeria. He added: 'I've just come from there. They are hiring extras'.

The Aussies thought that would do them, so off they went in their car. In Almeria they found a casting office where the extras were being hired. The guy asked the Aussies: 'What do you do, are you just a stand in or do you ride a horse?'

Astutely, Danny asked: 'What's the difference in pay?' The guy told them that being a stand in was worth the Spanish equivalent of four pounds ten shillings a day but if you rode a horse it was fourteen pounds ten a day. So, quick as a flash, Danny said, 'I'm a horse rider'.

Danny says he used to go to a few riding schools at Penrith to the west of Sydney when he was a kid. He said: 'This will be easy, I'm a horse rider'.

They signed up and got on the back of a truck which drove out to a nearby town where the movie scenes were being shot. On the way they started chatting to an American guy on the back of the truck and he asked: 'Are you a stand in or a rider?'

Danny replied: 'I'm a rider'.

The American then asked: 'Okay, have you used wires before?'

Not having a clue what he was talking about, Danny asked the American: 'What's a wire?'

The Yank looked at him in a funny way and replied: 'When you ride along you pull a wire which controls the front leg of the horse, so it rolls over front ways and you roll off. When you want the horse to rear up you pull another wire which pulls its back leg and it falls backwards'.

Danny immediately changed his mind. 'I'm a stand in', he declared.

According to the gossip Clint Eastwood would not sign up to the latest Sergio Leone movie and that was why he was absent. The makers of the film decided to shoot all the scenes they could without him. The rumour mill said that Clint Eastwood didn't want to be typecast, he wanted to go in a different direction.

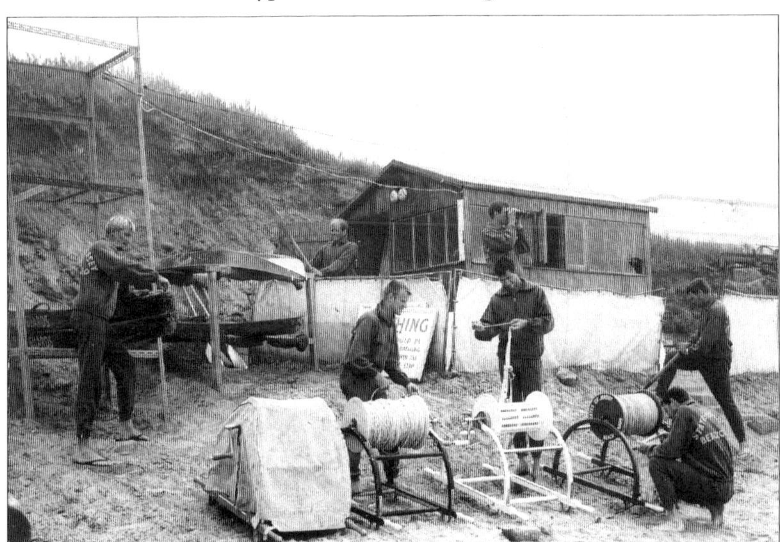

Beach Guard hut, c. 1965
Left to right, John Andrew, Peter Williams, Ian Peacock (with binoculars)
Front: John Roberts, Col Ambrosoli, Noel Bennet (kneeling) and Chris O'Connor
(Photo Courtesy of the Jersey Evening Post)

The actor Eli Wallach, who was there, was reportedly being paid three thousand US dollars a week and that was a lot of money in those days. Danny says by comparison: 'The three of us could live for ten bob a week - that included food, wine, accommodation, everything'. According to Danny, Eli Wallach used to have a party every night. He would get everybody, including the three Aussies, to come along and he would say: 'I don't care if Eastwood never comes'. Clint Eastwood didn't turn up. The boys had three weeks there as extras and then they went back to Jersey. It would appear that the movie never made it to the screen.

Beach guards Barry 'Cholly' Cardiff and Straw Andrew, along with four other Aussies including Frank 'Boofhead' Morton, took off for Europe at the end of the 1966 season. They bought an Austin Westminster station wagon for one hundred pounds. On a strict budget, they prepared thoroughly for the trip.

Cholly recalls: 'So, we bought a one hundredweight [45 kilogram] pack of rolled oats to eat for breakfast which we strapped on the roof. We borrowed a council tent and put that on the roof too. On our trip we all had allocated jobs – one was to set up the tent, Frank Morton and I were the chefs, and someone else got other jobs such as unloading the car'.

They crossed to France on the car ferry, had a bit of time in Paris looking around, then drove down to Portugal and continued south chasing the sun. They arrived at a camping site one night around ten thirty. They pulled up next to a car and everybody jumped out and quickly got to work as they were hungry and tired. Frank and Cholly went to rustle up something to eat and brought it back to cook.

The group had two Primus stoves. Cholly picked up a Primus and filled it with some methylated spirits but the flame went out after he lit it. Frank picked up a plastic bottle containing methylated spirits and said: 'It needs more metho'.

Cholly, seeing disaster about to happen, shouted: 'Don't do that'.

Too late! The bottle ignited and expanded and turned into a flamethrower. The flames went all over a maroon Jaguar car parked next to the Aussies' vehicle. As one side of the Jaguar was on fire, Cholly ripped his jumper off and tried to beat the flames out.

The woman in a caravan near the Jaguar rushed out and Cholly relates: 'She must have screamed for a minute and a half and gave us the greatest mouthful of abuse'.

The boys offered to pay for the damage and gave the woman and her husband their registration details. The fire also damaged a tarpaulin belonging to the couple so the next morning the boys went down to the town to find someone to repair the tarpaulin. They found a guy who said he could do it and he told them to pick it up the next day. When they got it back the following day Cholly says: 'The bloody bloke had sewn two thirds of a double bed sheet into the tarpaulin!' That was the repair.

Cunningly the boys folded the tarp up with the canvas part on the outside and gave it back to the couple. Off they went, relieved to get away from the scene of the fire. Strangely enough they never heard from the couple again. Cholly Cardiff says: 'They must have claimed it on their insurance. What a classic!'

Despite the fire, the boys wanted more heat, so they journeyed to Morocco. They finished up down in Agadir on the Atlantic coast. As it was all free camping they set up the tent and stayed.

Every morning they would have porridge and orange juice for breakfast. They used to take a big sheet across to the markets and the locals would fill it up with oranges which cost next to nothing. In the afternoon in the harbour the locals would fish for sardines, so the beach guards bought any that were excess. The six Aussies lived there for three months and in that time, they spent the princely sum of twenty-seven pounds each, that's nine quid a month. They were riding what Cholly believes to be the first surfboards to be seen down on that part of the coast.

The local rules were that the guys couldn't walk around without a shirt on and were not permitted to drink alcohol. A couple of the guys Cholly travelled with got into the weed. Cholly says there was one guy so high on pot he stuffed a whole lot of bananas into a bread roll and put it under his pillow to eat later. He was off his face on dope.

They left Morocco and took a ferry across the Mediterranean. Then they drove across the bottom of Europe to Monte Carlo and then on to Budapest in Hungary, part of the Communist Bloc in those days. They arrived in Budapest with three surfboards on the roof of the car. It was Liberation Day and Cholly says: 'The military was marching down the street doing the goose step. All of a sudden, these cops see us in this car with these three surfboards. They thought they were missiles, so we spent about an hour trying to explain what you did with a surfboard, that you put them in the water and stand on them. So, these guys were there with guns out, they had no English. We were trying to explain that these boards were for recreational use. It took a while, but they let us go eventually'.

On the return trip to Jersey they travelled to St Malo in France to board the ferry. Cholly describes it as being 'like a Monty Python film. Two of the guys had left earlier and flew back to Jersey and there were four of us left. The tent was there, the rolled oats were all finished but the car wouldn't start. It was dead. We got hold of the four corners of the big tent and anybody that had anything they wanted to keep tossed it in the middle. We got one on each corner and carted it on to the ferry and left the car where it was'.

9 This Sporting Life

'Then I got picked for first grade on the wing. Reg Gasnier was injured, he was out. Eddie Lumsden who normally played wing went into the centres and I went on to the wing.'

Extract from an interview with Duncan Page, an Australian lifeguard in the 1960s.

Although all of the young Australian men who worked as lifeguards in Jersey in the 1960s were fit, active and played sport, there were three that stood out from the pack. They didn't just play sport, they excelled in their chosen fields of rugby league, modern pentathlon, rugby union and surfing.

One of them was Duncan Page who spent a season in Jersey in 1960. A good runner and hurdler, swimmer and surf board rider, Duncan's sporting prowess gained him selection for two Olympic Games in the 1960s. As well, he was an accomplished rugby league player.

Duncan was a runner for as long as he can remember, and a good one at that. Through making the finals of the 220 and 440 yards hurdles at the 1954–55 Australian titles, Duncan was selected in the 1956 Olympics training squad for the 440 yards hurdles. However, two better performed athletes made the Olympic team for the Melbourne games.

Unfortunately, a bad accident cut short his hurdling career. Duncan says: 'There used to be a Labour Day sports event on Redfern Oval in Sydney which was a big competition in those days and I won the 880 yards race. But my foot went down in a hole on the grass track and I tore the ligaments in my ankle off the bone. So, for two years I was on crutches. As part of my rehabilitation I started to compete in surfing and surf club competitions. The reason why I joined North Cronulla surf club was to recover after that bad accident'.

This must have done the trick because he won the interstate beach sprint title at the Australian championships at Mooloolaba in Queensland in 1959. As a member of the North Cronulla team he also came second in the Australian beach relay at the same titles. Even though Duncan was a sprinter he also won a beach marathon at North Cronulla.

Duncan also enjoyed board riding. He had a part-time job working for four hours in the evening, so he could spend the daytime on the beach board riding.

The ten-foot boards were starting to become popular, he recalls. He, along with Ken Woods, took his board with him when he went to Jersey in 1960.

A chap named Mike Hurst, a rugby league player from Yorkshire, who saw Duncan playing touch football on the beach in Jersey thought he had the talent to play rugby league in England. At the end of the 1960 beach guard season Duncan went to trial with the Wakefield Trinity rugby league club in west Yorkshire. English rugby league was very strong in those days, and the Lancashire and Yorkshire Leagues were the most competitive. Coached by former English international Ken Trail, Wakefield Trinity had a good team. Duncan had a few trial games with Wakefield Trinity and Ken Trail said to him: 'We want you to play for us on the wing'. Duncan was pretty pleased with this because every one of the team members represented England bar one fellow who was a South African.

However, Duncan couldn't get a clearance from the Australian Rugby League to play. In 1960 the president of the Australian Rugby League, a chap called Bill Buckley, put a halt to Australians playing in England. The reason given was that when the Australian rugby league team went to England to play they received one third of the gate receipts for each game but when the English team came to Australia to play they got half of the gate receipts. Bill Buckley made a ruling that no Australian would be allowed to play in England until the gate receipts split was equitable at fifty/fifty.

Disconsolate, Duncan returned to Sydney for Christmas 1960. Determined to see where he might go in rugby league, he trialled for the St George club in the lead up to the 1961 season. Duncan recalls: 'Anybody in those days could turn up for a trial. I had three trials in the first part of 1961 then I played three games of reserve grade. Then I got picked for first grade on the wing. Reg Gasnier was injured, he was out. Eddie Lumsden, who normally played wing, went into the centres and I went on to the wing. Then the next week Reg was back so I played another game of reserves. I got picked again to play first grade against Balmain, but I had a bad bout of the flu and I couldn't get out of bed, so couldn't play'.

A couple of games later, playing on the wing in reserve grade against Manly at the Sydney Sports Ground, Duncan broke his leg in six places. It was a freak accident. A Manly player made a break and the St George fullback came across in cover and dived at his opponent close to where Duncan was positioned. At the same time the metal sprigs in Duncan's boot got caught in the ground and his leg started to twist. The St George fullback only managed to get one hand to the opposition player and all that did was to swing the fullback around like a pendulum. His body hit the back of Duncan's leg and it snapped like a twig.

After a couple of doctors at the ground set Duncan's leg in plaster he was sent home in a taxi. The next day a doctor who lived near Duncan came over to check on him. The doctor took one look at Duncan's leg and said: 'You'll have to go to hospital'. Off Duncan went to the St George hospital. The doctor there took the plaster off and reset the leg.

About two weeks later a precautionary X-ray was taken of the leg, which revealed a problem. Once again, the plaster came off and the leg was reset. It slowly healed but because of the mismanagement by the medical staff he couldn't run anywhere near as fast as he had done before the accident.

About eighteen months later Duncan says he was down in Kogarah and met the doctor who reset the leg. 'I had gotten to know the doctor pretty well by this time', he recalls. 'He said to me "You know, I've made a mistake with your leg". I was so naïve back in those days I didn't know any better or what to do about that'. That was the end of Duncan's rugby league career.

Duncan had always had an aspiration to compete in the Olympics in the 440-yard hurdles but of course that goal was unachievable given the damage to his leg. However, when one door closed, another opened. Duncan started thinking about the modern pentathlon which comprised the five disciplines of fencing, shooting, riding, swimming and cross country running.

He says: 'I had competed in a couple of modern pentathlon events in Victoria prior to breaking my leg and I ran a time [in the run component] one second behind the winning time in the 1956 Melbourne Olympics. The modern pentathlon run leg at that time was two and a half miles [4,000 metres] cross country. After I broke my leg and recovered I ran on the same course and ran three minutes slower for the distance. So, I knew my run leg was shot'.

Undeterred, Duncan decided to have a go. As a surf lifesaver Duncan could swim quite well but the other sports presented a challenge. He recalls: 'I was a pretty good rider, not so good at shooting and I couldn't fence'.

Around that time the United States sent an invitation for Australians to train in the US for the modern pentathlon events. Duncan and a fellow called Peter Macken (who had competed in the 1960 Rome Olympics for Australia) took up the offer and travelled to Fort Sam Houston in Texas to train. 'We had to pay our own way of course', Duncan recollects. 'Well, we met up with the American Olympic training squad of about thirty. They had a stable of horses and it was the best year of my life'. During their time in America they had access to a fencing coach, a riding coach and a shooting coach. It was a tremendous atmosphere in which to train and improve.

Although the facilities were fantastic, the pair had no money during that period and subsequently when they moved on to Europe to compete. As Duncan describes it, 'We were bums. In Europe we all had malnutrition, we had boils and sores'.

At the World Championships in 1967 in Switzerland the pair and another

Australian competitor named Don McMiken had to pay for their meals. They were so poor that they had to rely on the British and the American team members to bring them food out of the dining hall. Duncan recalls with disgust: 'There was an Australian Olympic official who was actually in the dining room, but he never spoke to any of us and he was being fed but we couldn't afford to eat'.

Duncan loved riding, although when he first started shooting his scores were not so good. But as the years went by he and his team mates got better. They went to Mexico for the world championships and from there they travelled to England. Duncan ended up competing for Australia in the 1964 Summer Olympics in Tokyo and in the 1968 Olympics in Mexico.

Because the modern pentathlon is a military type sport Duncan found that the pentathletes were able to stay at military bases. It was at Aldershot in England where he met a couple of Brits named Benjamin (Mick) Finnis and Jim Fox, both pentathletes who competed for Great Britain in the 1964 Olympics. Mick Finnis went to only one Olympics but Jim Fox, who was ten times modern pentathlon champion of Great Britain, competed in the 1964, 1968, 1972 and 1976 Olympic games and won a team gold medal in the 1976 Olympics in Montreal, Canada. He was later awarded the OBE and the MBE for his contributions to British sport. Duncan says: 'Jim Fox was a terrific fellow, just a nice guy. He was so nice that women used to climb up his bedroom balcony to try and get into his room'.

Jim Fox and Mick Finnis went to Jersey for a period and often trained with the lifeguards in the sand hills behind St Ouen's beach. They were so fast that they often did an extra three-kilometre loop on the run and still caught the Australians.

Duncan recalls Jim Fox helped to uncover a bizarre cheating attempt in the 1976 Olympics. A Russian pentathlete by the name of Boris Onischenko was found to have used a rigged épée in several of the fencing bouts. To score a fake hit he pressed down on a hidden pressure pad in his epée. However, it was Jim Fox who became suspicious of Onischenko, who ironically was rated as the best fencer in the Olympics and asked the officials to inspect his weapon. Eventually they found the hidden pressure pad and the Russian was disqualified and sent home in disgrace. Great Britain went on to win the gold medal.

Notwithstanding the problems his leg created, when everything fell into place Duncan did quite well as a competitor. He won the British Army on the Rhine championships in the 1960s. He says: 'But the course had to be flat in the run. I used to have to carry a walking stick around with me in the run to get up the hills. Even though I improved my swim times dramatically I got a frozen ankle which used to hang uselessly'.

During Duncan's time representing Australia in the Olympics the modern pentathlon team's best result was a fifth in 1964, an outstanding result given the quality of the opposition. Then in 1968 Duncan joined an exclusive group of Australians to compete in more than one event by fencing for Australia as well as the modern pentathlon. He says: 'My leg probably affected my fencing a bit. Australia doesn't really have a history of fencing. The Europeans start fencing when they are at school when they're young'.

Duncan Page retired from the modern pentathlon after the 1968 Olympics.

❊

A lifeguard who had made a name for himself playing rugby league in Australia in the early 1960s was John 'Straw' Andrew. At the age of eighteen as a fullback he got called up to play for Eastern Suburbs (now the Sydney Roosters) in the NSW competition. Although not a goal kicking fullback (typical in those days) Straw progressed steadily to the top grade, playing third grade in 1958, second grade in 1959 and then first grade in 1960.

Straw played in the first grade grand final against St George that year but Eastern Suburbs was beaten comprehensively. They had beaten St George about a month previously in a very close game by seven points to four. They kept St George from scoring a try in that game – Easts scored a try and kicked two goals. The legendary Jack Gibson was the captain of Eastern Suburbs that year. Eastern Suburbs was a very young side and Jack was one of the hard heads of the team.

Straw again played first grade for Eastern Suburbs in 1961. They just missed out on a finals berth, playing Canterbury-Bankstown in the last competition game and needing to win to make the finals. But the game finished in a five all draw, and they missed out by a solitary point.

In a shocking end to his career the next year Straw broke his neck playing on the Sydney Cricket Ground against Newtown in August 1962. Back in those days spear tackles were not illegal. During the first half one of the Easts' forwards named Neville Charlton, a very good back rower, got sent off after the opposition targeted him and he retaliated. Jack Gibson had left after a disagreement with Easts and went to Western Suburbs and Neville Charlton came to Eastern Suburbs. Charlton was in the mould of an early Artie Beetson (a talented player who represented Australia) but he succumbed to some niggling and got his marching orders from the referee.

A bit later in the first half two blokes lifted Straw in a tackle and drove him headfirst into the ground and that was that. With a trace of bitterness still in his voice Straw says: 'We were going very well, and we were on top of them. There were no replacements in those days, so I got carted off to hospital and later when I learnt that we had lost the game I couldn't believe it. I was in a bit hot form at the time. I'd got maybe a dozen tries that season - I'd scored three tries in one game as a running fullback. So, when I was taken off we were two down because no replacements were allowed'.

Straw Andrew broke the fourth, fifth and sixth cervical vertebrae in his neck. Back in those days (much the same as Ken Woods in the 1950s) the treatment was to put a weight on the back of the head after attaching it to the skull to pull the vertebrae back together. Anyway, after a couple of weeks the doctors found that the treatment wasn't working so they increased the weight to sixty pounds for six weeks but that didn't work either. Then they fused one of his vertebrae and took a bone from his hip to help repair the others. He was in hospital for six months and that was the end of the football (well not quite). The doctors told him not to play again. After he got out of hospital Straw says he had some restricted movement but says it never worried him too much – he could still surf and run and play contact sport although there was always a risk.

In 1966 while Straw was working as a beach guard the Huddersfield rugby league club in Northern England somehow found out that he had played first grade for Eastern Suburbs in Sydney. They sent one of their directors to Jersey in 1966 to ask Straw if he was interested in going to Huddersfield to trial and play. Of course, he said yes, despite the risk. The ban on Australians playing in England had been lifted by then. Huddersfield was one of the original rugby league towns where the game first started.

When the beach season ended he drove up to Huddersfield in the old Hillman that he owned. Club officials organised for him to stay with a group of Fijians that Huddersfield had signed up the previous year. Someone in the club thought the Fijians would be world beaters but Straw recalls they couldn't fire – they hated the cold. Huddersfield rented them a big house and, Straw recalls wryly, 'I moved in with them – what an education that was. They weren't bad blokes, but they were very primitive. They got an advance payment up front and they then spent it all on guitars and parties so within two months they had no money left. To top it off they weren't very good footballers, so they became a bit of an embarrassment to the club'.

Straw played first grade for Huddersfield at fullback. Straw recalls: 'We got twelve pounds for a win and five pounds for a loss. If we had a draw at home, we got paid the loss fee and if we had a draw away we got paid the win fee. We got paid on Tuesday night at training. You walked up to an office, knocked on a window and a shutter came up and you got paid in cash'.

Being a running fullback Straw found it hard going in northern England because of the weather – rain, sleet, snow, hard ground then soft ground. He got dropped to second grade because another full back who was a goal kicker was preferred.

Straw was then approached by a chap called Frank Dyson who was the England coach as well as coach of the Oldham rugby league team. Oldham was about seventeen miles to the south-west of Huddersfield, nestled in the Pennines chain of low ranges in central England.

Frank Dyson said to Straw: 'Come over to Oldham and play for us, we need a fullback'.

Straw went and played the rest of the season for Oldham. Straw made it clear to the Oldham officials that he was going back to the beach in Jersey at the end of the football season. Straw says: 'Oldham were about the same standard as Huddersfield. When I was playing in England the only time I was really worried was when I got dumped on my head [in a tackle] but thank goodness nothing happened'.

Straw found it to be a very entertaining experience playing rugby league in northern England and although he hated the cold he made a lot of good friends. He states: 'It was a hard life in those towns. Most of them worked in the mines or in the woollen mills. Playing football supplemented their income from work. Those people were the salt of the earth. They loved Huddersfield and Yorkshire. They were born and bred there and didn't want to go anywhere else'.

After his stint with Huddersfield and Oldham Straw retired from rugby league once more and resumed his beach guard activities. Perhaps Hilary, his wife-to-be, may have had something to do with this decision. More on her later.

Barry 'Cholly' Cardiff made a name for himself as a surf board rider in the 1960s. Not just content to ride big waves in Australia, Cholly joined the likes of Brian 'Midget' Farrelly in Hawaii in the early 1960s to ride the monster waves of the famous Sunset Beach.

As a young man Cholly set himself a goal – to surf in Hawaii. He managed to get a job as a Beach Inspector on the beach at Dee Why in Sydney during the Christmas holidays and school holidays. He also worked in the blossoming surfboard industry for Danny Keogh (who shaped the board that Midget Farrelly used to win at the first World Surfing Championships in 1964) with whom he went to school in Manly.

In 1961/62 the first lot of Australians, eighteen in total, journeyed to Hawaii to go surfing. A few of Cholly's mates, including Midget Farrelly and a guy named Tank Henry, left on the *Oriana*. They were very keen on surfing really big waves on the north shore beaches of the Hawaiian island of Oahu. Cholly, who hadn't saved enough money for that trip, went to see them off. As he enviously watched them leave he made a vow that, 'When this boat sails next year I'm going to be onboard'. He worked on the beach and did brickies labourer's work as well to earn the cash.

Sure enough, in September 1962 Cholly and a mate named Mick McMahon headed off to Hawaii on the *Oriana*, stopping at Auckland and Suva, then on to

Honolulu. Bob Evans (*Surfing World Magazine* editor), Midget Farrelly and the late Kelvin Platt flew there, sponsored by Ampol. Mick had been with the 1961 group and had a contact for accommodation with a fellow named Jose Angel who Mick met on the 1961 trip.

As luck would have it, within days the pair met big wave surfer and surfboard maker Bob Shepherd who offered them accommodation right on the famous Sunset Beach. Bob hit it off with the Aussies and Cholly says that fifty years later that friendship survives. They stayed in Hawaii for six to seven months, into 1963. That was the year when Midget Farrelly won the first international competition at Makaha Beach.

A female Australian journalist named Kerry Yates wrote an article on Cholly and Mick entitled 'Surf Safari in Hawaii' which was published in *The Australian Women's Weekly* on Christmas Day 1963.

The article describes the Japanese style bungalow on Sunset Beach where the surfers lived. It was a tough life – eighteen-foot waves on their doorstep when the surf was running. They each took two surf boards with them – one a shorter board for the smaller surf and the other a 'big gun' for the monster surf. They surfed the Banzai Pipeline, Makaha, Waimea Bay and of course Sunset. It was a dream come true.

To get around they boys purchased an old bomb of a car, paying the equivalent of thirty Australian pounds. Ironically, the only time it let them down was the day they were due to compete in the heats of the Makaha international championships. Lacking transport, they didn't make it to the event, although Australians Midget Farrelly, Bob Evans and Dave Jackman did. The boys were ecstatic to hear that Midget Farrelly had won. Speaking of Midget, the boys were bit players in a film made by Bob Evans called *The Midget Goes Hawaiian* which featured a sea turtle that Mick had earlier captured. Unfortunately, they didn't feature in the credits.

Other minor film roles followed in three surfing movies, one by Californian Bud Browne called *Gun Ho!*, another by Val Valentine called *Northside Story* and a third by Art Napoleon called *Ride the Wild Surf* which starred Fabian and Tab Hunter and featured footage of some really big surf (not that the stars rode it of course).

After returning home in 1963 Cholly was soon off again, this time to Santa Barbara, California. An American guy called Bob Cooper who came out to Australia got Cholly a job working for Yater surfboards (started by a guy named Rennie Yater). He was there for about eighteen months working and surfing.

Then he got a call from Straw Andrew who was in Jersey and who offered him a job as a beach guard. So off he went.

10   Wives' Tales 1960s

'Chris O'Connor (a beach guard) was supposed to be the best man but he couldn't make it. There was a friend of Straw's who played rugby with him for the Jersey Rugby Club, the half back, he happened to be walking through the plaza in St Helier at the time and Straw grabbed him as our witness.'

Extract from an interview with Hilary Andrew, who met and married John 'Straw' Andrew in Jersey in the 1960s.

Perhaps it was the birds and bees that created the atmosphere for love on the island, or maybe it was the easy-going lifestyle. Whatever it was, lasting romance blossomed for several of the beach guards. Romance which led to marriage that is, as opposed to short term entanglements of which by all accounts were plentiful. The following stories were related by ladies that met and fell in love with Australian beach guards in Jersey in the 1960s and subsequently accompanied their men to Australia to live.

In 1965 a young Irish woman named Hilary Parkes, along with her two sisters, went to Jersey from Belfast in Northern Ireland to work there during the summer season. Hilary and her sisters all left school at age fifteen and (at that stage) were not interested in pursuing further education. Hilary says: 'We sought change to a sun and fun-filled island supported by a working holiday. Jersey was a holiday island where university students and whoever went there on holidays and the tourism and the hotel industry thrived in the season'.

Hilary worked in restaurants and hotels seven days a week and, despite the workload, really enjoyed the island. She met a beach guard named John 'Straw' Andrew in a bar in the Chelsea Hotel in St Helier. At that time Hilary was working as a chambermaid. The pair quickly became an item and they were married in the Jersey registry office in 1967.

Hilary says: 'Chris O'Connor (a beach guard) was supposed to be the best man but he couldn't make it. There was a friend of Straw's who played rugby with him for the Jersey Rugby Club, the half back, he happened to be walking through the plaza in St Helier at the time and Straw grabbed him as our witness'.

Their daughter Amanda was born early the following year. The Chief Beach guard's pay was not enough to support a family so Hilary worked in a restaurant called the Golden Egg during the 1968 summer. Some friends looked after Amanda while she worked. Hilary says philosophically: 'It wasn't an ideal situation but that was what it was'.

The couple decided that the life in Jersey for a family was not for them, so they elected to go to Australia. Hilary recalls: 'Australia was a totally alien world to me when we arrived in January 1969. It was quite a shock – the attitudes were completely different. The first time Straw took me down to the beach at Maroubra the Beach Inspector was measuring the size of the bikinis on the women on the beach – they had to comply with a certain minimum measurement!'

Accustomed to being treated as an equal, Hilary felt Australia seemed to be male dominant back in those days compared to where she had come from. However, she adjusted most admirably to this different world. She says: 'When we got to Australia I worked as a telephonist, then had a second child, then I ended up going through education as a mature age student, then I went into teaching and ended up retiring as an Assistant Principal. So, in that sense Australia was very good to me and the opportunities I received in Australia were wonderful'.

Hilary started teacher training at Alexander Mackie Teachers College in Paddington in mid-1976 and finished in mid-1979. However, when she finished her teacher's qualification she was unable to get a job near to where they were living on the southern beaches of Sydney. She recalls that 1979 was the first year that teachers came out of the system unbonded, which meant that they were not tied to the NSW Department of Education or required to pay back their bond if they didn't work in the system for the number of years equal to the duration of teacher training. It also meant that there were no guaranteed jobs.

Hilary worked on a casual basis for two years and then was offered a non-permanent position in a school at Parramatta. If Hilary had told the NSW Department of Education that she wanted a permanent teaching position she could have been sent anywhere in NSW and she didn't want that. Straw was working as a baggage handler at Sydney airport and two incomes were important. They were living at Malabar in Sydney's south at the time and Hilary had to travel to Parramatta. Hilary says: 'I had a 15-month-old baby, Adam, at the time and it was extremely hard'.

She was eventually put on permanently at the school in Parramatta in about 1983. Then someone did something dreadful, not to her, but that changed her circumstances. She recalls: '... someone came along and burnt the school to the ground.'

Subsequently Hilary was able to get a job at a school in the eastern suburbs of Sydney which she says was wonderful. From there she studied for, and completed, a Bachelor of Education degree, followed by a Master's degree in Educational

Administration. In between Hilary and Straw had a third child, a son named Aiden, in 1982. After that she went into consultancy with the NSW Department of Education. Hilary says: 'The school system had a wonderful superannuation scheme and I was able to retire at fifty-five'.

The year after Hilary and Straw arrived in Australia one of Hilary's sisters came to live in Australia with her husband and daughter. Then her mother came out and then her older sister and they all settled in Australia. All three sisters undertook university studies under the adult education programs offered.

Adam Andrew, the son of Hilary and Straw, (who also worked as a beach guard in Jersey in 1989 and 1993) married an Irish girl in 2002 and they went back to Ireland for the wedding. Before that they had not been back in thirty-three years. Hilary says: 'We were from Belfast in Northern Ireland. It had changed so much – the place was rebuilt. I left before the Troubles (the conflict between the Catholic Irish and the Protestant British) had started and I didn't go back until after they were finished'.

The year 1965 is also the starting point for Vee Bradley's story. In that year Vee, a young woman originally from County Durham in the north-east of England, joined British European Airways (BEA) as a stewardess, or flight steward as the position is now known. BEA, at that time the largest airline in Europe, apart from the Soviet Aeroflot, was based at Heathrow to the west of London. Vee enjoyed flying as a stewardess and her job took her across Europe as the airline expanded.

Vee says: 'A couple of years later they wanted people to go to Jersey to work there. I had been there for a couple of times on holiday, so my friend Andrea and I went together, and we shared a flat firstly in St Helier and then we had a flat at Beaumont [a suburb to the west of St Helier] right on the beach. It was great'.

Andrea and Vee would regularly fly Jersey to London, London to Berlin or Munich with an overnight stop and then back to Jersey over a three or four-day period. They also flew Jersey to Guernsey, a 10 minute flight with an overnight stop.

Vee Cardiff recalls that there were lots of parties in Jersey with it being a tax-free location with cheap drinks. When she was in Jersey she didn't know much about the beach guards. Vee says: 'We probably moved in different circles – our crowd used to go to the Aero Club, I don't think that the lifeguards could get into there, and the Royal Yacht Hotel which was more a place where the airline people went to. The only one I knew was AJ, Alan Hardy, because he did those deck chairs (at Watersplash)'. AJ wasn't a beach guard, but he knew them all through running the deck chair concession at the Watersplash.

Early in autumn 1969 Vee was invited to a party on a boat in St Helier and that's where she first met Barry 'Cholly' Cardiff, a former beach guard who was by then working at the airport as a baggage handler. They must have hit it off (he managed to get her phone number) because Cholly called Vee during the following week and asked her if she would like to go out to dinner on the forthcoming Saturday as some beach guards were leaving Jersey at the end of the season. Vee's response was a cool: 'Oh yeah, that'll be fine'.

This was where fate decided to step in. On the Friday prior to the date Vee flew to London with the trip including a night stopover. She was due to depart Heathrow the next day on the 2.30 p.m. Vanguard (a turboprop aircraft) flight from London into Jersey, leaving her plenty of time to get ready for the date.

However, as Vee recounts: 'When we got to Jersey there was so much fog. Jersey was renowned for its fog; it was clamped. The captain tried to land, and he couldn't, he went round again and he couldn't. He went round the third time and the fog just dispersed so we landed. We were the only aircraft to land in Jersey that day and that's the night we went out for dinner'.

The nascent relationship saved, the couple started seeing each other regularly. Things progressed quickly – after going out for about nine months they decided to get married. The date was set for June 1970 because Vee's parents were coming over from England to Jersey for a week's holiday, so the pair decided to get married during their visit.

Not having much money, the pair decided to only have half a dozen people at the wedding. Vee's girlfriend Andrea was to be bridesmaid and a friend of Cholly's named John Pattinson (not a beach guard) the best man. However, things changed when a neighbour, a local lady named Corinne Le Marquand (more on her later), heard about the wedding. She lived across the road from Vee and Andrea and she owned the historic Windmill pub in St Peter. Corinne offered to have the reception at her home, a very nice house called Villa Lara. She provided champagne and somebody else organised the cake.

The number of guests at the wedding expanded to over twenty, including several beach guards, namely Jerry Shannos, John 'Ant' Roberts and Bruce Westwood. As Vee says: 'Everybody just turned up to the wedding. We had the most casual wedding'.

Because Vee was still working she had to take a few days off sick to get married. For their honeymoon they went to Malta because Vee could get cheap travel. She was working but they somehow found time to be together.

Later in 1970 Barry got a job at a place called Warren Farm in Wimbledon, England so Vee and Cholly moved to Wimbledon. He was a caretaker for a big house on a huge property and Vee was still working for BEA. They stayed at Wimbledon until the end of 1970 then decided to go to Australia.

Vee says: 'I took three months' unpaid leave from work when we came to Australia at the end of 1970. That was because I didn't know whether I was going to like it there or not. We got round the world tickets with Pan Am, who no longer exists, but I liked it here alright. We came to Dee Why [in Sydney]. For me Australia was the last place on earth I thought I would be in. I had lived in America for twelve months and I travelled a lot, but I never ever thought I would end up in Australia!'

Vee went back home and worked her notice and then came back in 1971. When she got back Vee worked as a casual in the restaurant at the Dee Why RSL. They lived at Avalon on Sydney's northern beaches and Cholly got a job at the airport with Qantas as a baggage handler.

Their eldest boy, Ashley (Ash), was born in 1972. When their son was three weeks old Cholly was offered his old job back at the Jersey airport. They were running a store at Mona Vale (not far from Avalon) at the time which wasn't all that successful, so they decided to go back. In Jersey they lived in a tiny cabin, but it just didn't work out with a little baby. They decided to go to England and stay with Vee's parents in Stoke-on-Trent.

Cholly was looking for work to make ends meet so Vee said to him: 'Have you ever thought about teaching?' Cholly thought that was a good idea and applied for a mature age student scholarship at Keele University near Newcastle-under-Lyme in England. Vee got a job and they moved into a council house. Their second son, Lauren or Loz for short, was born while Cholly was doing his three-year teacher training course.

About the time he finished teacher training the Australian government ran a campaign to encourage Australians to return home. The Cardiffs took up the offer - Cholly came back for free but Vee's fare cost about ten quid – and settled back in Dee Why. There they stayed and both sons live nearby.

11　A Permanent Base

Each year the head beach guard would submit an end-of-season report to the States of Jersey Tourism Department which contained an annual summary of the beach guard service as well as recommendations for improvements. This report originated in the early 1960s and was usually no more than three typed pages in length. It would cease to be written by the early 1970s.

The summary would provide details such as a wrap-up of the season's surf conditions, the number of rescues that took place, any drownings that occurred (normally not at the spots that were patrolled), the size of the crowds at the patrolled beaches and a repeated request (which was repeatedly ignored) to provide the beach guards with authority to properly police the increased number of surf board riders.

A section of the report headed 'Equipment' described the condition of the surf reels used on the beach and the box lines mounted in the vehicles, as well as several stretchers, a few first aid kits, surf skis, flag poles, the beach phones linking El Tico southwards and northwards along St Ouen's beach, the two-way radios, and the loud hailers for attracting attention on the beach.

In the end-of-season report for 1966 Chris O'Connor, who was in his final year on the beach, provided a recommendation that John 'Straw' Andrew be appointed as Head Beach guard for 1967. This was accepted.

Chris also commented on a momentous improvement in the beach guard service that year – the construction of what he described as a Life Saving Centre at El Tico on St Ouen's beach. This new building, which was to become known as the Lifeguard Tower, replaced the flimsy demountable shed that had been in use for most of the 1960s. This surely was a sign that the beach guards were going to be around in Jersey for a long time to come.

The call for the construction of the so-called Life Saving Centre had been contained in successive head beach guard annual reports and most of the beach guards had begun to believe that it would not be built for many years, if at all. As Chris O'Connor stated in his report, 'In the past years it has been the accepted thing for this Report to be concluded with a "gentle roast" and yet another request for that elusive Control Centre which, when I arrived on the island in 1963, seemed to be at least ten years off'.

The Lifeguard Tower was a facility with a ground floor and a small first floor lookout tower. The ground floor contained a changing room, a first aid room, a shower and a toilet and the lookout tower had large glass panels on three sides to permit viewing over the beach area. An open deck was situated next to the lookout tower. On one side of the building was an enclosed storage area to house lifesaving equipment.

The tower was a relatively modest building but, compared to the old demountable, the beach guards viewed it with pride and, as Straw Andrew wrote in his first report as head beach guard in 1967, 'The new control tower has just completed its first full season's use at St Ouen's and because of our increased membership, our extensive equipment and the larger crowds, it has proved its indispensability and value many times over'.

The Lifeguard Tower celebrated its fiftieth anniversary in 2016 and there is little doubt that the building, if it could talk, would be able to relate many stories about the goings-on inside its walls over the years. Perhaps it's just as well that it cannot!

Whilst the Jersey beach guards were consolidating their position as the pre-eminent surf lifesaving organisation on the island, unfortunately the Jersey Lifeguard Club, created on the Australian surf club voluntary membership model, was struggling. In 1966 the JLC changed its name to Jersey Surf Life Saving Club in keeping with the Australian tradition of surf lifesaving. However, the fast-growing pastime of surf board riding was denuding its membership to the extent that, at a Special General Meeting held on 10 January 1968, the decision was taken to wind the club up.

At some point in the mid-1960s the Jersey Surf Life Saving Club had moved from the wooden hut at El Tico to an old lifeboat house on the South Pier in St Helier, although they continued to provide voluntary patrols at St Ouen's beach on a Sunday afternoon. Indeed, Straw Andrew had commended the club for their Sunday patrols in his 1967 report. However, the Royal National Lifeboat Institute, which presumably owned the lifeboat house, had asked for its return so that the proposed inshore rescue service could be stationed there. The Jersey Surf Life Saving Club hierarchy could not find other suitable facilities which contributed to the decision to shut the club down. Those present at the meeting voted that the lifesaving equipment held by the club should be handed over to the States' beach guard service.

In closing the final meeting, the club's president expressed the feeling that the club had served its purpose, and that the sadness of the occasion was outweighed by the club's achievements.

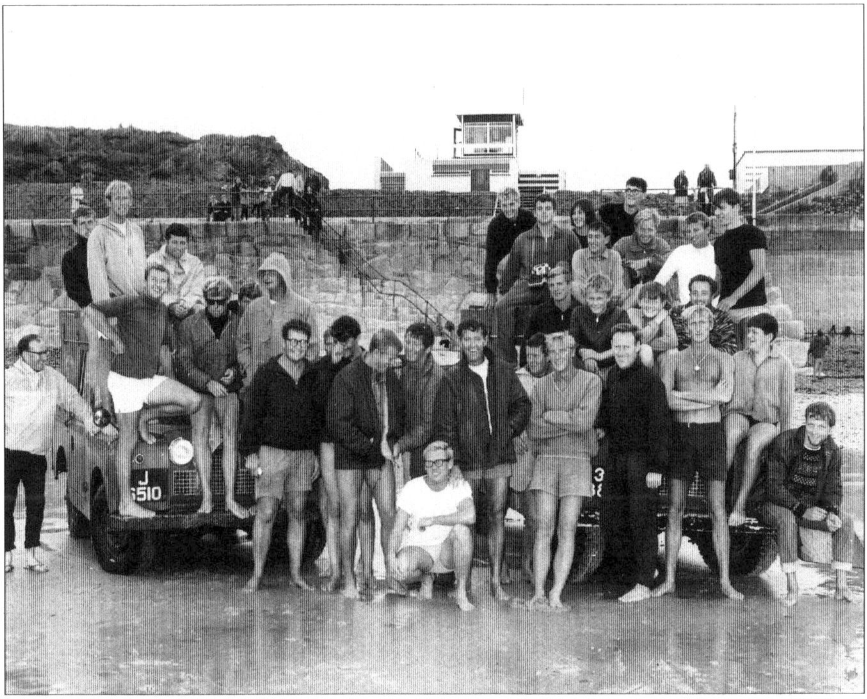

Surf Carnival at St Ouen's Beach c. 1967. The new Beach Guard Tower is shown in the background *(Photo courtesy of the* Jersey Evening Post)

These achievements were undoubtedly endorsed by the beach guards, of whom several had worked hard to train Bronze squads for the club in the 1960s. The acrimony and disruption caused by the beach guards' sacking in 1960 by the JLC's hierarchy had been forgotten, lost in the sands of history. The Australian run beach guard service was now the sole ruler of the beaches in Jersey.

12   The Golden Greek and Jughead

'The attraction of Jersey for me was the lifestyle; it kept on drawing me back.'

Extract from an interview with Jerry Shannos,
chief beach guard in Jersey from 1969 to 1988.

Jerry Shannos, a quiet, dark-haired young man of Greek heritage, arrived in Jersey in 1968 to work as a beach guard. With his muscular physique and dark good looks, Jerry quickly gained the sobriquet 'the Golden Greek': as with all Aussie nicknames it was only a little tongue in cheek. Jerry may have been quiet and unassuming, but in his younger days he had been a champion sportsman who held the Australian and New South Wales heavyweight weightlifting titles in 1961, 1962 and in 1966. He also represented Australia in the Commonwealth Games in Perth in 1962. This sport was a family affair as Jerry's older brother Arthur Shannos won a gold medal in weightlifting at the 1962 Commonwealth Games and represented Australia at Olympic level. Both were subsequently inducted into the NSW Hunter (region) Sporting Hall of Fame. A handy basketballer and Aussie Rules player, Jerry was a member of the now defunct South Newcastle surf club prior to going to Jersey.

Like many of his contemporaries, Jerry followed the urge to travel to Europe. Jerry says, 'I was having a beer in a pub in Newcastle East and got to talking to an Englishman. I told him I was thinking of going to England for a working holiday and that I had a surf club background and I was thinking of trying to get a job on the beach somewhere'. The Brit told Jerry that he came from a place called Bude in Cornwall and that an Australian guy called Alan Kennedy started the surf club there back in the fifties. 'He suggested I write to the Harbour Master, a guy called Fred Diamond and so I wrote to Fred and I had a job in Bude before I left Australia.'

At the end of the season Jerry travelled to Agadir in Morocco where as luck would have it he came across Straw Andrew who was wintering in Morocco. Straw offered him a job in Jersey, but Jerry already had a job at Bude, so he initially declined. But Straw, whom Jerry got on well with, talked him into coming to Jersey for the 1968 season. He must have liked it because he was to complete twenty seasons in

Jersey, taking over as Chief Beach guard from Straw Andrew in 1969 and finally relinquishing that position in 1988.

During a big storm that hit Jersey in the 1968 summer the beach guards at St Ouen's noticed what they initially thought was a shark cruising up and down in the water at the beach. It appeared injured and eventually became stranded in the shallows. It was then the beach guards discovered it was a swordfish. Jerry Shannos and a fellow beach guard named Tony Taylor from South Australia dragged it onto the beach using the Land Rover where unfortunately the swordfish expired. The head of the fish was subsequently mounted in the Jersey Museum.

Jerry joined the Australians living in the first Doghouse (in St Helier's Duhamel Street) and then moved into Doghouse No 2 in Old Street in 1972. He says, 'Something happened to the first one - I think Bill Duquemin decided to redevelop the place but we needed a bigger place anyway as we had more beach guards. The second Doghouse was not very far away from the first one. It was an old place that was owned by the States of Jersey government which was a bit derelict. They did it up a little bit for us, but it was still pretty basic. There were a couple of local women who cooked for us over the years, Kate was one of them. She was a nice girl, a good cook and didn't charge too much. I lived in the second Doghouse for a while, downstairs. Late at night the Midnight Marauders, we used to call them, would bang, bang, bang their way up the stairs after being out to the pubs and clubs'.

Tired of these antics, Jerry decided to move out and, being disposed towards thriftiness, moved into the Lifeguard Tower at El Tico. Jerry recalls, 'The building itself had a shower room in the front, a first aid room and another big room and a bathroom downstairs. You went upstairs to the tower by ladder to the viewing platform'. Jerry was to live there until his departure in 1988.

As chief beach guard, Jerry's role was to recruit the beach guards for each season and to run the service during the season. He invariably went back to Newcastle in the off-season where he worked for the Newcastle Council in the beaches and pools area. Jerry says, 'I used to get a lot of letters of application written by guys from surf clubs who wanted to come to Jersey, or local guys would come and see me – there was a lot of correspondence. Those young guys were keen to go to Jersey and use it as a launching pad to go on to Europe, to the continent after the season even though the pay was bloody awful. It is so sad that it's finished there'. Jerry was referring to the takeover by the Royal National Lifeboat Institute in 2011.

Jerry was also responsible for rostering the guys to the beach or the pools or for a day off. 'I had a deputy chief beach guard as well – Steve Porter, aka the Duke of Normandy, was my deputy for a while and also Brian Jones aka Jughead at one stage', recalls Jerry. Later his deputy became Paul Berghouse, who was to take over from

Jerry in 1988.

The shenanigans that the boys got up to were always a source of concern for any chief beach guard. Says Jerry, 'The chief beach guard was responsible for the conduct of the guys and some of them were a bit of a worry at times – a couple of the Sydney guys were a little bit wild and had to be reined in. A couple of the guys were locked up on some misdemeanour or other and we would have to bail them out. I played rugby for the Police side, so I had a good relationship with them, thank goodness'.

Whilst not exactly involved in a 'shenanigan', beach guard Dave Craig got his name in the *Jersey Evening Post* in September 1969 by winning a beer drinking competition at the Mermaid Tavern in St Peter. Dave downed 41 bottles of lager, or almost 21 pints, in an hour, eight bottles more than the runner-up. The JEP recorded Dave's tongue-in-cheek comment on this feat: 'I could have gone faster but the boys said I was so far in front that I eased off'. His prize was a half-gallon of whisky and he advised the newspaper that he and friends intended to drink it after playing a rugby match (presumably for the Jersey Rugby Club) in the Brittany town of Saint-Brieuc the following Saturday.

Whilst the beach guards were keen and skilled at their jobs, the equipment they were using by this time was not up to scratch. Recalls Jerry, 'When I started in Jersey the lifesaving equipment needed upgrading. There were some old rescue boards, but they were pretty useless. Over time we upgraded the equipment. We got ourselves a new jet ski in 1975 from somewhere in Europe, although we had a few problems with the motor, then an inflatable rubber rescue boat in 1977'. Jerry also was able to source some rescue boards from back home in Newcastle and persuaded the father of one of the beach guards, Mick Jones, to ship them over to Jersey.

An earlier example of a fault with the equipment occurred in the 1969 season during a rescue of four swimmers who got into trouble in the surf near the Watersplash. The *Jersey Evening Post* reported that the beach guards' rescue line became jammed and they had to get another one. Jerry Shannos was forced to deny that the swimmers were in danger and pointed out that they were saved and that no lives had been lost on the beach that summer.

Perhaps because of the 'misdemeanours' in 1971 Jerry decided to hire a new group of beach guards, eleven in all. Many were from surf clubs in or near Newcastle NSW, with the rest from Sydney, Perth, and even one from a surf club called Port Noarlunga, south of Adelaide in South Australia. Among the Newcastle contingent were Brian 'Jughead' Jones, Paul 'Wombat' Wallace, Peter 'Surg' Surgenor and Trevor Morton.

Jughead Jones recalls: 'In 1971 on the beach in Jersey we had eleven new guys and those twelve guys formed a bond which is still maintained to this day. We [the four previously mentioned] flew over in around April 1971 [from London where they had been working]. At this stage we thought we were pretty much world travellers and we were pretty relaxed about going to Jersey. We thought we would fit in well'.

A significant number of the new beach guards elected not to live in the Doghouse, then in Duhamel Street. Jughead says, 'John Le Fondre who owned El Tico was also the head of the Airport Authority and the Tourism Department – he was a bigwig in tourism by then. He owned a flat at St Aubin and we rented it. With me were Paul Wallace, Peter Surgenor and Trevor Morton. Bill Anderton, Tony Cassidy, Brian Holway, and Terry Swan joined Jerry Shannos at the Duhamel Street Doghouse. The others – Alex Penklis, Jim Reynolds, and Tony Taylor – lived elsewhere'.

For transport the beach guards had two Land Rovers – great vehicles according to Jughead – very efficient and very reliable. The Aussies were picked up from where they lived and dropped at St Brelade's, St Ouen's, Grève de Lecq on the north coast (a beach guard was there five days a week), or West Park pool in St Helier. There was one beach guard working at West Park near a deck chair concession run by AJ. At St Brelade's the beach guards operated out of the Land Rover – the old caravan from earlier years had gone. The two beach guards were located near the down ramp right next to another deck chair concession. At St Ouen's there were six beach guards. The remaining two were off duty. Jughead recalls, 'El Tico, the nightclub, was a shambles. It was old and dilapidated, rundown even, but with the Le Fondre family still operating out of it'.

At night the Land Rovers were returned to the depot above Fort Regent in St Helier. Jughead says with a smile, 'Occasionally we got them back slightly after knock off time. We'd go for a drink after work, usually to the Victoria Hotel in St Peter's and camouflage the Land Rovers by putting tree branches over them in an attempt to hide them. How silly – they were bright orange coloured and stuck out like the proverbial! After a drinking session we'd toss a coin to see who was going to drive the Land Rovers back to the depot. We'd drive along the beach at ten o'clock in the evening, perhaps some girls with us. The locals probably thought the beach guards had been working hard. We had no concept of the impact it might have had on the insurance coverage. Jerry would give us the occasional blast, but we never got into real strife'.

There were hundreds of pubs on the island and the boys managed to get to most of them. Jughead reminisces, 'The St Peter's pubs were at the top of the hill from St Ouen's beach and a handy port of call. The Oddfellows, the Old Court House, the Windmill, the St Brelade's Bay Hotel which we used to frequent after we'd done a shift. The Smugglers Inn, Moulin de Lecq, the Aero Club which was a more select establishment: Lloyds which was a little bit upper class, the Terminus, Pomme d'Or'.

The Aussies were a thirsty lot.

The beach guards' remuneration remained a festering sore point. They were poorly paid but were expected to manage the very large summer crowds and effect rescues when necessary. In 1971 Jerry and his fellow beach guards kicked up a stink about the pay, which was then about twelve pounds a week. As stated in an unnamed Australian newspaper at the time, sky rocketing prices were forcing them to moonlight as night club bouncers or barmen. This of course wasn't a recent occurrence – it had been going on for years. The newspaper clipping stated that the beach guards earned a tax-free forty-six dollars for a six-day week (about twenty-three pounds) and were asking for an eight dollar a week pay rise.

Jerry says: 'We fronted the head of the Jersey Tourism Department, Clarrie Dupré, a Senator, to ask for more money. I think they ended up giving us about four quid a week more – it wasn't very much. The government wasn't at all short of money, it's just that they didn't want to pay us too much. We were thinking of joining the Transport and General Workers Union at that time to press the pay case, but we were talked out of it because someone said we were an essential service'. The level of pay would continue to be a significant issue in the years to come.

Jughead recalls how he got a second source of income. 'The relatively small amount of money we were earning on the beach meant that a lot of us got second jobs. I became good friends with a lot of the Jersey Rugby Club guys. A lot of the rugby guys including Tony Hurford (more on him later) were working as bouncers or doormen in clubs and pubs on the island so I went to work with them'.

Jughead says, 'We worked in Behan's West Park, in Blimpers, the Chateau Plaisir, the Mediterranean, at the Royal in David Place with a guy called Colin Cook, Cookie. The Royal was a pub where the Jocks drank, and it was quite rugged. I worked in those places for quite a few years, right up until I left the island. We worked three to four nights a week. We could do that because we didn't start on the beach until 10 a.m.'.

There was always a conflict between the beach guards and the boardriders. The States of Jersey government introduced board registrations in the late 1960s or early 1970s. Boards had to have stickers and the beach guards were expected to police this. The Harbour Master used to come around and chase the boardriders without registered surfboards. Guys would take off – run into the surf and paddle out to sea - or bury their boards in the sand. Jerry Shannos recalls, 'We had no authority to confiscate boards like the beach inspectors back in Australia. Boardriders would hang around near the Watersplash which generally had the best surf. We had a patrol area set up at the Watersplash by that time. We took over from the lifeguards who were employed by Harry Swanson. The boards would come into the patrol area from both sides causing a lot of problems'. Eventually the Watersplash would become the domain of the boardriders and subsequently the windsurfers and kite surfers.

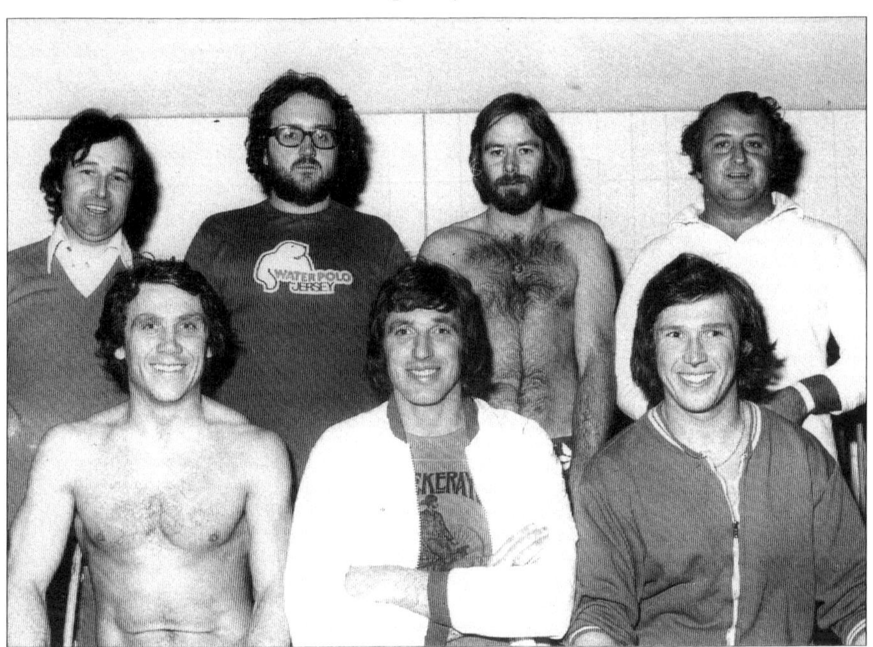

Swim Relay Team: Beach guards and locals form a relay team to compete in the Lions Club Annual Charity Swim at Fort Regent, early 1970s
Left to right, Rear: Brian Donaldson, Gerry Lozack, Peter Surgenor*, Tony Forbes
Front: Bobby Furness, Brian Jones*, David Blake *denotes beach guard
(Photo courtesy of the *Jersey Evening Post*)

The number of rescues continued to grow as the volume of holidaymakers increased during the late 1960s and into the 1970s. Jerry recalls, 'We used to average 50, 60, 70 rescues per year'. Most were close inshore, but several were much further out, and the occasional rescue involved pulling people up from the sea wall.

Not surprisingly the beach guards faced a challenge from the French tourists that came over to the island for holidays. Jughead says, 'They thought bathing in between the flags was a no-no. The frogs would go anywhere else but in the flags and they were being rescued left and right'.

Jughead recalls he was only involved with one death during his time in Jersey and that was during 1971 after the patrol had finished. He, Jerry and another beach guard named Jimmy Reynolds were having a shower at St Ouen's getting ready to go out for a drink. A young lad ran all the way up to the Lifeguard Tower from the beach opposite La Rocco Tower. A swimmer down there was in trouble.

Jughead says, 'We got him on to the beach and together we worked on him for quite a while on the edge of the water. He was blue in the face. Then the paramedics came but unfortunately he died'.

With the increasing tourist numbers, there were rescues on every beach. Tourists at low tide would walk out to Elizabeth Castle offshore from West Park and get trapped with the incoming tide and the beach guards would have to get them. A lot of rescues were because of the tidal surge. Jughead says, 'People would see swirling water which was a rip and then jump into it, they had no idea'.

Most of the rescues were close to shore. A lot of them occurred in the gutters (depressions in the sand) caused by the outgoing tide. Jughead observed that tourism increased at an unbelievable rate during his time in Jersey and there were at times thousands of people on the beaches.

In 1985 a rescue involving a local surfer named Gerry George took place at the Watersplash. It was after hours. Jerry Shannos says, 'I was living in the Lifeguard Tower and someone called me on the emergency phone. I rushed up there to find Gerry trying to keep some guy being slammed by the incoming tide against the sea wall, but they were both getting pretty battered. The fire service arrived, and they put a ladder down and the fellow climbed up the ladder. I threw a rope from one of the box lines down to Gerry and we got him out that way'.

One of the local characters Jerry fondly remembers was a woman named Corinne Le Marquand who had helped with Cholly and Vee Cardiff's wedding in 1970. She owned the Windmill Hotel and she was very good friends with the beach guards. She used to put on dinner at her house for the boys. She was blind in one eye and Jerry was in the kitchen this day carving the turkey. The boys were in the lounge room having a drink. Jerry was piling the turkey on a plate and she turned around and knocked the plate of turkey all over the floor. She commanded, 'Shut the fucking door', so Jerry slammed the door and they piled the turkey back on the plate and took it out and the guys ate it all up.

According to Jerry, Corinne claimed that her father started off De Beers diamonds in South Africa. Her father was Jewish, and he used to make and sell suits in Southern African countries, going door to door. One day he knocked on the door of a farm out in the bush. The old farmer said, 'Come in' and Corinne's father noticed a large rock which was being used as a door stop. He said to the farmer, 'How much do you want for your door stop, I quite like it'. The farmer replied: 'Make me a suit and you can have it', so he did. What the farmer hadn't realised was the rock was chock-a-block full of diamonds. The farmer's name was De Beer. Jerry says, 'It was a good story and whether it's the truth or not, who knows'.

Jerry isn't the only one to recall that Corinne Le Marquand had a liking for the younger guys. She always dressed like a younger woman. Apart from that, she was a very generous lady who was always inviting either the beach guards or others to the pub for parties.

Jerry heard a story about her hosting some rugby guys and their girlfriends at her house for dinner. It was winter, and it was snowing. When her guests made ready to leave after dinner she told them, 'You're not going to drive anywhere tonight, it's too dangerous'. But Corinne made the boys stay in a separate area to the girls. One of the guys who had his girlfriend there said to his mates, 'I'm not sleeping on my own', so he tiptoed down the corridor to where his girlfriend was. Corinne appeared out of the darkness and demanded, 'Where are you going?' He replied, 'To sleep with my girlfriend'. She said, 'If I don't get to do that, you don't either.

One night she invited Jerry, his girlfriend along with another beach guard named Steve Porter and his girlfriend Vicki for dinner. Steve Porter recalls that he was a bit reluctant because Vicki hadn't met Corinne at that stage and Steve was well aware that she would freely drop the F bomb in conversation. However, Steve says, 'She and Vicki got on just fine. The conversation got around to the war years when she was smuggling for the Resistance, things like legs of lamb – she was as cool as a cucumber'.

13   Ruck 'n' Roll

'The Jersey Rugby Club had a few big guys whereas the beach guards were a bit on the skinny side.'

Extract from an interview with Barry 'Cholly' Cardiff,
Australian beach guard in the 1960s.

Straw Andrew was a good enough athlete to be able to play rugby union as well as league. This was a distinct advantage for the sport-loving beach guards who had formed a good relationship with the mainstay of rugby on the island, the Jersey Rugby Club. Many of the JRC team members played touch football on the beach with the beach guards and through this a close bond was formed. This led to an annual game being played between the club and the beach guards at the start of the rugby season.

The first game between the beach guards and the Jersey Rugby Club was held in 1963. Ron Morton, who worked as a beach guard in 1963 and 1964, recalls that he challenged the club to a game whilst the boys were drinking with a Welshman nicknamed Taffy at the Adelphi hotel. Bill Lavarack and another South African from the Watersplash, possibly Cliff Honeysett, played for the beach guards. Ron, who had played fly half for the NSW Under 21 rugby team, was the captain. Bob Morris, Bob Paton, Ken Fawkner, Chris Connor, Noel Bennett, Bob Harris and Mike Gray were also in the beach guard side, as well as two Aussies, Ray McIver and Paul Bernasconi, who were not on the beach but lived in the Doghouse. Ron claims that the beach guard team beat the Jersey team on that occasion.

Rugby was first played in Jersey in the late 1870s, but it took another eighty years before a permanent home several kilometres east of El Tico was found. In 1961 a field was developed near the Jersey airport and the Jersey Rugby Club was formed. This was followed by a wooden clubhouse in 1964 which had a bar, a small kitchen but no restaurant, a couple of changing rooms and showers, a hall used for discos, and a members' lounge.

Rugby was the principal winter sport on the island and it was taken very seriously by the locals. Teams from Britain and France were invited over to play against the local team and the team would reciprocate by touring off the island. The standard was reasonably high in the 1960s, but more at the equivalent of second or third fifteen level in England.

In the second half of the 1960s Straw Andrew, who was still playing contact sports despite being warned against it by the doctors back in Australia, was head and shoulders above the rest of the beach guards as far as rugby ability was concerned. The beach guards were a hodgepodge lot of rugby union, rugby league and Aussie Rules players, very fit but generally not skilled at the finer points of what rugby buffs call 'the game made in heaven'. As Cholly Cardiff recalls: 'The Jersey Rugby Club had a few big guys whereas the beach guards were a bit on the skinny side. Bill Lavarack, a South African who worked at the Watersplash and then later as a part time beach guard, was an icon in Jersey rugby. If he creamed you it was like Gordon Tallis running over you'. Gordon Tallis is a former Queensland State of Origin and Australian rugby league forward who was renowned for his ferocious play in the 1990s and 2000s.

Although the Aussies, bolstered by a few ring-ins, would train hard and play enthusiastically, generally the matches between the Jersey Rugby Club and the beach guards would result in an 'honourable' defeat for the beach guards. After the game and a good singalong, the players would repair to the bar for many drinks and to swap stories about what might have happened if... Food and music was laid on, and the party would continue into the small hours.

The beach guards actually won three matches against the Jersey Rugby Club. The first has been already described. The second was in 1966 and the third was in 1977. All were famous victories but very much upsets. In the 1966 game the beach guards managed to secure the services of two very capable local players by the name of Arthur Wright and Brian Screen, both Welshmen who lived in Jersey. The pair played in the halves and they made all the difference. Straw Andrew, Cholly Cardiff and Col Ambrosoli played in that game.

During those days the president of the Jersey Rugby Club was a fellow named Bill Sugden. Bill would turn up to the game with a giant panda bear and jugs of beer for afterwards. After the game the jugs of beer would be drunk, together with a good singalong, with the panda bear pride of place. Well, the day the lifeguards won Col says with a laugh: 'When we got back to the sheds after the game there was no panda bear, no jugs of beer and no singing. They were quite dirty about the whole thing'.

Of course, this didn't last and before too long the beach guards and the club players were best mates again.

The standard of rugby played by the Jersey Rugby Club steadily improved into the early 1970s as the team was exposed to more games against better opposition. The island's charms attracted a number of good players from England, Wales, Ireland, Scotland, and Australia, not to mention Bill Lavarack from South Africa.

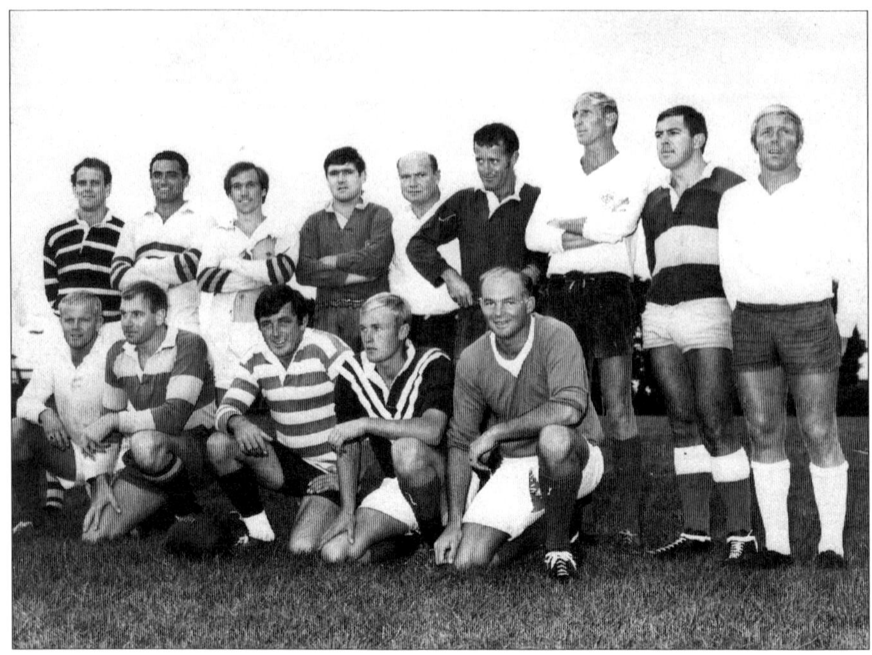

1968 Beach Guard Rugby Team: A number of Jersey locals help to make up the numbers of the team that played against the Jersey RFC at St Peter's.
Left to right Rear: Harry Scott, Jerry Shannos, Ian East, Gordon Rafferty, Jack Chandler, Barry Cardiff, John Andrew, Mick Parnell, Fred Grey,
Front Row: Danny Brosnan, Neil Hartley, Dennis MacInerney, Don Bailey, Barry Young
(Photo courtesy of the *Jersey Evening Post*)

Brian 'Jughead' Jones was a talented and keen rugby player who had played first grade for the Wanderers Club in the Newcastle (NSW) competition and had been playing for a club called Staines in England in 1970. Before long he started working in a second job with a fellow named Tony Hurford as a bouncer or doorman in various pubs and clubs. Tony, a Welshman, was a member of the Jersey Rugby Club and Jughead joined the club as a player in November 1971 after a brief holiday on completion of the beach guard season.

Tony Hurford had a strong connection to Australia through his great uncle, a man named John 'Slam' Sullivan, a Welsh boxer of some renown. Slam, who had got his nickname in his native Cardiff because, according to an article written about him by an Australian woman named Christine Talbot, he had the reputation of being able to knock out 'any loudmouth with one punch to the jaw'. Tony says that Slam had moved to Australia in 1913 after the death of his wife, leaving behind a daughter and son named Albert Patrick (called Pat), Tony's uncle. Slam worked in various jobs including as a swimming and boxing trainer and masseur. He established a reputation for being one of the best cornermen in Australian boxing and was associated with many champion boxers. Of note, Slam was employed by Sir Frank Packer as his masseur. Slam died in Sydney in 1964.

Working at a second job became a matter of course for Jughead and most of the beach guards to enable them to exist on more than a subsistence wage. He worked in establishments that have long gone, such as the renowned Behan's at the West Park Pavilion which attracted up to one thousand revellers at a time to watch world class acts in the 1970s including Slade, Susie Quattro and the Drifters. Others included Blimpers in St Helier, the Chateau Plaisir and the New Mediterranean on the Five Mile Road, and the Royal Hotel in St Helier.

Working with Jughead was a Jersey 'Bean' named Dave Blake who was also a rugby player. Dave complained that, when he was playing for the Jersey Rugby Club first XV, he was the only local in the team – all the rest were from England, Wales, South Africa and Australia! Dave found he had a good affinity with the Aussies because of the similar lifestyle. He had a strong fitness ethic, unlike most of his rugby mates, and would often train with the Aussies either running or swimming. Dave claims he was the smallest bouncer in Jersey but felt safe working alongside the larger Aussies. He recalls that the second-hand clothing shops in St Helier did a good trade selling used tuxedos to the guys working on the door.

Sunday night at the Rugby Club was the place to be, particularly when the annual Roman Night was held. Dave recalls an Aussie named Ricky McVicker (not a beach guard) being carried into the club on a litter dressed as a Roman Emperor and another time when the guys made a chariot and wheeled it into the Rugby Club.

One of the funniest stories that Dave can recall concerned a beach guard named Trevor Morton. Trevor was getting married and the boys put on a stag night for him. It was in the middle of winter. Someone made a proper ball and chain, quite heavy, which was locked onto Trevor's leg. Trevor had to carry this during visits to many pubs and he kept on dropping it, luckily not onto his feet, although he did drop it onto one unfortunate fellow's foot and broke it. Late in the evening the crowd took Trevor to Howard Davis park in St Helier, stripped him naked, chained him to the fence and adjourned to a nearby pub to watch the ensuing fun and games.

Trevor was eventually discovered by some passers-by who rang the police, but they didn't arrive for quite a while. By this time Trevor was blue from the cold and not very happy. The police took him to the station and cut the ball and chain off Trevor and booked him. Trevor was studying to be a lawyer at the time and thankfully he was let off with a warning.

Jughead went on to play five seasons with the Jersey Rugby Club, the last two as captain. After the lease on the St Aubin flat expired he, along with fellow Aussie Ricky McVicker, rented a couple of spare rooms from Tony Hurford and his wife Wendy who lived in a terraced house in St Helier. Jughead Jones played rugby until the next beach guard season and then started back on the beach. It was all amateur rugby, so he wasn't paid any money but, as he says cryptically, 'We got some benefits'. In the seventies the team played around forty games a season against some very good sides from England, Wales, Ireland, Scotland, and France. Jughead says with a smile: 'It was all very enjoyable – it became a big part of my life in Jersey'.

Traditionally the first game the rugby club's first XV played was against the Jersey beach guards. The beach guards who wanted to play (and not all of them did, although there was always a fair bit of peer pressure applied) were able to invite players from the Jersey Rugby Club or outside the club to play in their team so that there would be a competitive contest. The beach guards would invite a selected few guys to play with the team, mainly first graders. But the Jersey Rugby Club would occasionally veto the invitations. Back in 1975 and 1976 when Jughead Jones was captain, the club tried to stop him playing for the beach guards, but he said: 'No, that's not right'. The club's response was along the lines of: 'Well, you're the captain of the team, this fixture is on the official calendar, so you should play for us', but Jughead refused. Both times the club relented and allowed him to play for the beach guards. Despite this, the beach guards lost.

Ironically in September 1977, the first year after Jughead had left Jersey and returned to Australia, the beach guards beat the Jersey Rugby Club. The heading in the *Jersey Evening Post*'s article on the game says it all: 'Cook-a-hoop Australians'. There were nine beach guards in the team, namely Ross Ryan, Steve Porter, Paul Berghouse, Scott Wilson, Russell Evans, Greg Price, Jerry Shannos, and Mark Berghouse as well as Alan Wheeler, a former beach guard working as a lifeguard at one of the pools on the island. The South African Bill Lavarack, who was almost 45 years of age by then, also played for the beach guards as he was working part-time on the beach that year.

The team was coached by Jughead's mate Tony Hurford, a former coach of the rugby club's first grade team. Tony knew that the local team hadn't had a run out together and had cunningly organised a few trial matches for the beach guard team to work on their combinations.

The notable inclusion from outside the beach guard ranks was none other than 'the ageing but still most astute [Brian] Screen', the scrum half who had been a key factor in the previous beach guard victory a decade earlier. Brian Screen was about forty years old by then.

The *Jersey Evening Post*'s report says that the beach guards took it right up to the Jersey team in the first ten minutes 'to jolt the Island side out of their stride'. Playing fullback, Sydneysider Paul Berghouse, in his first year as a beach guard in Jersey, kicked two long range penalties in this period as a result of offside play by the rattled opposition. The Jersey team replied with a penalty goal of their own but only after ignoring several easy shots at goal from penalties and taking fruitless tap kicks. Beach guards Scott Wilson and Russell Evans who were playing in the centres were successful in snuffing out any opposing backline moves, and the score remained at six points to three in the beach guards' favour at half time.

The oranges in the break must have worked for the beach guard team because after ten minutes Brian Screen scooted through a yawning gap near the scrum base and made a run from halfway to close to the opposition try line. From the ensuing scrummage the beach guard team captain Greg Price managed to score. Paul Berghouse converted to make the score twelve points to three.

The prospect of an upset must have spurred the Jersey team on as they scored a good try but failed to convert, reducing the gap to five points. However, panic seemed to set in and three times in the last ten minutes the island team bombed near certain tries. When the referee blew the whistle to end the match the beach guards had triumphed twelve points to seven.

The beach guard team partied hard at the Rugby Club that night, celebrating victory.

The end of season rugby game in 1978 saw the beach guards being defeated by the Jersey Rugby Club, who were taking no chances following the 1977 shock loss. The club put a near full strength and very fit XV on the paddock and won 10 points to nil in blustery conditions.

In 1979, the beach guards arguably had a stronger team than either of the previous two years and they trained solidly under coach Tony Hurford for six weeks prior to the game. Recruited for the annual match was an Irishman named Kieran Conway who someone had spotted kicking a rugby ball on St Brelade's Beach. As it turned out Kieran had played in the first XV for the top English rugby clubs London Irish, Bedford and Gloucester as fly half or centre. Importantly, he was not known to the Jersey Club and fitted in at fly half outside Brian Screen.

Others who had good experience were fullback Paul Cramsie who had played first grade in Sydney for Eastern Suburbs and Leigh Anelzac, who worked as a lifeguard at the St Brelade's Bay Hotel. Leigh as a centre had represented Newcastle (Australia) in rugby league before heading overseas. Jonty Chappell was a young prop forward from Leeds who, like Kieran Conway, was in Jersey for a summer holiday.

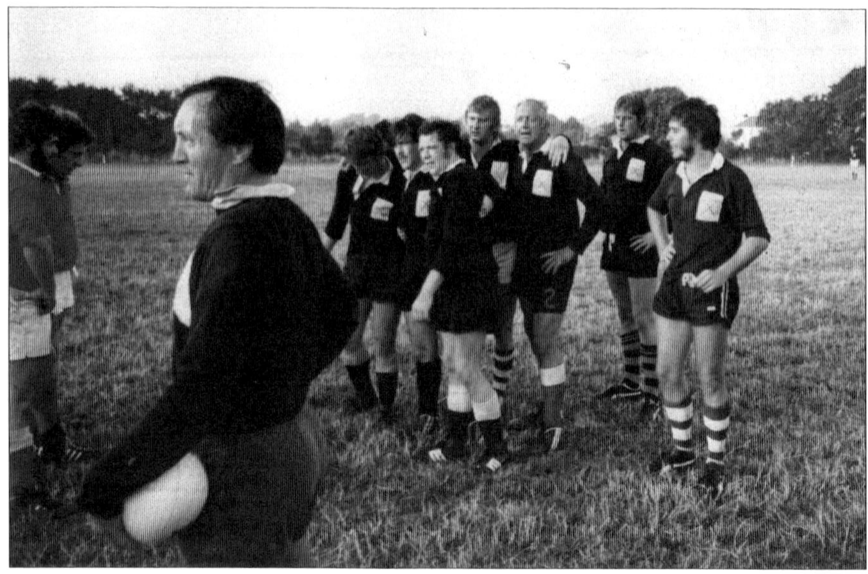

The 1977 beach guard rugby team, which had an upset win over Jersey RFC
Brian Screen with football as the beach guard scrum forms up.
Left to right, Front row: Terry Nicholson, Peter Hamon, Peter Noel (all from St Helier RFC Jersey)
2nd row: Bill Lavarack and Lindsey Mann, No 8 Wayne Bridges and flanker Greg Price.
(Photo courtesy of the *Jersey Evening Post*)

With Leigh Anelzac playing in the centres with Scott Wilson, Russell Evans moved to breakaway to pair with Guy Littler, who worked in Jersey as a beach guard during 1978 and 1979. Guy, a Novocastrian, had co-incidentally played breakaway with Brian 'Jughead' Jones in 1977 with Wanderers in Newcastle. Despite the strength of the beach guard team and their solid preparation, the Jersey first XV won a close encounter.

This is understood to have been the last game played between the beach guards and the Jersey Rugby Club. However, the close relationship between the beach guards and the Jersey Rugby Club continued, and the link with the beach guards has not been forgotten. On its website the club (now called the Jersey Reds) highlights 'the beach guard connection, with many Aussies having worked patrolling Jersey's beaches'.

14 The Duke of Normandy and Friends

'The first Sunday night we went to the Rugby Club and when we got home from the rugby club there were 17 women in the house looking to party. Harpo said, "How long is this been going on?"'

Stephen Porter, Jersey lifeguard 1973-1977,
describing his introduction to the Jersey and Doghouse lifestyle in 1973.

One Saturday in late 1972 three young Newcastle mates, Steve Porter, Kim Flower, and Michael Jones, were sitting in Souths Leagues Club having a beer or six. After a bit of discussion, the trio, like many other young Australians, decided to go overseas. Steve Porter recalls, 'We wanted to get out of the rut'. By this he meant the endless cycle of work, beer, chasing girls, ad infinitum. As members of Cooks Hill surf club, they knew about the beach guard work in Jersey and decided to apply through Jerry Shannos. They were successful.

In Steve's words, 'We went to Jersey to have a paid holiday with a bit of enjoyment'.

When they arrived in Jersey at the beginning of the 1973 season they lived in the second Doghouse on Old Street which was later demolished. Jersey made a quick positive impression on the trio. Steve says with a laugh, 'The first Sunday night we went to the Rugby Club and when we got home from the club there were seventeen women in the house looking to party. Harpo [Kim Flower] said, "How long has this been going on?"' For quite a while, Harpo, for quite a while.

The lads soon discovered that a lot of the beach guards that had been there for some time worked the doors of the pubs and discos to make some extra money. The owners liked Aussies on the door because if they employed locals they would let all their friends in. Thus, the Australians always had work. Steve says, 'Harpo and I didn't work at a second job that first year as we had some spare cash and didn't need to work. We would go to a disco where the boys were working and drink until it closed. What a lifestyle'.

Steve recalls that he had something like five nights at home in Old Street in the first five months – the rest of the time he and the others were out and about. A beach guard named Paul Wallace, aka the Wombat, took the new lads under his wing when they first got to Jersey. He had been there for three years. The lads bought an old car for the princely sum of twenty quid which they used to cruise around the island on days off. Steve says, 'Jersey was unusual because it had something like 500 registered bars on the island at that time. There were nine or ten cabaret spots and Jersey went from 50,000 people in winter to 500,000 in summer. There were something like 700 hire cars on the island. It [the off season] was a transformation that I only came to appreciate when I stayed over a winter and played rugby'.

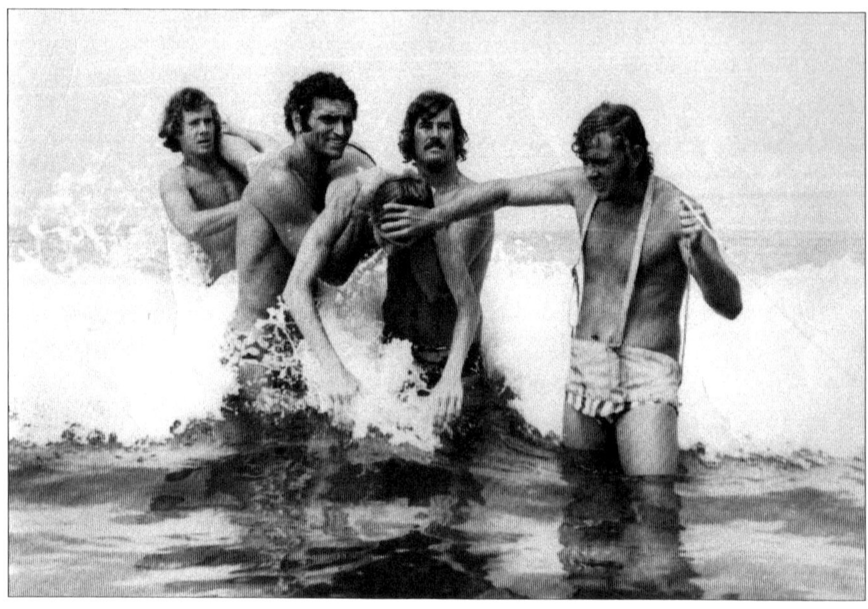

Demonstration of a Belt Rescue at St Ouen's Beach circa 1973
Left to right: Kim Flower, Jerry Shannos, Ian Fitzpatrick and Steve Porter. Patient Nick Lafolley (Jersey)   (Photo courtesy of the *Jersey Evening Post*)

Soon after arriving in Jersey Steve gained the nickname of 'the Duke of Normandy'. It came about in a rather roundabout way. The night before Harpo, Mick Jones and Steve were leaving for Jersey they went to Souths Leagues Club in Newcastle for a farewell drink. A woman they knew named Marcia Martini was working at reception. As they left the club the boys said goodbye to Marcia and told her they were going overseas. She said to them, 'Make sure that you send me a postcard'.

Sometime later in Jersey whilst he was sitting in the Land Rover waiting for a few of the beach guards, Steve wrote a card to Marcia. It said something like, 'Dear

Marcia, we have taken the island by storm', but Steve forgot to post it. A bit later one of the beach guards by the name of Ian Fitzpatrick, aka Captain Perfect, found the card and he quipped of Steve, 'Who does this bloke think he is – taking the island by storm – the last bloke that did that was the Duke of Normandy'. The name stuck.

Steve describes the beach guard job as, 'the drinking man's working hours'. They started work at 10 a.m. and finished at 6 p.m. After work with dinner consumed they went out to work on the door from 8 p.m. until 12:45 the next morning then, according to Steve, 'partied and made love until 4 a.m. and you still got five hours sleep before you had to go back to work'. They lived the high life all day every day.

Steve describes the daily routine. 'So, we would get up at 9 a.m. and have breakfast. Two guys would walk up to Fort Regent and bring the jeeps back to the Doghouse. We would leave at 9:30 and one jeep would drive to St Brelade's and the other to St Ouen's. Jerry Shannos had a second and third in charge and those three guys were always at St Ouen's. The other nine guys rotated with one guy at West Park at the pool and two others at St Brelade's. At various times we had guys working at Plémont, Harve Des Pas pool, and Grève de Lecq.'

Each season the Doghouse appointed a social organiser. In 1976 was Alan 'the Reverend' Walker, another Novocastrian. The Reverend's (Rev for short) principal responsibility was to ensure there was always enough beer ('Harry' Heineken at that time) available to fill the backyard fridge. The two beach guards rostered off each day had two jobs to do – one was to clean the kitchen and assist the cook if she needed something purchased from the shops, and the other was to restock the bar fridge. That was pretty much the extent of the house rules.

A number of the boys in the 1973 and 1974 seasons were working at a nightclub called Blimpers West Park at night on the door. It was owned by a guy named Hughie Behan who was alleged to have serious connections in the criminal underworld so, as Steve recalls, 'no-one fucked with him'. A fellow named John was the manager at Blimpers. John liked to knock around with the Aussies because there were always women on the scene.

One night at one of the beach guard parties at the Doghouse John asked where they got their grog from and Steve Porter told him that they got it from a nearby off-licence (bottle shop). John offered to supply them grog from Blimpers at a good rate which the beach guards eagerly accepted. Steve recalls, 'We would go and get it in one of the cars and pay him cash and everybody was happy. He would supply us with all sorts of grog. One night we even had a Moet champagne party – the girls loved it'.

One night the beach guards arrived at Blimpers to work on the door and Hughie Behan, the owner, started looking at them strangely. Someone asked him, 'Where's John?' Hughie replied coldly in his thick EastEnders's accent, 'Yeah, where the fuck is John?'

Apparently, John had absconded, and they found out he had never put the money the boys had given him for the grog in the till. Hughie took some convincing that the beach guards weren't in on the scam, but they told him the truth and he eventually accepted it. However, as Steve recalls, it was a bit tense for a while.

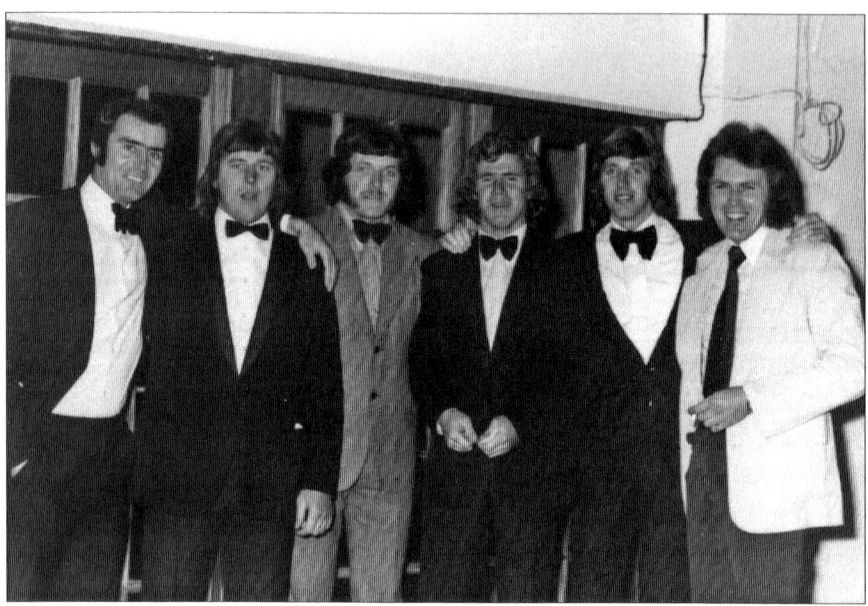

Working Nights on the Door at West Park Nightclub circa 1973
Left to right: Jamie Thomson, Denis Margeson, Ken McGready, Kim Flower, Brian Jones, Graham Newton   *(Unknown source)*

Hughie Behan employed two Scotsmen, Big Alex and Jamie, as full-time security at Blimpers. In 1973, twenty-year-old Ken Holloway, his brother Bob, Jughead Jones and Peter Surgenor, all beach guards, worked on the door part-time. One night that year Ken witnessed a fight over a girl between Hughie and Big Alex in the car park. Hughie Behan was very drunk and Big Alex thumped the shit out of him. Ken, who owned an old Jaguar motor car, didn't want to get involved and took off in a hurry.

Hughie, who was lying in a pool of blood, must have remembered the Jag but forgotten who he had fought with, because the next day Ken and some of the other beach guards were about to step out of the Lifeguard Tower at St Ouen's when Hughie screamed into the nearby car park in his car, jammed on the brakes and proceeded to threaten to shoot Ken, whom he had mistaken as his assailant.

Ken asserts that he wasn't too worried about the threat, although Jughead didn't help matters by declaring that Hughie was capable of carrying it out. Still, Ken got a bit of a sore neck, looking over his shoulder for a week or two.

Steve recalls that in either 1974 or 1975 the beach guards at St Ouen's got a call to rush to Plémont (a beach on the north-west part of the island) one morning because a kid had fallen off a cliff around from the beach and the tide was coming in fast. Steve asserts that he, as the one in charge of the beach guards at the scene, almost caused a disaster during the ensuing rescue of the injured lad.

Because the bay at Plémont was horseshoe shaped with the beach in the middle, the swiftly moving incoming tide swept in earlier at the ends of the horseshoe. Thus, the rocks at either end of the bay would be sealed off by the incoming tide quicker than the beach in the middle.

Steve was told that two kids were rock climbing on the bay around from Plémont and one fell down a cliff. He says, 'When we got there he was in some strife with broken bones and some spinal fractures. We took a surfboard down to the beach and walked around to where the kid was on the rocks'. The rescue party included several ambulance service people.

By this time the incoming tide was lapping up against the rocks where they were. Steve and the team were asked to wait while the airport rescue people tried to bring a zodiac (a rubber rescue boat) in to extract the youngster. However, the conditions were too rough for it to land and the kid was too badly injured to risk using that approach.

Steve says, 'It was my call, so I told them to go back. So, we put the kid flat on the surfboard and we had six guys each side of the surfboard holding him on with several [of those] supporting his neck. But the tide came in quickly as we started walking back around to the beach. Pretty soon the tide was up to the chests of the guys walking with the board. It was then that two ambulance guys who were with us started to panic because they couldn't swim. Thank goodness the bottom was sand and fairly smooth, but we had to jump up and down to keep our heads above the water'.

At this stage Steve thought they were in a lot of trouble. Not only did the beach guards have a kid with spinal fractures but they also may have had to rescue the two ambos. Luckily everyone managed to get around to the beach safely and the kid was carefully carried up the steps to the waiting ambulance. The kid survived but, unfortunately, he became a quadriplegic. Steve says, 'I think that was after that incident that we put a lifeguard at Plémont'.

In 1974 the States demolished the second Doghouse. Steve says sadly, 'It was a wonderful house - three stories, ten bedrooms and three bathrooms. Jerry Shannos had a flat in the bottom of the house, but he was driven out by the guys that year and that's when he started to live at St Ouen's in the lifeguard tower'.

The beach guards moved into the third Doghouse at 30 St Saviour's Road. The back entrance to the Doghouse was through a council car park. The Housing Department arranged for an entrance to be cut through the back wall to give the boys access because they couldn't park on St Saviour's Road. Recalls Steve with a grin, 'We would load and unload the Land Rovers there, plus it was great for bringing young ladies in and out of the Doghouse. We moved into there in 1974 and it was still going when I left in 1977'.

The Doghouse residents employed a girl at the St Saviour's Road Doghouse to cook for them because most of them were working at night and they only had a narrow window between 6:30 and 8 to get fed. She was a good cook and the boys ate well.

That Doghouse was located next door to the Continental Hotel which housed a disco called the Kon Tiki. A guy called Bob Furness, a rugby man, worked on the door, so the boys had no problem in gaining entrance. The Kon Tiki had an infamous nickname – the Bag's Ball – so called because it was popular with women aged from the mid-30s and above. Steve recalls, perhaps unkindly, 'If you missed out [on a woman] when you were out and around you could pop into the Kon Tiki and pick up a bag, otherwise known as a boiler'. Very non-PC in those days!

The third Doghouse gained notoriety in 1974 when it was the subject of a police raid. Two Australians who weren't working on the beach were living there with the beach guards. Steve tells the story. 'One of the guys [not a beach guard] came home drunk this night with his girl – I was actually in France with Harpo on an overnighter with some girls – and had an argument with a fellow outside the Doghouse. The guy punched the Aussie and knocked him into the gutter and started kicking him in the head. The girl stormed into the house and started screaming out for the beach guards. They came out and fixed up the fellow who was assaulting the Australian'.

Things quickly escalated from there. The guy who had been towelled up by the beach guards got up and ran back to where he was staying with a bunch of Scouse (Liverpool) guys. The Scousers come down to sort out the mess with the Australians and a melee ensued. Then the cops arrived.

Steve tells the story that was related to him: 'We had friends in the police force so one of the cops pushed the beach guards back into the Doghouse and told them to shut up and leave the sorting out to him. But that didn't work, and the beach guards were into it again so suddenly it was a riot and there were ten police cars and thirty cops [a possible exaggeration] outside the Doghouse. The girl who was with the drunken Australian started mouthing off and naming nicknames, so the cops grabbed the Aussies who were outside along with the Scousers and put them in jail'.

Early the next morning Harpo and Steve returned to Jersey on the hydrofoil and went back to the Doghouse. By this stage Steve was second in charge of the beach guards, reporting to Jerry Shannos. Steve says, 'One of the guys who was still there that hadn't been arrested told me only that some of the guys had already gone to work so I take three of them and proceed to St Ouen's, blissfully unaware of what had gone on'.

When Steve got to St Ouen's he told Jerry about the guys going to work. At 10:30 the phone rang at the Lifeguard Tower and Jerry answered it. He listened for a while, then he slammed down the phone and screamed at Steve, 'they're all in jail - what the fuck is going on?' Of course, Steve had no idea.

The boys had been kept in jail overnight and were charged with affray. Shaking his head, Steve recalls, 'The headline in the paper was something like "Sunday Bloody Sunday – Beach Guards Charged"'.

The boss of the Tourism Department was a nice guy and he spoke to Jerry and said that he would keep the incident as low profile as possible, although the cop in charge wanted to become a hero and take it further. The cops threatened to deport the Scousers, who wouldn't agree to let things settle down, but it quickly blew over. However, as a consequence of 'Sunday Bloody Sunday' Jerry really came down hard on the boys.

The summers of 1975 and 1976 weatherwise were two of the best summers on record in Jersey and indeed the rest of the UK. 1976 was the driest, warmest and sunniest summer in the 20th century in Britain (only surpassed by 1995 as the driest). Parts of the south-west of England went forty-five days without rain in July and August. Britain even appointed a Minister for Drought who suggested that people take a bath with a friend to save water. This provided perfect beach weather and perfect conditions for Jersey tourists. Steve claims the crew of beach guards in those years were great and because the guys were doing the right thing Jerry Shannos settled down and became less paranoid about their behaviour. They continued to work six nights a week at the pubs and discos but on Sundays the only establishments that were allowed to sell alcohol were the Aero Club (too posh for the beach guards) and the Rugby Cub.

The highlight of the week was Sunday night at the Jersey Rugby Club. The Aussies were made honorary members as several of the guys including Jughead were playing rugby with the club. The Rugby Club members used to go down to the beach every second Sunday when the tide was out to play touch football on the beach and then everyone would go back to the Rugby Club after knockoff at 6 p.m. It was a very

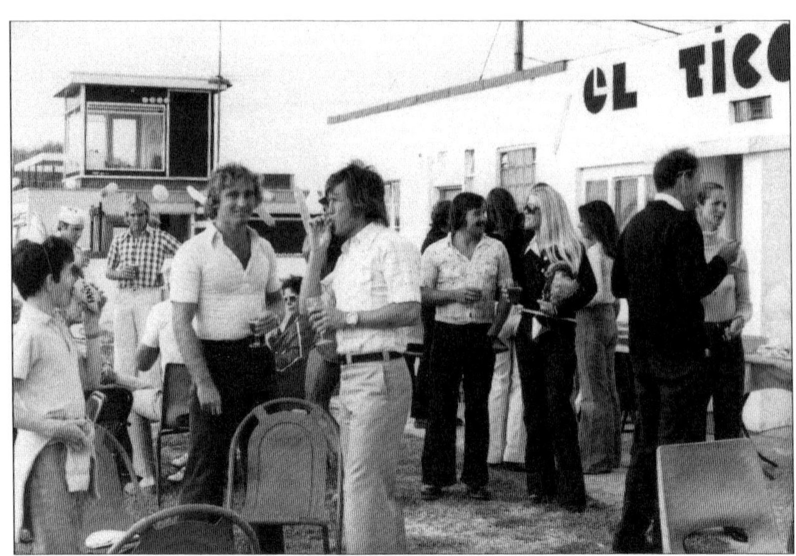

Beach party outside El Tico, 1975
Rex Neve with Dave Blake in centre. Peter Compton (check shirt behind), Barney Morris and Mandy (surname unknown) left of centre, Doc and Anne Lafolley on far right

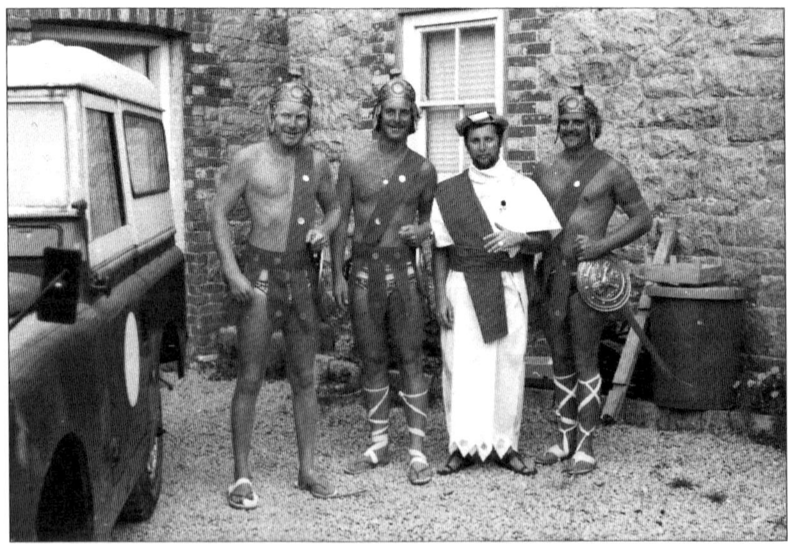

Roman Night Circa 1975
Left to right: Alan Wheeler, Michael Jones, Graeme Wolfenden and Steve Porter

(Both p hotos courtesy of Steve Porter}

close knit social arrangement. Then of course there was the Sunday night party back at the Doghouse.

The first after hours' place Steve worked at was a two-story disco/nightclub called The Deep which was housed above the foyer of the Forum Cinema in St Helier. Steve worked there with Ken Holloway (Hughie Behan's mate) in 1974. Then he and Harpo got what Steve asserts were arguably the best jobs on the island.

A guy owned two very respectable hotels, the Christina and the Somerville, in St Aubin's Bay. He normally only employed Portuguese and only from the Island of Madeira – they were all like family. The pair were the only non-Portuguese employees he put on and they were on the door. The hotels catered for the older crowd and as a consequence there wasn't too much action and in any event the Aussies were responsible for keeping the younger, rowdier crowd out. The owner wanted no trouble. Steve worked there for the next four years and Harpo for three.

Steve says the Christina Hotel was the spot that seemed to attract those married women who were inclined towards having discreet affairs. One night a well-known local married woman came in with a couple and a man who was not her husband. She came up to Steve and introduced the others and then whispered in his ear, 'I hope I can trust you'. Naively Steve hadn't caught on at that stage as to what was going on.

Shortly after the same woman fronted up to the Christina with another man. She said, 'Steve I'm not here tonight'. Steve by this time had wised up so he suggested that the couple went down to the bottom bar which was dark and discreet.

This happened again another night with the same pair. Later that evening Steve was at the door when he saw the woman's husband, whom Steve knew, walking across the car park towards the hotel. When the husband got to the door he said, 'Hello Steve, good to see you', and a quick-thinking Steve replied, 'Your mates are in the top bar', so off he went. Steve rushed down the steps to the bottom bar and got the woman's attention and touched the side of his nose like in the movie 'The Sting'. Quickly she got up with her companion and disappeared out the back door.

Steve thought that this was a one off but after it happened time and again with more married women and an equal number of married men, in his words he, 'became the confidant, the keeper of secrets, at the hotel'. He was amazed at how many married people in Jersey were having affairs. Jersey was notorious for marriage break ups although a lot of them had so much money, but they couldn't afford for the marriage to end because they would lose too much money. It was reported in the mid-seventies that there were more millionaires per capita on the island than any other island in the world.

For a period, Steve worked as a builder's labourer for a very wealthy chap who was renovating his house. Money was no object. He spent millions on the renovation. Steve and his co-workers had to pick up some granite window lintels for his house and they were going to take an old truck, but the owner said, 'no, let's use my Range Rover'. It was brand new. When Steve suggested that the lintels might cause damage to the car the man dismissively retorted, 'It's a Range Rover – it's a working vehicle and it should look like a working vehicle.

Doc Lafolley was a GP who looked after the beach guards medically, particularly when they suffered from what are politely referred to as social diseases. He would even bring the injections down to the Lifeguard Tower. He had two sons, Nick Lafolley (nicknamed Einstein) and Daniel. The Doc's wife Anne wanted the boys to be prim and proper, but the Doc liked them to associate with the beach guards because he wanted them to learn to act like men.

Steve recalls, 'How I know so much about the history of Jersey was through Einstein. When people came to visit us, we would take them for a ride around the island and a few drinks. Einstein would pester me to take him with us so eventually I agreed but told him that he should find something historical to talk about while we were driving around. I learned about the geology, the fungi, the flora and fauna, the Norse history, the Roman history, you name it – it was fascinating. The other brother Daniel was too young to get involved too much with us. Nick was 15 when I met him. Nick was a genius: a Mensa at 13, at 15 he was the Channel Island's fungi expert, recognised by Cambridge University'.

Einstein had plans to be a doctor like his father, but he was also interested in geology. Steve was coming back to Australia for a visit in 1976 and Einstein asked him if Steve could bring him back some rocks from Australia. As luck would have it, Steve knew some guys who were doing PhDs in geology, so they gave him a sample box of rocks which Steve took back to Jersey for Einstein. The lad was astounded that someone would do that for him, so he then decided to pursue a career in geology. He ended up in Africa, got involved in local politics and had a massive heart attack at age 35 and died. Very sad.

Steve became quite friendly with a Jersey copper, let's call him 'Pat' (using his real name would embarrass him). He was a guy who liked to come out to St Ouen's beach as part of his patrol and relax in the beach guards' area. He would shed his uniform and have a sun bake. Afterwards he would get dressed and go back on patrol.

In 1974 with the 'Sunday Bloody Sunday' incident hanging over the beach guards Steve says the boys tried to tone it down a bit, but of course that didn't last. One night there was a nude disco at the Doghouse. Unsurprisingly, things got a bit out of hand.

The next week Pat came out to the Lifeguard Tower to have a cup of tea. Accompanying him was a young probationary copper. Pat took his tie and shirt off and was sitting down relaxing with a cup of tea while the probationary copper remained in his uniform. The conversation got around to what had transpired over the weekend and the Doghouse came up.

The young copper got very excited and asked, 'Do you guys live at 30 St Saviour's Road? Steve and the boys answered, 'Yes, why?' The young copper said, 'We got a call to 30 St Saviour's Road last weekend. We looked through the window and there were all these nude women running everywhere!' Well Jerry Shannos spat the dummy, but Pat just laughed and laughed.

In 1974 Steve had played rugby in the off season and had suffered a broken jaw. It was New Year's Eve and a team from Petersham, a suburban Sydney side from Australia, came across to the island to play the Jersey side on New Year's Day. In the Petersham team were two guys from Newcastle (NSW) that Steve knew. He was in the bar at the Rugby Club when they arrived, and they had a good chat and quite a few beers. Come midnight on New Year's Eve it was snowing which was very rare for Jersey. Quite a few of the boys who were due to play the next day were out on the rugby field being sick – they had a lot of pints poured into them – part of the home team strategy. The bar closed, and Steve, not exactly sober, offered to give about eight of them a lift back to the Doghouse in his Ford Anglia.

It was snowing heavily as Steve drove slowly and erratically out of the Jersey Rugby Club. The windscreen wiper on the driver's side couldn't cope with the snow so Steve was hanging out the window pushing the windscreen wiper across the windscreen, trying to see.

Suddenly he spotted a cop car on the other side of the road watching the weaving path of the car. It waved him down and Steve pulled over, knowing that he had been sprung. A copper got out of the police car and walked across the road. Steve recognised the cop - it was Pat. He said sternly, 'What the fuck is going on, Duke? What are you doing? Get out of the car and the rest of you get out too'.

They all piled out, thinking they were history, Steve most of all. Pat pointed to four of the guys and said, 'You get in the police car'. At that point Steve was even more convinced they were nicked. Then Pat told the rest of them to get back in Steve's car. Pat got in the driver's seat and drove them home, followed by the police car. When they got to the Doghouse Pat got back in the police car and drove off. The two guys from Australia could not believe what had happened. Who had ever heard of the coppers driving home a bunch of drunks in their car? When Steve saw Pat at the lifeguard reunion in 2010 in Jersey he denied all knowledge of the incident.

On to the story of the Green Door, as told by Steve Porter. This story has several versions, depending on who relates it. The Green Door refers to a rather delicate subject, so discretion dictates that the subject of the story will be referred to as 'Jay'.

If, shock horror, Jay the beach guard had to get treatment for a certain social disease he had to go to the Pathology Department at the local hospital in St Helier. Pathology wasn't in the main part of the hospital; instead Jay would have had to walk out of the front entrance, proceed along the main street and enter through a green door. Of course, no-one wanted to be seen going through the Green Door. Certainly not Jay, who had an enviable reputation as a ladies' man.

It was the night of the beach guards' rage, a very popular event, the final party of the 1976 season. It was held at the Flamingo nightclub and it was by invitation only. The women outnumbered the men two to one. It was a big night with plenty of alcohol and food laid on. The highlight of the night was the award ceremony where the MC would present individual beach guards with imaginative awards commemorating a notable event from the season.

One of the beach guards said to Jay, 'You'll be lucky to pull a girl tonight'. This was like a red rag to a bull and Jay replied boastfully, 'Fuck off, I'm going to get three women and I'll get a photograph of myself with them on the bed nude'. Undeterred the beach guard said, 'I'll bet you ten quid that you can't get a woman tonight'. Jay accepted the bet thinking his mate was crazy.

Then the award ceremony began. One of the beach guards got a pair of boxing gloves because he was always wanting to fight somebody. Then it was Jay's turn. Numbly he stood there whilst he was presented with a small wooden door painted green and a 12-month supply of tablets. As soon as the crowd saw the Green Door they knew what it meant. The cry went up, 'Oh really?' Jay knew that he had lost the bet.

Jay's version is slightly different. He says, referring to what the MC said when he presented Jay with the green door award, 'This is to make sure that you know what it looks like in case you ever have to go there'. There's always another version of the 'truth'!

The beach guards would regularly buy old cars for ten or twenty quid and discard them when they broke down. Harpo and the Duke bought an old banger off the father-in-law of Mick Finnis (who features in an earlier chapter). The father-in-law was a Centenier. Although the car was a complete rust bucket, it still went.

About two weeks later the two Aussies were driving home after work. A woman in the car in front of them put her indicator on to turn left but changed her mind at the last minute and the pair ran straight up the back of her. In the aftermath of the prang the side wing fell off their car, as well as the back door. It was like the Keystone Cops.

A Bobby arrived, took one look at the car and was preparing to throw the book at Harpo and the Duke. He said, 'where did you get this car? Who owns it?'

Harpo replied blandly, 'We do, mate'.

The copper announced, 'This car is a wreck, it's not fit to be on the road'. He asked how long they had had owned it and Harpo said, 'Two weeks'. The copper said in an authoritive voice, 'I want the name of the person you got this wreck from'.

Harpo told him that it had belonged to Centenier [name withheld]. Well that shut the copper right up. After he thought about it the policeman said, 'Get all this pile of shit off the road and piss off'. They left the car there and someone had to come and tow it away.

Jughead Jones was the subject of another car story of the mid-1970s. Peter Surgenor and Jughead bought a vintage MG F-Type Magna. It cost them £200 each and it was a great car, in good nick. They bought it off a Jersey Bean. By this stage Jughead and Peter Surgenor were not working as beach guards but were partners in a construction business which was doing well. Jughead had the money to pay the guy, but unfortunately the old story about a fool and his money came to pass.

Just before Jughead was due to pay his share of the car, he and two friends went to the races at Dinard, just across the bay from St Malo on the French Brittany peninsula. They caught the ferry to St Malo and went to Dinard to the races by taxi.

Who would have thought it, but the boys fell under the influence of a couple of French girls and, in Jughead's words, 'They used us and abused us'. The lads went on to a casino that evening with the women. By two or three in the morning Jughead had no money left – he was completely broke. He had lost the £200 he had saved for the car. Of course, the women made themselves scarce when the money ran out. The three lads didn't even have enough money to get back to Jersey.

They drew straws and Jughead had to make the phone call to Jerry Shannos in the morning. Jughead laughs at the memory: 'I begged him to send us return tickets, so we could get back [to Jersey]'. Jerry went down to the Weighbridge in St Helier and bought some tickets for the three punters and sent them over on the ferry. That night they slept under a tarpaulin somewhere in St Malo before boarding the ferry the next morning.

Jughead recalls ruefully, 'Because I had no money to pay for the car I had to borrow it off Surg [Peter Surgenor] – he was pretty astute with money and had enough. I had to sell a block of land back in Newcastle, it was not worth much, to pay Surg back'.

Unfortunately for Jughead, another problem with a car was to result in him having to leave Jersey under a financial cloud. More on that later.

15 Wives' Tales 1970s

'We did mainly domestic flying. It was good fun because we had night stops at various destinations. BA flights out of Jersey were mainly to France and England. It was great; you could have a life, only a couple of night stopovers a week.'

Extract from an interview with Carol Jones, wife of Brian 'Jughead' Jones, describing her time as an air hostess with British Airways in the 1970s.

If there was one constant amongst the Australian beach guards, it was women. Romances blossomed and faded, many of them fleeting, but for some, it was true love. Romances that have endured to this day include John 'Ant' Roberts and his wife Enrica (a Jersey 'Bean'), Brian 'Jughead' Jones and his wife Carol (a 'foreigner' from England) and Steve 'The Duke' Porter and his wife Vicki (another 'foreigner' from England). Another romance between Bill Lavarack and his Jersey 'Bean' partner Ida resulted in marriage, but sadly Bill passed away in the early 1990s in Jersey.

Enrica Moltrasio was born in Jersey. Her father was Italian, and her mother very much a Jersey Bean – her maiden name was Le Sueur, a long-established Jersey surname. Enrica's father was a businessman which was to hold her in good stead when it came to employment after she left school in Form 5 (Year 11). She had done her O levels (School Certificate equivalent) the previous year and, as Enrica recounts, 'Because I was mucking around my father told me that it was time to leave and get a job'.

Enrica's father got her employment firstly with one of his customers, a publishing company, then subsequently for St Helier Garages, another of her father's customers. She says it wasn't difficult to get work back then because the economy was booming. Then she moved to a company called Grove Financial Services because they paid more money.

Enrica met John 'Ant' Roberts at St Ouen's beach in the summer of 1970. She says it was the attraction of him being a beach guard and the fact that she and her friends used to go to the nightclub at El Tico where the beach guards were based.

Her father asked Enrica one day who she was going out with and her mother said: 'You know, the lifeguard' and her father said: 'Well, I hope it wasn't the one in the paper the other day', referring to one of the Aussies who had been arrested for peeing in the street or some similar misdemeanour. Enrica thought that Ant was a nice-looking fellow and being Australian he was a bit different to everyone that she knew.

Enrica remembers people commenting that Ant had the broadest accent of all the Australians. She can remember Ant saying to her at a nightclub one evening,' You want a Southa?' She thought, 'I don't know what to say to that' but she said, 'okay' and then found out it was a South of France, a dance! Ant used a lot of abbreviated slang.

Enrica recalls being down at St Ouen's beach with a girlfriend one day and Ant and a few beach guards came along in a jeep. Ant asked the girls, 'Do you want to come for a jump?' Puzzled, Enrica's girlfriend turned to her and asked, 'What did he say?' and Enrica replied, 'I'm not sure but let's go anyway, it'll be fun', so they got in the jeep and tore off towards La Rocco Tower to jump off the tower into the water. They climbed up the rocks and jumped off. It was great fun.

The relationship between Enrica and Ant grew to the point where, when Enrica's parents moved to Italy, she stayed behind in Jersey. Ant had decided not to continue as a beach guard and in 1971 began working for a Jersey architectural firm. Ant described himself as a 'halfitect' as he had earlier studied architecture at the University of New South Wales but didn't complete his degree. The relationship between the pair deepened to the point where they made the momentous decision to live in Australia. At the end of 1972 Enrica and Ant went to Italy to have a holiday with Enrica's family and for Enrica to say her farewells. Following this the pair took off into the unknown (for Enrica).

They arrived in Australia at the end of January 1973 and went to the Gold Coast in Queensland because Ant had a job offer there. Enrica and Ant got married in 1975.

As there was a very deep recession in Australia at the time – there was no work at all - they went to South Africa where Ant got an architectural related job in Johannesburg with a mining company called Anglo-American and Enrica Roberts did secretarial temping work. After about three months Ant was offered a job with Anglo-American in Namibia (south west Africa) at a large diamond mine. Two children came along in the four and a half years they lived in Namibia, Claire in July 1975 and John Jr in December 1977. The expat scene was pretty good: although there was only one other Australian at the mine, there were a lot of engineers from England and some from other parts of Africa including Rhodesia (now Zimbabwe).

Enrica says, 'It was a great place to have children. Most of the couples decided to have children while they were there. It had good infrastructure including an excellent private hospital. There were plenty of social activities – there was a lake for sailing, I was secretary of the riding club, and there was a golf course – with Anglo

American money was no object. It was all a bit surreal; housing was provided, so no mortgage to have to worry about'.

All good things come to an end and in 1979 they returned to Australia. They lived on the Queensland Gold Coast briefly, with Ant employed by the same architectural firm he had worked in before he left Australia. Soon after Ant was asked to go north to the beautiful beachside town of Noosa, to open an architectural office. Enrica and Ant have lived in Noosa ever since. Back in 1979 the infrastructure was poor – only one school, but since then the population has almost quadrupled, changing everything.

Of note, both their children went to Jersey to work. Claire was there from 1999 for nearly four years jointly managing the La Bastille restaurant in St Helier with Anna Truelove, a Jersey relative. John Jr was there for ten years from 2001 to 2011 as the chef at the Old Courthouse Hotel in St Aubin.

Carol Johnson was born in Newcastle upon Tyne in England which, she says, 'is ironic because I live in Newcastle, Australia now'. Carol was an army brat, her father having served in World War II and staying on in the military after the cessation of hostilities. Like many military families, the Johnsons travelled around a lot. They lived in York, Salisbury, had three years in Malaya, and two years in West Berlin. By the time she became a teenager Carol was well accustomed to travelling.

When Carol's father retired from the British Army in the early 1960s the family went to live in Norwich which was where her mother was born. Carol did her last bit of schooling there but, as she says, 'All I wanted to do was travel. I couldn't care less about school or anything else. I wanted to leave and go overseas at fifteen, but my mother said: "No way, you're not going anywhere". I thought I was old enough'.

During those army years she went to so many schools her education suffered, although she wasn't really interested in school anyway. She says: 'At school all they wanted me to do was to go to work in a factory somewhere, but I wasn't going to do that. In those days at school you were never encouraged to get on'.

Carol says: 'I wanted to be like all the other girls - go to high school and be really smart. But I was never going to get there. I certainly wasn't going to stay in Norwich'. Carol thought to herself: 'I'm not staying here, they don't do anything except get married'. She wanted to live. Travelling was her way of escaping. She was up for adventure and left school at fifteen.

As a first step Carol got a job in Marks and Spencer for a little while but she hated it. She says: 'They put me on the frozen foods and I wanted to be a window dresser'.

She left Marks and Spencer and went to work in an office doing clerical work but that didn't suit her either. Then she met a lovely lady who was always talking about Jersey. When Carol was working in Marks and Spencer one of the ladies that worked with her said: 'You should get to know my daughter, she wants to travel'. The daughter and Carol got together and that was the start of their adventure.

Carol desperately wanted to go overseas but as she wasn't yet eighteen the only place she could go to without a passport was Jersey. Carol's girlfriend was a year older than her and they decided to go together. The parents of Carol's girlfriend were very supportive about her going to Jersey but Carol's father in particular was not that keen, being quite protective of his daughter. Somehow Carol managed to talk him around.

They went to Jersey in 1969, Carol being four months short of eighteen. Carol's mum took her down to the bus stop and she met her girlfriend at the next stop. Then, blissfully unaware of the peril they might have put themselves into, they started hitch hiking and made it to Weymouth on the south coast of England and got the ferry over to Jersey. After they got off the ferry they went to the employment office and registered for employment.

One of the clerks asked Carol if he could help her and she said to the man: 'Can you give us a job? What jobs are going?' He replied: 'Oh no, you go out and find a job and come back and see me'.

Carol was horrified – she didn't know she had to do that. Perhaps taking pity on her, the clerk said to her: 'Anyway, what sort of work do you want to do?' Carol said: 'I don't know, maybe something to do with photography'. The clerk advised: 'Go and try Lynn's Photography (in St Helier)'. Carol got a job there and the girls stayed in Jersey for the summer season.

Jersey was the gateway to Europe. Carol's father ended up sending her passport over to Jersey when she turned eighteen and she and her girlfriend took off and hitchhiked around Europe. She says: 'We never thought anybody would do that but once we got to Europe we found everybody was doing it'.

After their European adventure they went back to Norwich and worked there for a while before returning to Jersey the following summer season (1970). A guy Carol used to work with in 1969 got her a job in another photography and printing business. Carol says fondly: 'I just loved it. I loved all the interest of photography'.

She worked in Jersey during the 1970 season and at the end of the season Carol and her girlfriend went back to Europe. After that she ended up in London where she worked in another photographic business for a while.

Then came a significant change in jobs. In 1971 Carol got a job as a stewardess with Channel Airways, a UK based airline specialising in charter flights. She says: 'I thought I'd give being a stewardess a go and see how that worked out. I was attracted to the glamour of the job but more particularly I was attracted to the free travel'. No argument there.

Channel Airways operated out of Stanstead Airport, north of London. Carol absolutely loved the job. Her first flight was as a supernumerary and she said to the girl she was with, 'I've never flown before', and she said, 'What?' Carol said, 'I've never been in a plane before. She said, 'My God'. Carol said, 'It's okay, I'll be fine'. And she was. Carol was never airsick. She says: 'I had so much confidence, I didn't care. All I could think about was that I was going to go all over Europe'.

However, ten months later Channel Airways went broke. The seasonality of their major source of income – charter flights – created a cash flow crisis that was their undoing. Carol was out of a job.

Undeterred, she took herself back to Norwich for a while and worked in a record shop, an experience she describes as 'crap'. Carol says: 'So I decided right, time to go off to Spain now. I went there with a couple of girlfriends. We worked in Majorca for six months [in the summer of 1972]. I didn't speak a word of Spanish but that didn't matter, we got by. I actually ended up working in a nightclub in Majorca taking photographs of patrons, going out the back printing them, then bringing them back inside and selling them. And I got paid for that. I had such fun there, I didn't care as long as it paid for my rent'.

After Spain Carol ventured up to Scotland, but only for six weeks. She recalls with a shudder: 'I just couldn't live there, it was too cold for me. I worked in a hotel as a receptionist with my girlfriend. That was her forte, but it certainly wasn't mine'.

From there she went back to Jersey and managed to get a stewardess job with British Airways at the end of 1972, her previous Channel Airways experience holding her in good stead. She says: 'We did mainly domestic flying. It was good fun because we had night stops at various destinations. BA flights out of Jersey were mainly to France and England. It was great; you could have a life, only a couple of night stopovers a week. If I had had been working out of Heathrow, your life would have become the airline. What I really cared about was that I got lots of holidays and I made most the most of that'.

Carol moved around a bit, living in St Helier, St Mary's, and St Brelade's. Socially she used to frequent the Old Court House hotel, which was her favourite place. She and her friends had a good social life; there were plenty of things going on. Carol says: 'I preferred Jersey in the winter when all the tourists had gone home. You had your circle of friends and it wasn't so crowded'.

Carol's jet setting lifestyle continued unabated, even when she first met the Australian man she was to marry, Brian 'Jughead' Jones, in the early part of 1976. At that time, she was 'going steady' with another fellow but that relationship began to fall apart. Carol decided to go off to Durban in South Africa with a female friend with whom she used to fly. They stayed with a guy called Big Con (a Jersey Rugby Club member). Big Con was forty and Carol and her girlfriend were about twenty-three. Carol says, 'He was like a dad to us. He was lovely'.

Big Con knew Carol's ex-boyfriend and he asked, 'What's going on?' Carol said, 'I'm not really interested in him anymore. If I go out with anyone I'll go out with that Jughead because I like the look of him'. Carol had seen Jughead a few times when she was out and about, including at the Rugby Club, but they hadn't spoken. Carol says candidly, 'Even so, I had the hots for him. What I liked about him was the fact that he wasn't chasing the women, they were chasing him!'

When Carol returned to Jersey some rugby club friends, obviously worded in by Big Con, conspired to get them together. Carol's flatmate saw her coming home from the airport and she rang Jughead and said, 'Carol's just come home. Why don't you give her a call?' He did.

Carol recalls with a smile: 'I was shattered after coming back from Durban with the jet lag and I'd gone to bed. I got this phone call and he said "It's Jughead here" and I thought "Oooh". He asked me to come up to the Rugby Club, so I did. I got dressed even though I was jetlagged. I had a great tan from the sun in Durban and I wanted to make sure he saw it. We met at the Rugby Club and it was the first time I'd spoken to him'.

When she set eyes on Jughead Carol's first thought was, 'My God, his face is so scarred'. Jughead had played rugby that day and the other team must have used his head as the football as he had a lot of stitches in his face. Carol says: 'Anyway I had a nice night. I knew Peter Surgenor (a close friend of Jughead's) from the beach so I was quite at home up there at the rugby club'.

The next time Jughead asked Carol out also involved the rugby club. He was captain of the rugby team and the club committee and the captain were going to France for the day. It was in April 1976, at the end of the rugby season.

Jughead asked Carol: 'Would you like to come to France for the day?' Of course, she said yes. They flew over to France to have lunch and a day out. It was a pretty impressive date, at least in the beginning.

Carol recalls with a laugh: 'We went to this lovely restaurant for lunch. All the rugby wives and girlfriends were really lovely to me. I hadn't met most of them before'.

During the lunch Carol felt really sorry for Jughead – everyone was having wine and they made Jughead do the chug a lug. On the way back in the coach Jughead was sick all over Carol! She laughs: 'I was wearing a white outfit and he vomited claret all over me. The girls got me outside the bus and were wiping me down. He was very embarrassed, but I thought it was hilarious. Mind you, if he did it to me now I'd kill him. That was our first date. Apart from that, the trip to St Malo was lovely'.

Soon after this Carol realised that Jughead was still involved with another woman, although Jughead told Carol that the relationship was over as far as he was concerned. The other woman was away at the time, but Carol said to Jughead: 'I'm not getting involved in this'. Coincidentally, at that same time Carol's flatmate couldn't make up her mind whether she was going to stay in a relationship with a married man and he couldn't make up his mind whether to go with her or stay with his wife. Not wanting to get involved in a complex relationship, Carol parted ways with Jughead.

To his credit Jughead sorted out the problem with the former girlfriend and it was less than a month afterwards that he and Carol got back together again. Their first date was on April 16th and their relationship quickly became full on – they were an item.

For a while everything looked rosy. Carol had a good job with British Airways and a great lifestyle. She was quite happy to stay in Jersey. The building business that Jughead and a friend from the rugby club were partners in was going well. Jughead had every intention of continuing to play rugby in Jersey as the captain of the team. But life has a habit of going pear-shaped when you least expect it.

The woman that Jughead had broken off with had owned a very nice MGB car and Jughead had purchased the car from her during their time together. She was also the bookkeeper for the business in which Jughead was a partner. Obviously not happy about the relationship breaking up, the woman dobbed Jughead into the Internal Revenue for non-payment of taxes. This coincided with the business finishing a big contract with nothing further in the pipeline. Because Jughead did not have the money to pay the tax owing, he lost the MGB. What's more, there was a possibility that his work visa might be taken away because he had a black mark against him after the taxation problem.

During all this Jughead had been considering returning to Australia for a short visit in October 1976. He hadn't seen his parents for some time. He asked Carol if she wanted to go to Australia with him for a month or so. She said yes.

With the financial problem rearing its head it became a real decision point for the couple. What to do – to go to Australia temporarily then to come back to Jersey, or to go to Australia permanently. They had a long talk about what to do. Jughead felt that he needed to get a proper job in Australia if option two was going to work.

Carol says 'I never really wanted to go to Australia. I wanted to go to New Zealand for a visit. Why? Because everybody wanted to go to Australia and I wanted to be different'.

Carol wasn't going to give up her job and go to Australia 'willy-nilly'. She says:

'I had to know that Jugs was serious about this. So, I did everything right. I didn't even give my parents a thought, I was so in love. My dad was pretty good about it. He loved Australians because he used to fight with them in Tobruk in World War II. So, he liked the idea that I was going to end up with an Australian. My mother said to me "You've done to me what I did to my mother", but she was talking about the fact that she left her mother for three years when we lived in Malaya. I've been here in Australia for forty years now, that's the difference. I was so independent, I never thought about what they might think. I always respected my father, but I always wanted to prove him wrong'.

Carol's father went over to Jersey for a weekend to meet Jughead and they did a bit of drinking over several days and Carol's dad got on famously with him. Her father loved the beach guards and the way they went about enjoying themselves. Jughead buttered him up.

Carol and Jughead went to Australia for six weeks as a test. They travelled around, went up to Queensland and then Carol made the decision that she would immigrate. That must have been a very difficult decision, but Carol met the challenge with her usual optimism. She had to return to Britain to complete the paperwork.

Just before Carol was due to return to Britain, Jughead took her to dinner at the home of a friend in Newcastle. Carol met a pregnant lady who said to her: 'Why don't you apply for a job at British Airways here in Newcastle because I'm leaving?' The woman provided the details and Carol went for an interview. The guy that interviewed her was, she says, 'a lovely man'. He said to Carol: 'You have to go back and immigrate which is going to take a bit of time. I can't offer you the job because I need someone now. But I'm moving out of the unit where I'm living, into a house in Merewether. I can offer you and your partner this unit'.

Carol didn't get the job, but she came out of the interview with an apartment for them to live in. Jughead moved into it while she was away.

Carol was in Britain for nearly ten weeks. She recalls: 'It was very difficult to do all the documentation to immigrate. I had to prove that I was engaged to be married, which I was. Jughead said before I left "You go and get a ring and we'll get engaged" and we did, just like that. Nothing has changed!' They had set the date for April 1977.

Saturday 16 December 1976 started out to be a very happy day. Carol was arriving by plane in Sydney. Jughead had driven down to Sydney from Newcastle the previous day and had stayed with his ex-beach guard mate Peter Surgenor who was going to be his best man. Peter Surgenor, or Surg as he was called, lived in the upscale eastern suburbs area of Vaucluse and was an electrician. Surg had just rekindled a romance with his ex-girlfriend and was pretty happy about that.

Jughead and Surg went for a run in the morning but Surg had to go and do an electrical job in an old terrace house in a nearby suburb. During the run Jughead arranged to meet Surg on Saturday afternoon after he had picked up Carol from the airport. Carol and Jughead were to stay with Surg that night.

Jughead was duly reunited with Carol and they went off to meet with Surg, but he wasn't at the rendezvous. Puzzled but not overly alarmed the couple drove to Surg's unit in Vaucluse but he wasn't there either and they couldn't get in because Jughead didn't have a key. Carol was pretty jet lagged so they went to Coogee for a quick drink and then drove back to Newcastle.

At about three o'clock on the Sunday morning there was a bang on the door at their unit. When Jughead opened the door, his sister stood there crying her eyes out. Jughead naturally assumed that something must have happened to his father or mother, but it was Peter Surgenor. He had been accidently electrocuted the day before in the old house that he had been working on. Jughead and Carol were absolutely devastated over this terrible news. Such was the high regard in which Surg was held, people came back from Jersey for the funeral.

Despite their terrible loss, the couple had to press on. Carol obtained a job straightaway at a business in Newcastle called Greenleaf Photography Studios. She worked there for five years doing black and white photography. When the owner went into advertising Carol took over his job and did all the studio and external portraits.

Carol and Jughead decided to postpone their April 1977 wedding date because they had no money. Fortuitously Carol managed to get an extension on her visa. They waited for another six months and in that time Carol's parents were able to arrange to come to Australia for the wedding. They were married in November 1977 in a very English-style church in the Newcastle coastal suburb of Merewether and their reception was at the old Alcron restaurant in the city centre. They could only afford to invite forty guests.

Carol Jones says: 'Our wedding was like a reunion. Jughead's (new) best man was Nicky Gill from Swansea Belmont surf club. Most of the males were lifeguards. There were a couple of rugby guys from the Wanderers club [in Newcastle]. I had my three best friends come to the wedding, one lived in Sydney. I ended up making my wedding dress because we had no money and then my husband went out and bought a suit!' Oh, that Jughead.

Carol and Jughead had two boys, born in 1982 and 1985. Their sons now run the family business. Carol sums up her story: 'Jersey has been a big part of our life - all sorts of people lived there ranging from the very rich who used it as a tax haven to the lifeguards who had nothing to the rugby players who provided a lot of social and sporting enjoyment'.

✸

Vicki Jones was born in Surrey, England. Her parents immigrated to Canada, but they came back to Britain when Vicki was four because her father couldn't get a job. They settled at Moreton on Thames and she grew up there. When she left school, Vicki went to London to work in the hotel system.

When she was 19 she worked in London at the Metropolitan hotel with a girl called Lyn who was from Jersey. Lyn wanted to go home but hated flying, so Vicki went to Jersey by herself and got a job in hotel reception in 1975 before the summer season started. Vicki was there on her own for a while and felt lonely, so she convinced Lyn to come home. They worked and lived in the L'Horizon hotel which was the one and only five-star hotel in Jersey. Vicki recounts one of the oddities about Jersey: 'The funniest thing about Jersey was that you couldn't pronounce any of the road signs – all Norman French'.

That's where the two friends came across the beach guards, at St Brelade's beach. Vicki went out with a beach guard named Mickey Jones (a mate of Steve's from Newcastle) for a short while. Then she met Steve at the 1975 beach guards' rage (their annual farewell party) and, says Vicki, 'I refused to go home with him, but he persevered'.

Steve had already committed to returning to Newcastle for the northern winter of 1975 - 76 and Vicki stayed in Jersey. When Steve came back to Jersey in early 1976 they got back together, and the rest is history. The pair went out for the summer of 1976. Vicki was still living at the hotel during that time. Vicki says nostalgically, 'We had the two best years weatherwise in Jersey in 1975 and 1976. It was just magic'.

Vicki was candid when she talked about the man she was to marry: 'I'm not sure what attracted me to Steve – he was fun, and we had the best time of our lives in Jersey – we had an absolute ball. I used to finish work at 10 p.m. and go and meet him up at the Cristina Hotel when he was working on the door. We would have the run of the bar. I think we never got home before 2 a.m'.

At the end of the 1976 season Steve optimistically told Vicki that he was going to go home and make a lot of money for them – 'another lie!' she says with a laugh. When she heard Steve's intentions Vicki declared, 'I'm not hanging around here – I'm going to Canada', and she went to Canada for the winter to work.

Steve came back to Newcastle with the objective of making some money in the wool business, but it collapsed, and he was out of work by Christmas. His father ran the wool stores in the Newcastle suburb of Cooks Hill and Steve worked for him. For a start there was overtime every night, but the Japanese pulled out of the market and the wool price took a dive. Steve finished up working at the BHP under a false name as a labourer because he had been on staff there and he couldn't use his real name.

Steve went back to the beach for the 1977 season and Vicki returned from Canada. Vicki says, 'At that stage we knew we were going to get married. We lived with Lyn in a place in St Saviour's parish. We bought an old Morris Minor car – the year before that we had a Sunbeam Rapier. When the Morris went up the hill we had to fill up the radiator. We had some terrible cars'.

In 1977, when the pair came back to Jersey Vicki started work at the Water's Edge Hotel in Bouley Bay, on the island's northern shore. She was working at reception with a Swiss girl named Bridget and her German boyfriend was a chef who ran the kitchen, so Vicki managed to get a share of the leftover food. She would take it home and she and Steve would have a picnic, sitting up in bed at two o'clock in the morning and eating beautiful soufflés. Vicki says, 'I used to ring up and make reservations at posh restaurants saying it's the head chef at the Water's Edge Hotel wishing to dine at your establishment. Those two were the witnesses at our wedding'.

Vicki and Steve decided to get married because Steve wasn't going to settle in the UK. As Vicki says, 'He didn't want to live anywhere where he couldn't wear stubbies and thongs'. Steve said to Vicki, 'We are going to have to live in Australia' and she said, 'Well, if I'm going to live there, I'm going to get married here so that all our friends and family can come to the wedding'. Vicki was aware that being married to an Australian made it much easier for her to immigrate to Australia.

Vicki Porter's 1977 wedding photo shows her and Steve standing in the middle of a bevy of beach guards with St Ouen's beach in the background. Vicki was resplendent in a long white gown, Steve, wearing a beard and longish hair, looked like a shorter version of Barry Gibb of the Bee Gees. Flared trousers were the order of the day, and everyone had a big grin on their face. No doubt the party would have been spectacular.

The pair arrived in Sydney via a two-day stopover in Singapore. Vicki hated Singapore – she found it too hot and humid – not surprising after Britain. On the plane into Sydney Steve, not one to mollycoddle his new bride, gave Vicki an Australian newspaper and told her, 'Find yourself a job'. Vicki looked through the ads and she asked Steve, 'what is TAA [short for Trans Australian Airlines]?' She says, 'There was a job for a telephonist and it was the only job I could do'.

Steve said dismissively, 'You'll never get a job with them, everyone will be after that job'. Undeterred, Vicki rang TAA when they got to Sydney and she got an interview and started the week after.

The married couple initially stayed at Maroubra with the former beach guard Ken Holloway. Then they got a flat in Coogee and lived there for a year. The flat was unfurnished, so they borrowed some money from Ken Holloway and went out and bought a fridge, a bed, a lounge and a coffee table. Ken provided a few saucepans.

Vicki recalls, 'We bought an old VW Beetle for $500 and that's how we started our married life in Sydney'.

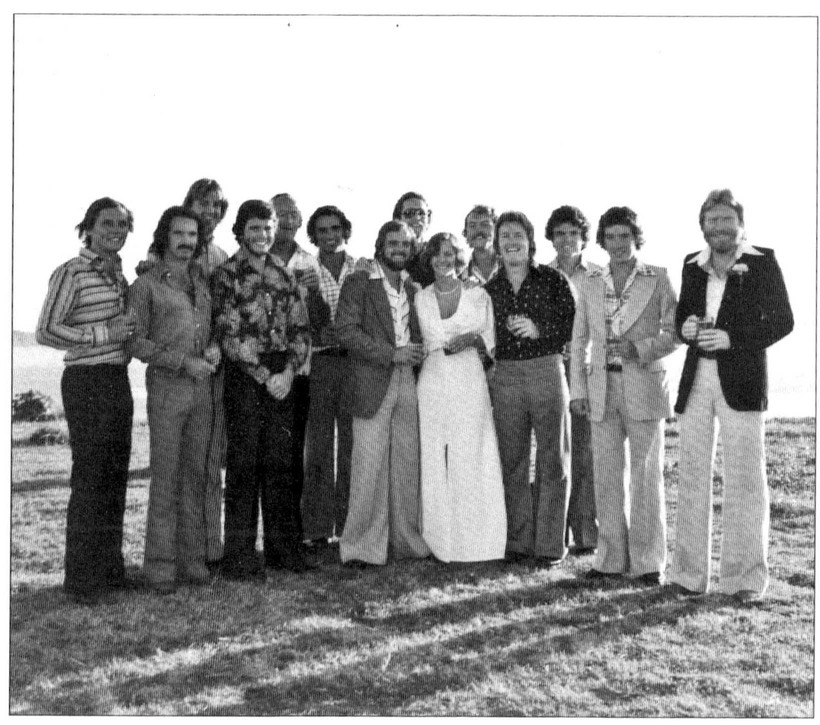

Vicki and Steve Porter's Wedding St Ouen's 1977
Left to right: Bruce Stanger, Scott Wilson, Wayne Bridges, Greg Price, Bill Lavarack, Jerry Shannos, Steve and Vicki Porter, Hugh Secomb, Russell Evans, Paul Berghouse, Mark Berghouse, Ross Ryan, Alan Wheeler   *(Photo courtesy of Steve Porter)*

After a year they bought a house in Maroubra – Steve's uncle left him some money which they used as a deposit. TAA then became Australian Airlines which eventually became Qantas Domestic. Two children followed, Chanelle in 1983 and Aaron in 1985. Vicki worked in the TAA office in central Sydney and TAA trained her as a ticket seller. They visited Steve's home town Newcastle regularly and, says Vicki, 'I was hoping for a transfer to Newcastle, but they didn't have any positions, so I finished up with TAA'. She had been with the airline for eight years.

Vicki was quite keen on her adopted country. 'I liked the Australian lifestyle. We really got into sports in Sydney – I swam, ran, went to the gym, everything. The only time I missed home was the first Christmas. Steve worked all day and came home drunk'. One can imagine that Steve would have been on the receiving end of some very pointed comments from Vicki that evening.

Despite her love of Australia, Vicki didn't ignore her roots. 'I went home to England frequently because I got a bit of cheap travel [working for an airline would have been handy] and I took the kids back home with me'.

By the time it came to move to Newcastle, Vicki says, 'I had friends up here and I had a job up here and it was a different lifestyle for us and the kids. We made friends with the local people who had kids around our kids' age, so the social scene was good'.

Vicki sums up her decision to accompany Steve halfway around the world: 'I've never regretted coming to Australia or to Newcastle, and I'd do it again. I would only change one thing – buy more property. We were the offspring of a generation that came through the war and didn't have anything. We didn't buy anything on credit and were not risk takers. In Jersey we didn't earn a lot and spent it all, so we had no money when we got to Australia.

Ida Laffoley, a Jersey woman born and bred, met Bill Lavarack in the early 1960s soon after he arrived in Jersey from South Africa. Ida, who had two children from a previous marriage, used to go out on the town with her brother and kept on bumping into Bill at various nightclubs along the beachfront at St Ouen's as well as the Rugby Club. As well as enjoying the bands playing at these venues she was attracted to Bill because he was a real 'man's man'.

Slowly things got more serious between Bill and Ida even though Bill was reluctant to be tied down in a relationship. He liked to party, and Ida was tolerant of this.

They had a break for a period when Bill went back to South Africa. Ida volunteered to go with him, but Bill didn't want the responsibility of being a father to her children back in South Africa, so they split up. However, Bill found that he couldn't live without Ida and decided to return to Jersey. Interestingly, Bill and Ida's kids got on really well so perhaps it was Bill's fear of being tied down that led to his decision to go home. Anyway, Bill eventually stepped up to the plate with the kids.

When Bill returned to Jersey things settled back into a similar routine, although by now Ida was getting a little impatient with Bill about commitment. She says, 'We went out for about seven years and I said to Bill, "This is ridiculous, I want a little bit of stability". He didn't particularly want to get married, so I said, "I will make a promise to you. I will not try to change you. I just need a permanent roof over my children's head". "Fine", he said, "I will provide that roof", and that's what he did'.

Ida and Bill got married in 1970. The wedding itself was a very quiet affair because

Bill didn't want a big fuss. However, as people found out they wanted to celebrate so they started buying champagne for the couple. Bill's response was, 'Christ, this is bloody good, isn't it?'

Ida found that with Bill the old saying, 'if you can't beat them you might as well join them', rang true. With Bill working on the beach part time from the mid-1970s until the early 1980s she used to put on dinner parties for the beach guards – a home away from home sort of thing. Ida and Bill were living in Beaumont at the time. Ida says wistfully, 'We always had such fun. I used to do paella. The boys had never had that sort of food'.

Ida's meals became so popular that when Steve Porter and Vicki Jones decided to get married they came to see Ida at work one day to tell her they were getting engaged. Ida offered her congratulations and they asked Ida if they could have their engagement party at her place, with paella. Ida replied, 'certainly!' Ida remembers the wedding at El Tico, particularly the photographs of the sunset over the water which she described as 'truly wonderful'.

Ida was working for a firm of tutoring accountants when she met Bill. The job entailed handling the administration for accountancy examinations. Later in the 1960s she moved to the Royal Bank of Scotland where her work involved sending different currencies to all parts of the world for clients. Ida says fondly, 'I loved that job, it was very interesting. The bank retired me when I was 60 and then they asked me to come back because there was no one else who could do the work. I went back for another year and then retired again'.

Bill was diagnosed with heart problems in the late 1980s and he went to London for a triple bypass operation. He was 56 or 57 at the time. The doctors told Ida that they had never seen a heart shaped like his. It was totally misshapen because it was trying to compensate for the blockages caused by his lifestyle. He also had a very high threshold of pain. The doctors believed that some time in the 1980s he had a massive heart attack and he wasn't even aware of it. The beach guards at the time joked that if Bill had fallen over they would have thought he was just drunk.

Ida says quietly, 'The doctors told him it was the quality of life not the quantity from then on. However, it was very difficult to get him to try and take it easy, he was having none of it. He decided he might as well live the life that he wanted to live if he hadn't got long to go'.

He had another big turn in 1992 and he was admitted to hospital. The staff used to call Ida matron because she went to see him first thing in the morning and she demanded to know what the news was about him.

One evening when Ida went to the hospital to check on Bill she didn't like the look of him, so she told the nurses that she was staying. The staff curtained off the bed next to Bill, so Ida had somewhere to rest. What happened next was like something out of a novel.

It was about seven o'clock the following morning and Bill got up and wanted to go to the toilet, so Ida helped him. When he came out Ida's daughter Jackie had just arrived, and Bill said, 'Jackie, there's a white light'. Ida immediately shoved a chair under him and told her daughter to go and get the crash team and her sister who was in reception. Bill was admitted into intensive care and, in Ida's words, 'they worked a bloody miracle and got him back'.

The surgeon told Bill and Ida that Bill was not going to last a lot longer and, unfortunately, he was correct, although it didn't happen until the following year. Ida remembers it like it was yesterday It was Monday 6 September 1993. She recalls, 'I'd taken the day off to go to the doctor with Bill and then we were going to go to lunch with one of the Aussies. We stopped to look at a catamaran regatta and he went and chatted to a few people. I saw him walk up this incline which was unusual for him, given he was very short of breath. Bill went to the bathroom and he was very happy, whistling. The next minute I heard him shout "Oooh" and bang he was down and that was it. I didn't know whether to do CPR, phone the ambulance, or what. The ambulance was there in less than five minutes, but he was gone. He died a month shy of his 61st birthday. His funeral was like a party, a celebration of his life'.

Ida still lives in Jersey. Her daughters are married and live there as well. She smiles when she recounts the times she and Bill had with the beach guards: 'The Aussies were curious and outgoing and wanted to meet as many people as possible, and everybody wanted to meet them as well.'

16 Noddy, Berghouse and John Wayne

'My approach to them was this – why buy the book when you can go to the library. So, I didn't make any lasting attachments.'

Extract from an interview with Jim 'Noddy' Reeves, long term Australian beach guard where he describes his approach to various female acquaintances during his Jersey time.

Other than Jerry Shannos, two other Australians were to feature as the longest serving beach guards/lifeguards in Jersey. They were Jim 'Noddy' Reeves and Paul Berghouse. Another, Wayne 'Bridgie' Bridges, aka John Wayne, made his mark in Jersey over a five-year period from 1976 to 1980.

Jim Reeves got the nickname Noddy because when he got to Jersey in 1976 he was jet lagged and kept falling asleep, including when talking to a girl at a disco one night soon after he arrived. He didn't say what she thought of that. Before that he had the nickname 'Jatz' from Swansea Belmont surf club – short for Jatz crackers. The reader can figure out why.

Jim was born in Sydney but moved north with his parents to the southern Newcastle beachside suburb of Belmont in about 1957 or 1958. He left high school at the end of year 12 in 1971 and worked as a labourer at the very large Australian steel making company called the Broken Hill Proprietary (BHP) for a short period and then got a job working in a plumbing supply firm. He tried to enter the Australian Navy in 1973 but failed the medical because of colour blindness. Noddy wanted to be a clearance diver, which required very high levels of fitness. Apart from the colour blindness issues he was in perfect physical health, so he was very disappointed. It was back to work in the plumbing supplies business in the Newcastle suburb of New Lambton.

Jim joined Swansea Belmont surf club in 1967 to do his Qualifying certificate, then his Bronze medallion in 1968. He rowed surf boats as a junior. The surf club background gave him the qualifications and experience to apply for Jersey through Jerry Shannos for the 1976 season. Steve Porter, Alan 'the Reverend' Walker and Jim all flew over from Australia together.

Noddy lived in the St Saviour's Road Doghouse that year. A tall, good looking fellow, Jim had an interesting angle on that fact that there were lots of girls hanging around during his many years in Jersey. He says with a smile, 'My approach to them was this – why buy the book when you can go to the library. So, I didn't make any lasting attachments'. Well, not for many years at least.

At the end of the 1976 season after a trip to the Munich beer festival with a couple of the boys Jim went back to Newcastle. After a brief stint working in a warehouse he went back to his old plumbing supplies job. Jim returned to Jersey in 1978 but not to the beach, instead he worked in the Metropole Hotel in St Helier as the pool lifeguard. They provided accommodation which was a bonus. He wanted to be on the beach but, as he explains, 'I couldn't get a spot because Jerry and I didn't exactly see eye to eye. At night time I did a bit of door work with the boys'. Jim didn't expand on what he and Jerry didn't see eye-to-eye on.

Paul Berghouse left Australia in 1976 when he was 22 to start what he calls his world adventures. He had met Jerry Shannos before he left Australia in 1976. Jerry advised him that the beach guard season would have already started by the time he got to the UK (in 1976) but to get in touch with him and Jerry would see how things were – there might be a few positions on the beach left. Paul's travels initially took him up through South East Asia, across to India, down through South Africa then up to Kenya. He arrived in London midway through June 1976 which was too late for Jersey, so he worked as a lifeguard in a swimming pool in the East End of London and enjoyed a bit of the London culture scene.

Paul says he went overseas on a working holiday primarily to play rugby. He had arranged through the Sydney rugby club Randwick to have a run out with the Richmond club in London but when he arrived in London it was their off-season. So that went out the window because Paul wanted to travel. At the end of 1976 Paul did a bit of traveling around the Mediterranean then got in touch with Jerry. He offered Paul a position on the beach. Paul's brother Mark came over to Jersey as well in late April 1977 and he worked on the beach as well. Paul and his brother lived in the St Saviour's Road Doghouse.

With fellow lifeguards Wayne Bridges and Russell Evans, Paul stayed in Jersey after the 1977 season. There he very much enjoyed the social set up in Jersey and played with the Jersey Rugby Club. Obviously, the famous win by the beach guards over the club in 1977 and Paul's goal kicking abilities were a factor.

Paul recalls the victory with a laugh, 'I must admit that it took a while for the local team to adjust to the defeat by the lifeguards – they didn't take the loss very well. They hadn't been training and they just threw a side together because they thought it would just be a training run. A half an hour after the game finished there were only us and one of their guys left having a drink'.

The Jersey Rugby Club learnt from the experience. Paul says, 'The strange thing is that in 1979 we played them again and we had a pretty decent side, in fact a much better side then in 1977, and we lost. In 1979 they took it seriously, they weren't going to be ambushed again. I don't recall playing against the Jersey Rugby Club ever again'.

The annual game against the beach guards faded into oblivion because there weren't enough beach guards coming to Jersey with sufficient experience to play rugby. Even so, Paul continued his interest with rugby and notes that in those days in the UK there wasn't a regular competition of home and away games leading to finals. That was the case in Australia but in the UK the rugby season consisted of a series of knockout competitions and if a team was defeated then that was it. However, Paul observed there were a lot of games that were played, termed 'friendlies', which were just as intense but without playing for competition points. The Jersey Rugby Club would play 'friendlies' against teams that came over at the weekend.

Paul thinks that the amateur status of rugby played a big part in this arrangement prior to the early 1980s. After that rugby union in Britain started what they called a League which was not a knockout. Courage Breweries were the initial sponsors and teams started to play in individual Leagues for competition points with finals.

Wayne Bridges had just turned 20 when he arrived in Jersey in 1976. Recruited by Jerry Shannos and although very young, Wayne stood six feet four inches tall, had a thick mop of brown-blond hair and, in his words, 'very green'. Intending to stay only one season, he was to remain in Jersey for five years. Wayne recalls with a grin, 'Jersey was a big experience for me. I grew up overnight. I found the people that we hung around with in Jersey to be fantastic and they really looked after me. The nucleus of those people came from the Rugby Club and that then expanded out through the island'.

Despite his tender years, Wayne was soon initiated into the ways of the beach guards. Part of the initiation was meeting Bill Lavarack. Wayne takes up the story. 'When I first arrived in Jersey I went up to the Rugby Club and met Noddy and got on the drink. Noddy was doing his usual trick of sleeping standing up. They had a whole week of John Wayne movies on at the time. When I first met Bill Lavarack that night I was with Noddy and we were introduced as Jim and Wayne. Bill said, "Ah, John Wayne" so I got that nickname'.

John Wayne continues: 'I used to have the Monday and Tuesday off every second week. We went to the Rugby Club on the first of my nights off and Bill was there. Ida had let him come out to have a drink with us. Hughie Behan, the local heavy, was also there with an entourage of women. I knew Hughie because I was working at

Blimpers West Park that he owned. Huey turned to me and said, "Hey John Wayne, is there a party at the Doghouse?" and I said, "Hang on". Then I went and had a word with the Duke and he said, "Yeah, that's okay', so about three quarters of the Rugby Club came back to the Doghouse. After a while we ran out of beer. Hughie heard about it and he said, "Hang on a minute" and he jumped into his Rolls Royce and drove down to West Park and filled the back of the Roller with grog, then drove back to the party and off we went'.

'The next morning it was still my day off, together with Harpo and the Beast [Peter Compton, another Newcastle beach guard]. When we got up in the morning feeling more than hungover all we could hear was tinkle, tinkle on the floor of the loungeroom. Bill was asleep underneath the pile of beer bottles. When he woke up he wanted to keep on drinking, so we decided to go down the road and have a beer with him. But the boys set me up. They said, "Hey Bill, take Bridgie for a drink", so he did. We started drinking pints then we got onto pints with Scotch chasers for Bill and Gin chasers for me. Then we decided to do a pub crawl. There was one pub called the Prince of Wales. We crashed through the doors and Bill knew the owner who was sitting in the corner, so he went to speak to him. I went to the bar to order but as I leant over the bar I [accidentally] took out two rows of glasses. I said to the bartender, "Mate, you can give us a pint each and we'll be on our way, otherwise it might get a bit nasty". He looked over at the manager and the manager nodded so we had a pint and left.'

'On the way home there was a pretty rough pub called the Rising Sun. If you didn't have a scar they'd give you one! Bill said, "Let's go in and have a fight". I said, "Bill, let's go home and I'll wrestle you there". We eventually got back to the Doghouse and as we came through the front door the Duke laughingly shouted out that they had put out a search party for us.'

'As I came in I was bouncing off the walls in slow motion, so they ended up putting me to bed. When I woke up the next morning they said, "Bridgie, you are officially a member of Bill's Monday Club".'

The beach guards at the time were experiencing a similar wave of local resentment to that which occurred in the mid-1960s. For example, some of the reporters with the *Jersey Evening Post* took every opportunity to depict the beach guards in a poor light. Bridgie says, 'There were a few defining moments that happened during the time there. One concerned the local farmers. Most of the farmers also liked to do a spot of fishing but they would normally treat us with disdain if we gave them advice on the surf conditions'.

One day in about 1978 or 1979 Bridgie was sitting up in the glass tower at St Ouen's with one of the beach guards who was checking out the girls on the beach with a pair of binoculars. The beach guard just happened to look up through the top of his binoculars and saw a boat being overturned at l'Etacq, so the pair went down and told Jerry. He decided to launch the rubber ducky. However, because of the surf the only place it could be launched was down at Le Braye slip. Jerry motioned to Bridgie to jump in the rubber ducky which had been playing up a little bit over the past week.

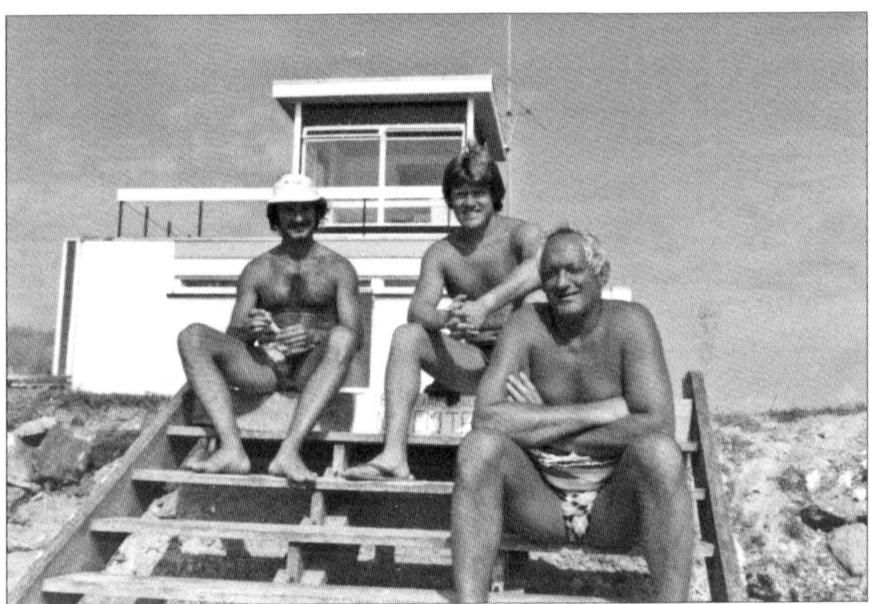

Keeping a Watchful Eye at St Ouen's Beach Circa 1978
Left to right: Scott Wilson, Paul Berghouse and Bill Lavarack

Bridgie continues. 'Jerry jumped in and turned the motor over. There was a big sea running and we had to go through a series of reef breaks to get down to where the boat had overturned. We were right out the front of the tower when the motor conked out. As Jerry was fiddling with the motor I got on the radio and spoke to the tower and said, "Can you get the air sea rescue going, we might need some backup here". Their reply was, "Don't worry about the air sea rescue, have a look behind you". I turned around and there were several sets of waves coming as big as a block of flats. I sang out to Jerry and I thought we were gone. Suddenly the engine kicked over, then died, then kicked over again, then kept going.'

'We got out through the break and drove down to where the overturned boat was. There was a bloke hanging onto it. We said, "Hey mate, is there anybody out here with you?" and he said, "Yes, look for my uncle". We did a few laps, but the overturned boat started to get washed towards the break, so we went back. Jerry dived in and got the fellow to the rubber ducky. As I was pulling him into the boat I spotted the other fellow nearby. I told Jerry, so we headed over to where the guy was. I dived in to get the bloke and brought him back to the duck. Jerry was trying to help me get the fellow into the duck, but he had forgotten to release the throttle and my toes were getting a manicure from the propeller.'

'Anyway, we got him in to the boat and started to work on him whilst trying to control his nephew. Apparently, they had a little Jack Russell dog with them in the boat, but the dog managed to swim towards shore. When we got to the beach the boys came down in Jerry's car and a crowd had gathered around. We started to work on the uncle again. A man pushed through the crowd and told us he was a neurosurgeon, so he helped. However, the doctor soon pronounced the uncle dead. We found out later that the uncle was riddled with cancer and his nephew was taking him out for one last fish.'

'This incident was on a Friday. On Sunday afternoon I was sitting in the tower and I could hear the noise of a lot of cars pulling into the car park. Jerry went outside to have a look and called us out. There were a large group of farmers who came down to thank Jerry and the boys for our efforts in getting the two men to shore.'

'From that point onwards, we would be driving between beaches down the back roads and the farmers would toot the horn on their tractors and give us a wave and would come up and say hello in the pub. The incident made the paper and that seemed to break the ice with the locals.'

Bridgie recalls a funny incident that occurred one afternoon when some of the beach guards were driving back to St Helier after work. Mick Sylvester, who features a bit later in this book, had showed Wayne how to backfire the Jeep, which Mick used to do to clear the carbon off the plugs. As Wayne relates, 'After he showed me how to do it he said later it was the worst thing he ever did, because I kept on doing it.'

The boys were driving along the dual carriageway on the south of the island. Wayne was driving, Robbie Shaw, a very fit older beach guard, was sitting in the middle and big Mick was in the back. A bloke pulled up alongside the Landrover at the traffic lights in a red convertible Mercedes Benz with white leather, two English Sheepdogs in the back and this gorgeous blonde bombshell in the front with him. She looked over and smiled at the boys. Bridgie says the bloke wasn't too amused at this. As the lights turned green he took off.

Wayne pulled up alongside the Mercedes at the next set of lights and that happened for three sets of lights. As Wayne says, 'By this time the guy has got the shits with us. We then came up to the roundabout in front of the Tourism Department and stopped again for the lights. When the light went orange, I put the jeep into gear and took off and beat the Mercedes into the tunnel. He was right on our tail and I backfired the jeep. Well, the dogs jumped out of the back of the car and took off. Robbie was laughing that hard that his stomach muscles were jumping up and down and tears we're coming out of his eyes'.

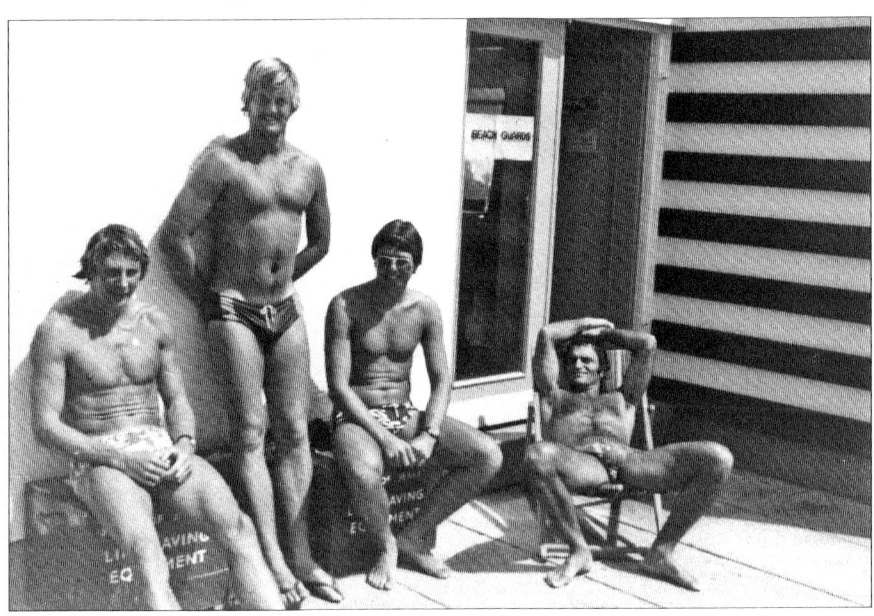

Enjoying Some Afternoon Sun at St Ouen's Circa 1978
Left to right: Tim Joyce, Wayne Bridges, Guy Littler and Jerry Shannos

In 1980 Wayne was joined by his younger brother Steven Bridges on the beach. Steven, only 20 years old, says he also grew up quickly that year. He did have on problem – no-one knew him as Steve. He recalls with a laugh: 'During my time in Jersey no-one ever used my name – they referred to me as Junior or Wayne's brother – no-one ever knew my first name. By the time I got there Wayne had been there for a few seasons and he was number two [to Jerry] and everybody on the island liked him so they liked me too. But I was always known as Junior'.

Steve, or Junior rather, was a typical testosterone propelled young man and chased girls, so much so that his brother said to him, 'Why don't you go for quality, not quantity?' Steve laughs. 'As if I was going to take any notice of him as a horny 20-year-old.'

The brothers would have stayed longer in Jersey, but fate stepped in. Steve says sadly: 'I had turned 21 over there when we got the phone call about our mother. We came home and had a bad 12 months. Mum had cancer and had a brain operation. Our mother ended up dying in 1982. After that I went off the rails a bit'.

Wayne went on to work in the ship building business, but Steve says: 'I went back in 1984 because I had unfinished business in Jersey'. Steve's girlfriend convinced him to come back to Newcastle at the end of 1984 season. Then he joined the police force where he stayed for 25 years.

By the early 1980s Wayne Bridges, who was Jerry's second in charge, and Russell Evans (third in charge) had left the island so Jerry shifted their responsibilities on to beach guards like Paul Berghouse who had been there for a while. The administrative side of the beach guard service changed also due to an increased level of paperwork demanded by the Harbours Department. Paul says that Jerry didn't seem too keen on that, so Paul did all the reports, rosters and other material as Jerry's second in charge until Jerry left in 1988. Paul says Jerry was quite relaxed about who went to which beach – he left it up to the beach guards to decide. However, Paul decided to put it all into roster form, so everyone knew exactly which beach they were to turn up to, and when.

Back in the mid-1970s Paul recalls they were paying about five or six quid a week for rent in the Doghouse. As he wasn't the boss, Paul doesn't know to what extent back then the Jersey Tourism Department was involved with the Housing Department concerning the location of the Doghouses or the rent payable. However, as everyone would attest, the housing itself was of a very basic standard. Moreover, the pay scale remained quite low – none of the lifeguards went to Jersey to make money. The fun for the blokes was living in the Doghouse with their mates.

Most, but not all, had had their fill of the Jersey lifestyle after several seasons. It was only a hard core few of the Aussies that stayed on and on, such as Jerry, Jim and Paul – for whatever reason they enjoyed the place too much to leave. Paul says he loved working on the beach, working on the door and having fun in the nightclubs. Wisely he got a coach driving licence during the winter of 1978 to make himself more employable in the off-season. In 1977 Paul recalls the Aussies were paid about 46 or 47 quid a week. He says, 'You could survive on it but not save much money. We were probably picking up five quid in tips a night on the door so with three or four nights that put an extra 20 quid in your pocket'.

Paul's first trip back to Australia was in 1982 when he took his future wife Yvonne to Australia to introduce her to Paul's mother. Paul met Yvonne on Anzac Day 1979 at a restaurant in St Helier. He was there with some visiting Australians and Yvonne was working at the restaurant as a waitress. Yvonne, Scottish by birth, came over to Jersey to work and play like a lot of other people. Jersey was in full swing in those days. Paul tried to chat her up but got absolutely nowhere – the first time, the second time and, he says, about ten times thereafter. However, once he had made her initial acquaintance at the restaurant he kept on running into her at nightclubs and in various pubs. Undaunted, Paul kept on asking her out, but she kept on knocking him back. She had heard about those loudmouth Australian lifeguards and wanted nothing to do with them. All her girlfriends were urging her to go out with Paul, saying he was a nice guy.

Eventually she agreed to go out with Paul and that was that, well almost. Paul had arranged to take her out on the first date and then promptly forgot about it. He turned up at a nightclub soon afterwards and Yvonne was there, and she was looking daggers at him. She said to Paul, 'You've had your chance and you blew it' and then walked away. However, things got resolved and they're still together. Paul says sheepishly, 'We got married in 1993 but were engaged in 1982 – a very long engagement'. Yvonne eventually moved into the fashion industry in Jersey, something which she was trained for.

Jim Reeves again returned to Australia at the end of the 1978 season because of a family illness. Then he went back to Jersey for the 1979 season and worked at the Merton Hotel, a big hotel with a 33-metre pool and a 10-metre diving tower. He continued to work with the boys at night time and party with them.

The beach guards in 1978 went to another Doghouse (number 4), again in Old Street, St Helier. Like St Saviour's Road it wasn't particularly flash. Then in 1979 they moved to Doghouse no 5 in Raleigh Avenue, about 700 metres away as the crow flies from Old Street. All the Doghouses belonged to the States of Jersey.

The pool at the Metropole wasn't so busy but there were quite a few hotel guests who used the pool at the Merton. Jim says being a pool lifeguard was a rather boring job although a guy drowned in the Metropole pool after hours one night.

Jim actually made a rescue at the Metropole in 1978. A guest went to the bottom of the pool – he was quite a big fella and Jim dived in and got him to the side of the pool. He was trying to push him out when a woman came by and asked Jim if the guy was in trouble. He sarcastically replied, 'Oh no, I do this for fun all the time'. Jim managed to get him onto the pool deck and he asked someone to, 'go and get someone to ring an ambulance'. In the meantime, Jim put the victim in the recovery position and checked all his vitals. Suddenly the fellow sat up and appeared to be fine. Jim concluded he must have had some sort of a fit. Jim went into the hotel to tell them not to worry about the ambulance where the staff informed him that one wasn't being despatched because 'I wasn't a doctor'. Too bad if the guest had been in real trouble.

Once again Jim went back to Australia after the end of the 1979 season because he had a girlfriend back home and she had told him that he should go and do what he wanted to do and then come back. However, the relationship didn't work out. Jim soon after was offered a job with a firm called Ace Gutters in Newcastle who were opening the plumbing part of their business. He eventually ended up being the manager of the brassware department.

Then in 1980 a beach inspector position came up with Lake Macquarie council and Jim applied for it and got the job. The manager at Ace Gutters offered him $100 a week more to stay but Jim said to him, 'Don't worry mate, I've already accepted $100 less to go'. Jim says he wanted that job because he loved the beach lifestyle.

Jim worked as a relief Beach Inspector for a start and he stayed on the beach until early 1985 and then decided to back to Jersey for the summer of 1985. A mate of his who had worked in Jersey in 1983 suggested they both apply, and they were successful. Jerry Shannos was still running the beach guard service. Notwithstanding the disagreement between Jerry and Jim in 1976, Jerry must have figured out that Jim was older (and perhaps wiser) and undoubtedly took into account Jim had been working professionally on the beach for five years so he took Jim on once more.

However, when Jim 'Noddy' Reeves got back to Jersey in 1985 he noticed things had started to change.

Part 3: THE WINDS OF CHANGE

Mid-1980s – Early 2000s

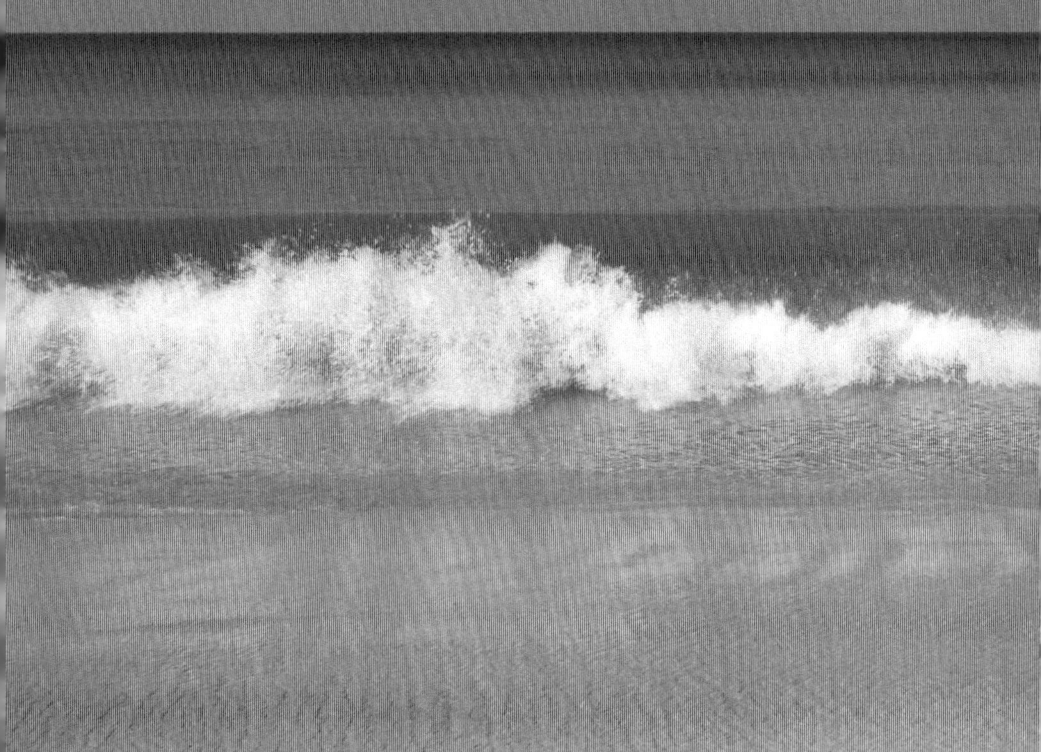

17 The Rules Tighten

'So, unless you had a work permit other than on the beach you couldn't work elsewhere. If you got caught working [outside the beach] you would be in breach of your immigration status.'

Extract from an interview with Jim Reeves, long time Australian beach guard/lifeguard.

In Jersey by 1985 transformation was indeed happening. As a holiday destination which in the 1960s and 1970s had enjoyed a massive seasonal influx of tourists, Jersey was now facing stiffening competition from countries around the Mediterranean such as Spain, Greece, and Egypt. They were cheaper destinations with guaranteed sunshine and a burgeoning discount airline market meant they were increasingly easier to get to. Jersey was still quite a busy place but not like it was in 1976. Jim Reeves recalls, 'At that time [1976], when you looked from the beach to the airport there were planes always landing and taking off – it was one of the busiest airports going. But things gradually quietened down – the beach was more taken over by the locals'.

The island being a tax haven, there were still people driving around in tasty cars and buying big houses and properties. There was one fellow who was famous for his parties which were held in a massive barn on his farm. They would start about 1:30 in the morning. Jim went to one of them because he was working on the door of a nightclub and met the fellow. Everybody that went to the party had to take a bottle of alcohol. There would be about 300 or 400 people at the party and Jim describes them as 'pretty wild'.

As far as the beach guards were concerned in 1985 they were still as boisterous as they had ever been. The numbers were much the same – about a dozen on the beach and unchanged routines – same working hours, beaches and pools. West Park Pool ceased to be part of the roster in the late 1980s. Its popularity declined and, in any event, being a tidal pool, the beach guards only patrolled when the tide was out. When Jim left in 2010 West Park had become a surfboard area with flags and buffer zones because the surfboards had taken over. Boardriding popularity had massively increased into the eighties and continued to do so up until when Jim finally left for the last time in 2010.

Many of the boardriders in Jersey weren't very good but there were some who had real talent. Barry Jenkins was one of the first boardriders, along with Gordon Burgess. The States of Jersey put a big red marking on the sea wall at St Ouen's to delineate the board riding area from the area for body surfing, not that the board riders took much notice. The boardriders started around the Watersplash then eventually went south of El Tico and around to St Brelade's when the surf was too big on the west coast.

At the end of 1985 Jim and a couple of mates had a few weeks in Greece then flew to South Africa and stayed there until April 1986. It was at the height of the apartheid period, but Jim says, 'We never felt threatened. It was safe enough although there was trouble the day we landed in Johannesburg. They had had the first riot ever of black people in the business district of Johannesburg because the authorities had executed three black people. We got lost in Johannesburg and ended up in the black train station. A bloke came up to us and said "Excuse me, you're in the wrong station. Yours is over there". We were quite amazed when we walked down the street and the black fellas would say "Hello boss" and we would look around until we realised they were talking to us'.

The beach guards lived for three months in Durban in a couple of apartments that came with their own maid. It was very cheap living. The poor maid couldn't work the boys out because they weren't the usual white people she was used to. They liked to have a joke with her. She worked six days a week and the local blokes at the nearby pub advised the boys, 'Don't spoil her – make sure you leave a mess in the kitchen and the apartment looking like a tip'. It was cheaper for them to go to the pub every night to eat than to cook. On Sunday nights the pub was shut so they used to invite everybody around for a BBQ and a party.

Joyce the maid would come in on Monday morning and the boys would be sitting there with hangovers and they would plead with her not to make too much noise, they had a headache. She replied in a mock scolding voice, 'Joyce has headache too – you boys make a big mess, you very bad boys'. It took her about three weeks to even start to talk to them.

Then they moved apartments and the next maid's name was Constance. When the boys left Durban to drive to Cape Town Joyce and Constance came to see them off. Joyce said, 'Constance and I have bought two pairs of new shoes each'. The boys asked what for and she said, 'One pair of shoes is for Cape Town and the other one is for London because we coming with you'. Jim said, 'In London in April you might need more than a pair of shoes – you will be freezing'. They never went with the boys. That was their dream, but it never happened.

In 1985 the beach guard pay was a lot better than 1976 but the boys still needed to work in the evening to get enough money to live on. Jim says, 'We would have been on about a hundred and something pounds a week by the time 1985 came along.

1985 was the first time the beach guards lived in a Doghouse that wasn't in St Helier. Doghouse no 6, named Bellevue, was located near St Brelade's Bay in a suburb called St Aubin. It was the place where everybody wanted to be on a Sunday night because the nearby Old Court House pub really jumped.

The St Aubin Doghouse accommodation was pretty reasonable compared to the other Doghouses. It was a three-storey terrace place with six bedrooms situated right next to the Church of England minister's residence. The minister, who was friendly to the beach guards, ended up going to Australia to work in the Mount Newman mining area in Western Australia with his wife and five kids under the age of 10. Jim says sadly, 'Unfortunately she died and left him with the five children'.

In 1987 Paul Berghouse told Noddy that the States government was going to clamp down on the beach guards' driver's licences – they now needed a Jersey driver's licence to work. But the government wouldn't recognise Australian driver's licences so Noddy had to sit for a test. He was taken aback, '33 years of age and I had to sit for a driving test'. Resigned to his fate, Noddy made all the arrangements including borrowing a car. Noddy asked Paul if he should run it past Jerry. 'No', he was told, 'just go to St Brelade's [on duty] and duck away from there'.

When he got to St Brelade's Mick Sylvester, the guy who was on duty with Noddy, was very much hung over. It was a miserable rainy day and Mick started to drink on the job – a hair of the dog (or two) – a big no-no. Jerry came to St Brelade's to check on the pair (he obviously didn't take too much notice of Mick) and just after Jerry left Noddy had to go and do his driving test. He took off.

Coincidentally, Noddy's passport was running out and an Australia House official told him that as he lived quite a distance from London they would post it to him. It hadn't arrived, so he rang them twice and the second time he was told he would have to pick it up. Noddy had arranged to take the next day off after the driving test to travel to London and pick up his passport. In the meantime, says Noddy, 'Jerry had some grand plan for me to pick up some information in Australia House about a car he wanted to take back to Australia and make some money out of it'. In other words, sell it. But he hadn't spoken to Noddy in much detail about what he wanted.

After Noddy left, Jerry radioed St Brelade's to talk to him about getting the car information, but Mick made an excuse about Noddy not being there. Jerry, obviously keen to speak to Noddy, called back and Mick made another excuse. Jerry called back a third time and Mick owned up and told him that Noddy wasn't there, so Noddy was sprung. Noddy sighs and says, 'I should have just owned up to him and got the time off. Mick tried to call me at the Doghouse before I did the test, but I missed the call'.

Noddy did the test and passed. When he got back to the Doghouse one of the boys asked him, 'What's it like being an ex-lifeguard?' Noddy called Jerry who blew up. He told Noddy angrily, 'You come and see me when you get back from London'. However, luckily for Noddy the boys had told him what information Jerry was after in London.

In London, despite Australia House stuffing him around quite considerably, Noddy managed to get his passport and the information for Jerry. On return to Jersey the next day Noddy went to see Jerry in the Lifeguard Tower and he started to read Noddy the riot act. A knock on the door interrupted Jerry and two coppers came in for a cup of tea. Jerry said to Noddy, 'I'll speak to you later'. After the coppers left Jerry went for his daily run and swim and to check the beaches. While he was away Noddy put all the paperwork Jerry was after on his desk. Noddy says with a smile, 'I never heard another thing about my transgression after that'.

One of the beach guards by the name of Chris Redler, a great guy but not very capable on the drink, was at the Old Court House hotel one night in 1987. He was very drunk and was lying on the stairs that led up to the restaurant. Jerry came down out of the restaurant and found him and Chris was saying, 'Just walk over me, I don't give a shit'. He didn't come back the next year.

Another beach guard called Darryl Hadfield was always having run ins with Jerry. Darryl was a very staunch unionist. Jerry always claimed the Lifeguard Tower at St Ouen's as his house, but Darryl insisted that was the beach guard's workplace. Darryl decided to get himself in the good books with Jerry one day and to wash the jeep. He went inside and grabbed a bit of cloth to clean the jeep. When Jerry came back the jeep was sparkling inside and out. The problem was that Darryl had used Jerry's pillowcase, which he thought was a rag, to wash the jeep. Of course, Jerry blew up and Darryl was in the shit again.

✿

The late 1980s saw a tightening of the government rules and regulations concerning working in Jersey. Until then the beach guards continued to moonlight as doormen, but things changed as the result of changes to the work permit rules.

Jim Reeves recalls, 'So unless you had a work permit you couldn't work elsewhere other than on the beach. If you got caught working [outside the beach] you would be in breach of your immigration status. The only way to get around that was to apply for a special work permit or to have patriality status'. This didn't go down too well with many of the beach guards but there wasn't much they could do about it so most, apart from one, abided by the new rules.

As Noddy recalls, 'There was only one guy who couldn't cope with the idea of not working on the door – Mick Sylvester. Mick was a big guy and working on the door gave him the chance to talk to girls. The States [government] was promising a big change in the remuneration so that the pay would be adequate to allow us just to work on the beach. Mick continued to work on the door and he got caught twice. In the meantime, he had a break up with a girlfriend and he got done for drunk driving. The day he was supposed to go to court he never appeared at work or at court. He just got on a plane and flew out. It was probably the best move he could make because he was going to be deported anyway'.

Things were changing, and fast. One of the changes was the employment of the first Jersey Bean as a beach guard.

18 The First Jersey Bean

'He turned up at the beach with tinted hair and earrings and Jerry Shannos said, "Start Monday and lose the jewellery"'.

Extract from an interview with Jim 'Noddy' Reeves in which he describes Gordon Callendar's start as a beach guard.

In the mid-1980s a young man named Gordon Callendar became the first native born Jersey person to be successful in getting a job as a beach guard. Gordon's employment resulted from pressure being applied by the States' Tourism Department, although to be fair to Gordon he was a good candidate, apart from the choice of hairdo and jewellery.

Gordon started on the beach in 1986, while Jerry Shannos was still head beach guard. There would be only two Jersey Beans employed to work as beach guards/lifeguards (the latter name was to be adopted later) during the fifty plus years the Australians were in charge of running the service.

At the age of sixteen as a Jersey student, Gordon was lucky enough to get a scholarship to an international school on mainland Britain called the Atlantic College. The college was located in the Vale of Glamorgan, a county borough in South Wales. Coincidentally, Atlantic College was founded in 1962 by none other than Dr Kurt Hahn, who had previously set up Gordonstoun School in Scotland and had had an association with Adrian Curlewis during the first year of the beach guard service in Jersey in 1958. The ethos of Atlantic College was very much about academic excellence combined with activities that were aimed at providing service to the community.

Gordon was a keen swimmer as a youth and that helped in getting the scholarship. He says, 'I was very pleased to go there and one of the things that they offered was surf lifesaving. Atlantic College's claim to fame was that they invented the Rigid Inflatable Rescue Boat [RIB]. The RNLI [Royal National Lifeboat Institution] adopted it and it went from there. I did my surf lifesaving qualifications with Atlantic College as part of their outdoor programs'.

Once he had completed college at age eighteen he was planning to have a year off before going to university. He decided to look for a summer job in Jersey. Gordon recalls, 'I wrote to hotels and the Tourism Department seeking a lifeguard job. I got given a job with the lifeguard service. I had to meet Jerry Shannos. I found Jerry to be very straightforward but not overly friendly; however, when you got to know him that was his nature. I think he was quite suspicious at first – he didn't really know too much about what life surf lifesaving training I had even though I had a Bronze medallion and an Advanced Resuscitation Certificate plus experience in RIBs from Atlantic College. I wasn't sure that I overly impressed him, but I got the job. Jerry put me through the standard fitness test before he was satisfied that I could become a lifeguard. At the end of my first year at Atlantic College I spent a month on the beach patrolling in South Wales. The beach used to get a decent surf at times'.

Gordon frankly admits that he didn't know how much pressure was put on by the Tourism Department to employ a local on the beach. Although there was a rumour going around that pressure had been brought to bear by Gordon's father, Gordon emphatically denies this. He says that his father was not politically inclined and had no relationship with the Tourism Department. Gordon says, 'The lifeguards were a little curious about me, but I think they could see I had the skills to do the job, so we got on fine'.

Noddy Reeves has a humorous recollection about when Gordon started as a beach guard. 'There was a local guy named Gordon Callander who was put on by the States of Jersey. He turned up at the beach with tinted hair and earrings and Jerry Shannos said, "Start Monday and lose the jewellery"'.

Paul Berghouse was quite happy with Gordon working as a beach guard. He recalls, 'Gordon Callander did very well for a young bloke. He was a champion pool swimmer. To his credit he stood back and took it all in and he learnt a lot from the lifeguards'.

The biggest challenge Gordon faced was to make sure he socialised with the Aussies because he was living at home, not in the Doghouse. Although still at a tender age, he was determined to give it a go. He says, 'At the end of the first week of work it was time to go out for a pint or six with the boys. The lifeguards had a reputation for being good on the beach but also as enjoying a pint. My parents said go out and enjoy yourself and whatever time you are finished ring and we will come and pick you up regardless of what state you're in. I think I was in a bit of a state after my first night out. I made sure that I bought a round when it was my turn and kept up the pace as best I could. It was very entertaining, but I can't remember a lot of it. I always went out on weekends with the boys after that'.

During the northern winter of 1986-87 Gordon travelled to Australia and stayed at Palm Beach in Sydney for three or four months with Mick Sylvester (a former beach guard who had left rather than face court for working at night without a permit and for drink driving). He was the lifeguard at Palm Beach. Gordon recalls,

'Mick very kindly made arrangements for me to stay at the [Palm Beach] surf club and do patrols on the beach. There was enough partying going on around Palm Beach to satisfy an eighteen-year-old. I got a job in the cafe next door to the surf club. Everyone was very friendly and accepting of me'.

Gordon retuned to Jersey and went back on the beach for the 1987 season. He then went to university in Edinburgh to study medicine. Both of his parents were Scottish and had moved to Jersey in 1965 before Gordon was born. His parents weren't that keen on his choice of city: 'They come from Glasgow and were a bit suspicious of Edinburgh'. Very Scottish!

During the long university holidays in summer Gordon continued working on the beach as, he says, 'Jerry by then was quite accepting of me'. He worked shorter seasons in 1988 and 1989 which Gordon claimed suited both Jerry and Paul Berghouse (who had taken over by then) because they didn't have to source someone from Australia.

The States of Jersey had provided the service with a car for transport as well as the Land Rovers. Gordon recalls, 'The first year I was on the beach we drove an old Ford car – a Cortina or Granada – and we used to work at Plémont which is a little tiny beach at the top of the island. It had a gravel car park and we always used to fishtail the car through the gravel on the way out after work. Unfortunately, when I did it the driveshaft broke and I had to ring Jerry up and tell him that I broke in the car. He was not very impressed. I would occasionally get the Land Rovers bogged down in the soft sand on St Ouen's beach. On one occasion Jerry came down and tried to take the radios off because the tide was coming in and he didn't want them to be destroyed. He was always pretty understanding but he didn't always see the funny side of it'.

Gordon recounts another story about the car. 'The States brought in seat belt laws in Jersey. Jerry used to get in the car and insert a piece of wood into the seat belt fastener to pretend he had buckled up. One day I had to pick someone up from the far end of the beach and a police car followed me and pulled me up. I didn't have a seatbelt on because I couldn't buckle it up'.

Despite a few run-ins with Jerry Shannos, Gordon got on well with him. 'Overall I found Jerry to be very fair and a very fit man. He knew what was going on with the lifeguards, whether it was on the beach or after work, and he knew when they did well or the reverse'.

Gordon had to stop working on the beach after the 1989 season because he was going into the third year of his medical training which had become quite intensive. He recalls fondly, 'I really enjoyed my time on the beach – great people, great fun. People took it seriously but there was still time for a few laughs. And it was a great way to meet girls. I loved Sunday nights at the Doghouse, the St Aubin's wine bar and the Old Court House hotel and then to the Rugby Club. There were very strict licensing laws in the late 1980s. If you went to anywhere after 11 p.m. you had to have food which was essentially a plate of chips. None of us joined the Rugby Club as members but it was easy to get signed in. Traditionally Monday in Jersey was the quietest day on the beach because it was the changeover day for the tourists in the hotels'.

Gordon says that Jersey has had a peculiar tourism history. Part of the tourist boom came from British Rail employees who received free travel to anywhere in Britain on the network which included the ferries. A lot of people would look to find the most exotic place in Britain they could go and Jersey was their choice. Also, a lot of honeymooners used Jersey as a tourist destination. The number of hotel beds grew enormously but the tourist boom started to tail off in the mid-1980s as people started to elect to go elsewhere.

He recalls, 'Twenty years ago Britain had a thing called Air Miles where you got points for filling up your car with petrol or buying things at the shops etc. At one point Jersey was one of the most popular short break attractions using Air Miles. No-one ever earned enough points to fly to America or Asia. Now tourism is mostly from older people who come in the shoulder season. When I was growing up, St Brelade's beach, which was near where we lived would be so heavily populated with people you could hardly see the sand. Also, big changes occurred in the economic scene with finance becoming the dominant employer and prices rose'.

Gordon provided an interesting insight into the itinerant working situation on the island. 'People who came to Jersey to work during the season were only allowed to live in bedsits. The facilities allowable in a room were very limited so the pubs flourished because there was nowhere else to go at night apart from sitting in your room looking at the wall. They were allowed a single gas ring and a sink – anything else and it wasn't a bedsit. So, the pubs became the social centre for the summer employees'.

Interestingly, Gordon also noted that during the Australian lifeguard service period there was no surf lifesaving education for school groups or anyone else. He feels that this could have been useful. He says, 'It never ceased to amaze me that local Jersey people, despite growing up near the sea, rarely knew about the sea in any way shape or form. I remember getting someone out of the water using a rescue board – a local. Initially he said, "I'm fine, I'm a local". So, I sat next to him for a while and then asked him how he was. He told me again that he was fine, so I sat there for a bit longer. Then he said, "Maybe you can give me a bit of a hand"'.

When Gordon graduated with a medical degree in 1992 he worked in Jersey on and off. He did a six-month job in Jersey into 1993 and another one in 1994. Then he returned to Australia and worked in the NSW Central Coast city of Gosford for a year. After that he went back to Jersey for twelve months, then to the British mainland for another twelve months and then eventually settled in Jersey at the end of 1997 where he continues to work as a doctor.

Gordon sums up his time on the beach. 'The lifeguarding experience was great. I was very fortunate to do it and I made a lot of friends. Most importantly the service was done properly'.

19   Same, Same, but Different

'When I came back in 1987 for my brother's wedding I saw how the helicopter rescue service was building up in Newcastle. They were starting to put on people as well as more volunteers. I had been a volunteer with the rescue helicopter before I went away to Jersey in 1986 and I had a rescue certificate.'

Extract from an interview with Peter Martine,
Australian beach guard mid to late 1980s.

The number of Australians employed as beach guards in Jersey who were not professional lifeguards started to dwindle from the mid-1980s. However, one who was not a professional was a young Newcastle man named Peter 'Squirrel' Martine who, after finishing up in Jersey in 1989 went home to Newcastle and got into a much more unusual form of rescue – by helicopter.

Peter Martine already had an indirect connection to Jersey, although he wasn't aware of it. Peter is the son of Marcia Martine, the lady who worked in the early 1970s at Souths Leagues Club in Newcastle and who inadvertently played a role in gaining Steve Porter, the Duke of Normandy, his nickname when he forgot to send a postcard to her back in 1973. Peter was a member of the same surf club as Steve, Cooks Hill.

At age 22, Peter had finished his apprenticeship as a pastry cook and was seeking some adventure in his life. He was contemplating going touring over to Western Australia in a converted 12-seater bus when a friend by the name of Graham 'Max' Murlind told Peter that he intended to apply for a job as a lifeguard in Jersey. Max asked Peter if he was interested so they wrote to Head Beach guard Jerry Shannos. Peter says, 'I was Chief Instructor at Cooks Hill surf club at that time, so I was well qualified. We had no idea of the pay rates or what the job involved. Anyway, Jerry rang me up and said, "I might have a position for you" so I said "Great". I rang up Max, but he hadn't been offered a job'.

Undeterred, Max decided to go to Jersey anyway, deciding to look for a job as a lifeguard at one of the hotel pools. They left Australia in April 1986, had a month touring through the USA then they went to London to have a look around.

They arrived in Jersey in May 1986. Peter lived in the St Aubin's Doghouse which, he describes, 'was a great place to stay'. A few of the beach guards including Noddy

Reeves welcomed him. The house was on four levels and he shared a room on the bottom floor street side with another beach guard named Gavin Skeffington (Skeff). It was about two weeks to go before the season started and the other beach guards were trickling in.

The fitness requirement dictated that the beach guards had to go up to the heated pool at Fort Regent to do an 800-metre swimming test which they all passed. The beach guards had a deal with the pool management which allowed them to train for free. The pool opened at six in the morning and the Aussies did laps from about seven, then returned to the Doghouse for breakfast where they were picked up in one of the jeeps to go to work. Although the beach guards didn't get paid until the season started they were able to live in the Doghouse for free until then. Max stayed there as well.

Soon after they got to the Doghouse a beach guard named Mick Sylvester who had been there for a few seasons took Max and Peter for a walk and a chat to clue them in. The three sat down on a bench around the corner from the Doghouse and Mick gave the newcomers a rundown on what to expect on the island. Peter says, 'His words were on the lines of, "You're here to do a job and to have a good time. The pubs and clubs are great but when you're on the beach you're a professional". He told us that we would have plenty of parties at the Doghouse and as Australian lifeguards on the island we would get invited to quite a few parties as well'.

Peter recalls that people liked having the beach guards around. They were aware that the tourism scene in Jersey was slowing down – they heard that from the locals, the people putting out the deckchairs and those working in the cafes on the waterfront. Peter says, 'During my time there were a lot of Swedes, Germans and French tourists coming to Jersey and spending their holidays there. The weather wasn't fantastic in my time – you'll be lucky to get a couple of days of 26 - 27 degrees [Celsius]'.

Peter was involved in a rescue one day in 1986 at St Brelade's. It was a very cold day, so cold that the two beach guards on duty had driven up and down the beach in the Land Rover to get the heater going to warm up. They were sitting in their tracksuits, Peter with a towel around him to keep warm. There was no one in sight until a woman who Peter estimates was in her 50s walked down onto the beach from the promenade in her swimsuit. In she went.

The tide was going out and the Aussies were keeping an eye on her as she started to bounce up and down in the water. At first, they thought she was just cold but then she started to struggle. Peter's mate said to him, 'You're going to have to go and get her because I haven't got my Speedos on'.

As the other beach guard got the rescue board off the Land Rover, Peter ran to the water's edge with a rescue tube. He says with a shudder, 'As soon as my feet hit the water I almost fell over with the cold. I had to keep running to get to the deeper water where she was, about 30 metres out. I dived into knee deep water and it was like diving onto a concrete block - the water temperature was only about 9 or 10 degrees, absolutely freezing. I got to her and grabbed her, and she said, "Thank you, thank you". I pulled her in and we asked her what she was doing in the water and she said, "I'm on holidays from England staying at a hotel nearby and I thought I'd come down and have a swim"'. Not a good idea.

Because the beach guard wages were not very flash, 'just enough to buy your food and some nights out but not to save very much', Peter got a second job through connections of Noddy Reeves and Paul Berghouse as a doorman at the Hotel de l'Europe in St Helier, earning 10 quid a night cash in hand. He and Skeff shared the job, working from 6 p.m. to 1 a.m. The clientele was, in the main, people staying in the hotel. Their job was to keep out anybody else that wasn't living there or wasn't a local.

He recalls that the cost of living in the mid to late 1980s wasn't too bad – the beer was still cheap, and the beach guards didn't eat out a lot. The number of Doghouse parties had dropped considerably by this time. Peter Martine says, 'We would probably have only one party a month'. The beach guards teamed up in pairs to buy food and cook it. Peter says, 'Skeff and I paired up and put in 50 quid a week for a food kitty. Each pair had their own section in the kitchen. Skeff wasn't a very good cook so I did most of the cooking and he cleaned up'.

Peter recalls with a laugh an incident one night at the hotel with a drunken Scotsman. The elderly owner liked to sit just behind reception every night because, Peter thinks, it was to give him something to do. A fellow began to play up in the bar area; Peter could hear the fellow swearing and carrying on, so he went in to see what was up.

Peter says, 'This Scottish guy was blowing up at a lady and another fellow, so I said, "Mate, what's the problem?" He was drunk and argumentative, and he said to me, "What are you going to do about it? Piss off"'.

The Scotsman was bigger than Peter and Peter wasn't that keen on getting into a brawl, so he replied in a polite but firm tone, 'I'm not going to do much, I'm just going to ask you to leave'. The Scotsman came back aggressively, 'So what?' Peter politely said to him, 'Do you live here?' The reply was, 'No'. Peter, getting a bit tired of this, said, 'Mate, the local police here love getting mainlanders and locking them up. All I have to do is to get someone to call the police and you'll be in the clink for a couple of nights'. The drunk said aggressively, 'Go on then'.

The drunken Scotsman started to get in Peter's face. Peter got worried he was going to be head butted so he put his arm up in the fellow's throat. Peter says, 'He was that drunk he could hardly stand up, so I kept walking him backwards and walked him to the door and pushed him out through it. He didn't come back and that's why I got an extra two pounds a night!'

Jerry Shannos kept his distance from the beach guards out of hours and, Peter Martine says, 'tended to turn a blind eye to what we were doing in the Doghouse. He didn't want to know unless we got into strife. He said to us, "Don't play up because we've got to preserve what we've got here" which was fair enough. We hardly ever saw him apart from at work. He relied on Noddy to keep us under control'.

During the off-season Peter Martine and his fellow Aussies followed the lead of countless other beach guards before him and took off to explore Europe until their money ran out. Then they would look for work to tide them over until the next season in Jersey started. For Peter this happened at the end of the 1986, 1987 and 1988 seasons.

At the end of the 1988 season he and friends travelled through Greece, Turkey and Africa. Peter, along with an Aussie beach guard named Rex Horsley who had started in Jersey in 1987, heard from a contact about a company that employed people in Sweden building large food silos to feed the pigs out in the country. Before they left Jersey they successfully applied for jobs in Sweden, to start in February 1989.

Needing work to make ends meet after their European travels, they did what most Aussies do when confronted with the same problem – they went looking. Earlier Peter had met a girl in Turkey (as one does) and she said she used to work at a French ski resort called Meribel. It was located in the French Alps near the Swiss border and was quite popular with the English. So off they went to France in October 1988.

Rex got a job as a glassie (collecting glasses) at a bar. Peter initially found it difficult to find employment. He had found accommodation through an Australian bloke whom he somehow managed to meet while standing on a corner in the freezing cold as it was snowing hard. Peter must have been looking lost because the Aussie said, 'A bloke I know has a unit', so Peter bunked in there for 60 quid a week.

Then he started looking for a job. Peter laughs as he says, 'I just kept going to the pub every day. It was run by a Pom and I got to know him, and he told me one day that the cleaners had quit so I volunteered for the job. By that stage I was within two weeks of running out of money – I'd been there about a month'.

The cleaning job gave him enough money to pay the rent plus a bit more left over. Then one day the manager of the pub told Peter that the dishwasher had quit so he asked the manager, 'What's the go there?' He replied, 'You get accommodation, a lift pass, all your food plus 30 quid a week'.

When Peter asked for the job, the fellow said, 'Who do I get to clean the pub?' Peter said, 'I don't care, I want that dishwasher job'. He shared the job with another young guy. The restaurant wasn't all that busy, so the work wasn't very hard. Peter and Rex stayed there until it was time to go to build silos.

The pair had to go to Bath in England first for an interview then the company paid their way to Gothenburg, on the Swedish west coast. There they met up with a Kiwi guy and they drove around a series of farms at the southern end of Sweden towing an 18-foot trailer which they lived in. There was a husband and wife team and four or five labourers to build the silos. Peter says, 'The weather was freezing - you'll be working out in the fields and it will be sleeting, trying to do up these big bolts. We stuck it out because the pay was good, and we got all our food paid for and we weren't spending any money'.

Eventually the cold became too much, and the pair returned to Jersey. That season turned out to be Peter's last. Peter says, 'I could have kept going back [to Jersey] year after year, but I came to the realisation that I needed to do something else with my life. It would have been easy to continue on and I can see why Noddy did it'.

That something proved to be, as the saying commonly used in Thailand and Bali goes, 'same, same, but different'. As Peter explains, 'When I came back in 1987 for my brother's wedding I saw how the helicopter rescue service was building up in Newcastle. They were starting to put on people as well as more volunteers. I had been a volunteer with the rescue helicopter before I went away to Jersey in 1986 and I had a rescue certificate. I did a few volunteer shifts in 1987. There was a rescue crewman spot available as a volunteer when I returned in late 1989 so I worked a few shifts a week. I got a job back at Coles then my brothers got the contract to run a bistro at Newcastle University and I helped them out. I was still volunteering but I then got some casual work with the helicopter service then a full-time job came up and I got it. It was perfect timing because the contract expired at the university'.

Peter was involved in a lot of incidents in his time with the helicopter rescue service. One occurred in May 1994. The service had been called up to the jail in Cessnock (in the NSW Hunter Valley west of Newcastle) because someone had been stabbed and had died of their wounds.

The crew was heading back to base from that job when they got a call to fly to the nearby Luskintyre airport at Rutherford as there had been a plane crash. In the helo was the pilot, an air crewman, a rescue crewman (Peter) and two paramedics. As they neared the aerodrome they could see the smoke from the wreckage, but they didn't know how serious the crash was at that stage.

Upon landing near the crash, the crew could see that a male had been thrown out of an old Tiger Moth bi-plane. He turned out to be the pilot and he was barely alive. Peter recalls with a shudder, 'It was the most horrific thing that I had ever seen – he was black from head to toe. The plane must have exploded on impact and he was charcoal'. The paramedics did their best to save him. They got an IV line in somewhere around his foot because the rest of his body was too badly burned to find a vein. The man's hair, his nose, his eyelids, his ears, were all burnt off'.

The helicopter crew were told that the plane had been putting on a stunt show for a Variety type event. The Tiger Moth had done a run at low level and had apparently stalled. It went straight into the ground. None of the rescue helicopter crew were aware that there was also a woman involved in the crash – she was a wing walker, reminiscent of the 1920s stunt flying. Peter says, 'While the paramedics were attending [the pilot] I went for a walk over to the aircraft. The fire was out by then, so I looked at the wreckage and realised that there was another person in the aircraft remains. The woman was still attached to the top of the wing, but she was dead – no skin left. I went back and told the paramedics who took a look as well but there was nothing they could do for her'. Horrific stuff indeed.

The pilot was loaded into the helicopter and flown to Newcastle's John Hunter hospital, but he died on the way.

Peter says the most exciting rescues were the water rescues. They were always urgent and so if the rescue was within about 15-20 minutes' flying time of their Newcastle base the helicopter would launch without the paramedics who were stationed elsewhere. The paramedics would make their own way to the closest point of land to meet the helicopter if the patient needed medical assistance.

The water rescue that stands out in Peter's mind was in the early 2000s at Frazer Park on the coast some 30 kilometres south of Newcastle, an area notoriously dangerous in big seas. Three men had made their way down to a rock platform in a large horseshoe shaped inlet to have a look at the big surf when they were washed into the water by a huge wave. A large cave sits beneath the cliffs at the curve of the horseshoe. As a safety precaution life rings were positioned on the rock platform and someone had thrown them into the water in an attempt to help the men washed off the rocks.

After an emergency launch the helicopter crew flew down to Frazer Park. They knew exactly where the men would be because, as Peter says, 'people were always going in there'. The helicopter arrived overhead, and the crew spotted two of the men being pounded by the big seas but there was no sign of the third man. As the rescue crewman, Peter was quickly winched down into the water on the wire. He was in full garb: flippers, helmet, snorkel, mask, full thickness wetsuit and harness. He got to the first bloke without too much problem although they were hit by a couple of big waves before the lift. Up they went on the winch and into the cabin went the first man. Peter went back down and got the second bloke secured. Peter asked him, 'Weren't there three of you?' He replied, 'My mate has swum into the cave'. Peter got him out of the water and into the helo. He was all tangled in a rope attached to the life ring, but the crew managed to disentangle him and get him into the helo safely.

The pilot then backed the helo off and the crew were able to spot the third man inside the cave. The waves were pounding into the cave like a big shore dump and the tide was coming in, so conditions were only going to deteriorate. Peter says with a grin, 'We had a discussion on how we were going to get him out of the cave. The idea of me coming off the wire to go into the cave was discounted because of the danger. So, we came up with a plan'.

Peter was winched down into the surf just short of the cave and the helo dropped as low as it could to give him some slack on the wire. He surfed into the cave on the back of a wave, still attached to the wire and managed to reach the man without mishap. Peter told him, 'We have to get out of here'. The fellow dubiously replied, 'What, back out there?' With no time to waste, Peter stated the obvious, 'How else are you going to get out of here?' That settled the argument.

Peter put the harness on him and just as they were ready to launch into the water a big wave hit them both and washed them right up to the back of the cave. The helo crew lost sight of the pair which, although Peter didn't know it, concerned them greatly. But there was nothing the crew could do – it was up to Peter.

Peter, still attached to the man, carefully moved towards the cave entrance again and despite being hit by a few more waves, 'I launched us into the water and gave the thumbs up and the helo dragged us out and when it was safe to do so we were winched up to the helo. The three blokes were fine, only a few scrapes, very lucky'.

Another incident in bad weather and very rough seas occurred one day in the early 2000s. The service got a call that someone had gone overboard from a motor cruiser off Port Stephens, about 40 kilometres northeast of Newcastle. Two men had motored out of Newcastle harbour to go fishing but the weather quickly deteriorated. A Mayday call was received from one of the men that his mate had gone overboard. The conditions by this time were so horrendous they were the only ones still out at sea. Peter says, 'It was easily a three to four metre swell running. Apparently, they had hit a wave and one was at the stern and the other on the flying bridge, neither with a lifeline attached. The fellow on the flying bridge had gone overboard'.

As the helicopter got close to the cruiser, the crew was able to make radio contact with the man still onboard. He told the aircrew that he could see his mate bobbing up intermittently in the water about 50 metres ahead of the boat. By the time the helicopter got to the cruiser the man had been in the water for quite a while. Peter says, 'We discussed how we were going to try to get him. The waves were too big for me to stay on the wire because I would have been lifted up and smashed down as the swells passed. The helo was going to then back off and wait for me to call it in'. So, they decided that Peter would come of the wire – a very dangerous move – but there was no other choice.

Peter was winched down as close as possible to the fellow in the water. Releasing the clip, he dropped into the water. In the confused water conditions Peter couldn't see the man for a moment but then he spotted him only a few metres away. Peter says sadly, 'I swam hard and got to him, but he was dead. He was tangled up in rope that his mate had thrown to him to try to pull him in. Because he was non-responsive it took a lot of effort to get the harness on him'.

While Peter was struggling to get the dead man into the harness one of the paramedics onboard the helicopter thought he saw a couple of sharks circling. Peter, thank goodness, didn't know this. Finally, Peter was ready to be winched up, so he gave the thumbs up and the wire came down and he clipped on. Up he went with the body and the crew got him into the helo. The helicopter immediately headed for land and touched down at an oval at the town of Nelson Bay. There the paramedics found that the man had bled out because he had severe lacerations on his legs. It turned out that when his mate had tried to get him back on the boat with the rope he had been chopped up by the propeller.

On the eve of Valentine's Day in 1993 Peter was on call at home. He had just started to prepare for a BBQ with Tina, his new girlfriend and whom he was later to marry when his pager went off. Someone had fallen down a waterfall up at Barrington Tops, a rugged mountainous area northwest of Newcastle. Peter recalls, 'We had the old French Dauphin helicopter at that stage, the first twin engine aircraft the Service had ever had. The site was northwest of the Barrington Guesthouse. It was about 7.30 p.m. and drizzling with rain. We pinpointed where the incident was but as we were a bit heavy with fuel the decision was taken to offload a bit of weight, stretchers and the like, from the aircraft. We decided to land in a large paddock near the Barrington Guesthouse to do this'.

The helicopter came in low over the paddock and the pilot decided to fly up towards a gate neat the guesthouse. Peter was sitting in the front of the helo next to the pilot with the air crewman sitting between them. They all had their eyes peeled for obstructions because they were so low. Peter suddenly saw something and shouted out, 'Wires, wires', but it was too late – the helicopter hit an electrical wire leading to the guesthouse. It immediately snapped and wrapped around the rotor blades which shattered - Peter says it sounded like the noise made by a wounded bull

– and the aircraft went down. Thankfully the pilot kept his cool and held the aircraft straight and on level keel as they dropped like a rock from about 20 metres above the ground. The Dauphin hit the ground hard and transmission oil started to pour out of the engine. Unsurprisingly, they got out smartly. The skids were spread apart, the transmission had been ripped out and the blades were wrecked. The aircraft was a write-off.

Shaken but otherwise unharmed, the aircrew walked up to Barrington Guesthouse which had lost electrical power because of the crash. The two paramedics ended up walking in to the fellow who had fallen but he was dead. Co-incidentally, when Peter got up to the guesthouse a voice called out, 'Squirrel, what are you doing here?' It was Jack Merlin, the older brother of Max, the bloke he went to Jersey with.

Peter stayed with the helicopter rescue service until 2014, enjoying many other adventures. He now works as an assistant in nursing at a private hospital near Newcastle.

Of his time in Jersey, Peter states, 'If I had my time again I'd do it all over again. The camaraderie was fantastic, and I might not see those blokes too often now, but we still have a very strong relationship. Living with people and travelling with them, it was a great time. I don't think we played up as much as the earlier blokes, but we still had a lot of fun'.

20   The Changing of the Guard

'My idea was to try to modernise the service to make it a facsimile of the service in Australia so that when the Australian lifeguards arrived in Jersey it would be a seamless continuation of the service they had provided back home.'

Extract from an interview with Paul Berghouse,
Head Beach guard/Lifeguard from 1988 to 2010

The late 1980s saw some significant changes in the world order. Mikhail Gorbachev, the General Secretary of the Soviet Union, began a program of glasnost and perestroika in recognition of Eastern Bloc economic decline and an emerging sense of nationalism in the USSR's satellite states. Momentous events followed, such as the fall of the Berlin Wall separating East and West Berlin and the emergence of democratic movements in Poland, Hungary, Czechoslovakia, and Romania. The tragic outcome of the Tiananmen Square protests in Beijing put considerable pressure on the Chinese Communist government that up until then had allowed limited economic and political reform in the post-Mao era.

In Australia in 1986 a significant geo-political event took place when the country achieved full independence from Britain. The Australia Act 1986 removed the right for the British government to become involved in Australian domestic affairs, whether federal or state. Britain turned more to Europe, to the European Union for trade, whilst Australia turned to Eastern Asia. However, Australia continued to 'export' young fit beach guards/lifeguards to Jersey.

By the early 1990s Jersey's population growth, rampant in the 1960s, 1970s and 1980s, had begun to slow markedly. In fact, in the last decade of the 20th century the population growth was only 3.7%. The summer months saw the usual increase in the itinerant population as foreign workers flocked to jobs in cafes, hotels and restaurants. Gradually the Italian and Spanish workers were replaced by Portuguese because of the opportunity to earn more money in Jersey than at home.

However, during the 1990s Jersey began to lose its attractiveness to the Portuguese as their own country began to benefit from its membership of the European Union. Gradually the gap was filled by Polish workers for the same reason that brought the Portuguese.

Tourism peaked in Jersey in the 1970s, and its steady decline reflected a similar fate which befell more traditional Jersey industries centred on cattle, knitting, oysters, cider, fishing and potatoes. Only finance continued to thrive. Tourism changed from longer stay, beach type holidays to short stays in good standard accommodation. The number of tourist beds fell steadily as the cheaper Billy Butlin (holiday camp) style of vacation began to decline in popularity in the UK. This period also saw a rapid rise in property prices and, although the population rise was not as great as earlier, the demand for local accommodation meant that it was often more lucrative to close hotels and restructure or rebuild them into residential accommodation to derive year-round income from the rental market in place of seasonal income from tourism.

The rise of the well-paid bankers and financial advisors also had the effect of driving up prices for goods and services, as well as property, which had reached parity with the prices paid in London. The locals, unless they were in the public service or finance sectors, could not afford to buy property.

The finance industry in Jersey had become the star of the economy, and in the thirty years since the 1960s the States government income had risen by a stunning 500 percent. However, things in this sector were not all rosy. The industry's deregulated nature resulted in numerous financial scandals involving misappropriation of monies. A high-profile example of this involved a foreign exchange trader from the Union Bank of Switzerland who used Bank Cantrade, a Jersey based subsidiary, to defraud investors out of some £26 million. Money laundering was also a lucrative source of income for those less scrupulous in the finance sector.

The 1970s and 1980s had seen a rapid build-up of so-called 'shell' companies, organisations that had no assets or operations, usually set up for tax evasion or tax avoidance purposes. These shell companies had nominee shareholders and often nominee directors, third parties registered as a shareholder or director in order to shield the actual shareholder or director from public scrutiny.

Notable examples of obfuscation of the ownership of funds within Jersey registered financial entities included hiding the Soviet Communist Party's money during the last days of the Soviet Union, and the murky way in which the post-Soviet era Russian oligarchs hid their assets. Even when the South African government wanted to avoid sanctions connected to their apartheid policy, they hid their money in Jersey.

This state of affairs continued until into the 1990s, at which time the States government was pressured to introduce tighter controls. The new laws and a raft of controlling legislation that supported them resulted in the use of nominee directorships, set up to hide the real ownership of companies or stocks and shares, becoming less attractive. The new legislation imposed a significant increase in the fiducial responsibilities and liabilities of directors. This meant that making easy money earning directors' fees as a nominee became much less lucrative and appreciably more onerous. However, the finance and legal experts were quick to change their approach and the trust company (a legal entity set up to manage the transfer of assets to a beneficial party) became the new financial vehicle for tax avoidance.

For the beach guards, such tax larks played no role in their day-to-day lives. They were at the bottom of the pyramid pay-wise and their no-frills accommodation was subsidised by the States government. Importantly, enough locals and tourists, albeit the latter in lesser numbers, were still using the island's beaches and bathing spots to justify their jobs. Of particular interest to the beach guards was the fact that there were still more females than males on the island.

But things that related to their sphere of interest began to change. The first was the abrupt departure of the head beach guard, Jerry Shannos, midway through the 1988 season. As Noddy says, 'Jerry's departure was a bit of a secret – he just disappeared. He told Paul [Berghouse] he was going and off he went'. The Aussies were shocked, and rumours spread like wildfire, most wildly inaccurate, some with a grain of truth. Paul Berghouse assumed the mantle in Jerry's place.

Jerry Shannos had his reasons for the abrupt departure. 'The reason why I decided to pull the plug in Jersey was that my father had died, and my mother got ill so I made a decision to come back to Newcastle. I was lucky enough to get a full-time job with the [Newcastle] Council in the pools as a superintendent'.

There was speculation amongst the Australians that perhaps Jerry had fallen foul of the tax man, but Paul Berghouse says that was false – a tax situation did arise (not unusual given the fact that taxes in Jersey were calculated and paid well after the money was earned), but Jerry had left before it came up.

Paul's assumption of the role of head beach guard caused other changes. One of the first things he did was to carry out an audit of the current lifesaving equipment. He asked the more senior beach guards that had been there for a while, in particular Jim Reeves and Peter Martine, for their input. The results of the audit became the catalyst for proposals to the Tourism Department for new equipment including IRBs and new rescue boards.

Paul says, 'My idea was to try to modernise the service to make it a facsimile of the service in Australia so that when the Australian lifeguards arrived in Jersey it would be a seamless continuation of the service they had provided back home. We put in place emergency action plans, standard operational procedures and a lot of other documentation. It took me months and months to get all that stuff together because they had never been written before'.

Paul contrasts the situation pre and post Jerry Shannos. 'The difference between Jerry's time and mine was that Jerry was able to run the lifeguard service almost as his own private fiefdom whereas I faced a different arrangement. Jerry had a special relationship with the people who were running Tourism at the time, particularly his immediate supervisor. They worked together for many, many years. In 1987 or 1988 that supervisor retired and a fellow by the name of Nigel Philpott took over the running of the service. He was not old school like his predecessor, he wanted to know the ins and outs of how everything ran. It became obvious that the old system was going to go out the window. Wayne Bridges [in the late 1970s and early 1980s] and I ran the operational aspects of the lifeguard service, but Jerry was in charge of the overall management and administration. Nigel Philpott was eventually replaced by a guy called John Williams who wasn't too popular with the lifeguards, but he was very helpful in sorting out where the funding was coming from. At that stage I became very interested in trying to sort out why the lifeguards weren't employed as normal workers under the Jersey system. It possibly was because the old system had been running for a long time under the radar'.

Paul continues: 'In conjunction with blokes like Jim Reeves we started to take the lifeguard service onto a much more professional standard. We required the lifeguards to be able to meet the gold medal standard of the Surf Lifesaving Association including professional qualifications. The level changed from the basic surf club standard in my day to a professional standard'.

Things were indeed changing. The good old days of beach guards being able to get a job in Jersey based on their surf club skills and qualifications were largely over. The vast majority of the beach guards who were recruited in the 1990s and beyond had professional lifeguard experience gained on the beaches back in Australia. In recognition of their professional status the beach guard moniker changed to lifeguard. The era of the 'professional' Jersey lifeguard service had begun.

21   In the Swim

'Prior to going there [to Jersey] I had won a number of Australian still water and surf titles.'

Extract from an interview with Mark Scully,
Australian lifeguard from 1988 to 1995.

The employment in 1988 of 28-year-old Mark 'Scull' Scully as a Jersey lifeguard exemplified the introduction of a more professional approach to the service. As well as being a part-time lifeguard back home in Australia, Mark's CV contained a few notable achievements – he had won a number of Australian still water and surf titles. Mark could swim very well indeed.

After joining Swansea Belmont Surf Club as a cadet (under 15), Mark had won his first Australian surf title when he was 14. He followed this up by winning the under 18 title, then the Australian surf teams race in 1977. He was also placed 2nd and 3rd in the 1978 and 79 Australian open surf races. Keen to train with top quality competitors, Mark subsequently joined Sydney's Freshwater Surf Club where he again won a gold medal in the Australian surf teams race in 1986.

Mark says modestly, 'My swimming ability was as a result of a lot of hard work. I was introduced to the beach by my father and grandfather who were members of Cooks Hill surf club in Newcastle. I chose to join Swansea Belmont [south of Newcastle] because I had mates in the club that I trained with in the pool. There were a lot of swimmers doing surf skills in Swansea Belmont at the time, many of whom were older than me and passed on their knowledge. There was good mateship but also good rivalry between the members of the squad'.

Mark had the distinction of being awarded a swimming scholarship to study at the University of Hawaii in the late 1970s, soon after he left school. As well as tasting success in the surf, Mark was a very strong still water swimmer. In 1978 at the Australian swimming titles leading up to the Commonwealth Games in Canada he placed second in the 800 freestyle, second in the 1500 metres freestyle, third in the 400m freestyle to two Olympians and fourth in the 200 metres freestyle. Despite these results Mark didn't make the Commonwealth Games team, but his efforts drew the attention of the University of Hawaii. Mark says that two Australian swimmers who were attending the university knew him quite well and must have put in a good word.

'The university believed I could be useful in helping them to win points in competitive swimming against other American universities. I had to do an entrance exam and I got a scholarship. I really enjoyed the time in Hawaii. I made a lot of mates and I still see them. For the past six years between May and August I have been back to visit them for a week. We have a reunion and BBQs. I also compete in ocean swims in my age group. I still manage to place in the top three even though I only train part-time these days.' The only downside was that for the next four and a half years Mark couldn't compete in Australia at state and national titles during those times because he had exams in Hawaii.

Mark decided to apply to work as a lifeguard in Jersey because at 28 he considered himself past his prime as a still water swimmer. He put his name down for Jersey with Jerry Shannos, but Jerry said that he thought there were no vacancies for 1988. He said if anybody pulled out he would let Mark know. Mark was pleased to receive a phone call from Jerry soon after. He and another Novocastrian called John Rowlatt from Stockton Surf Club became the rookies for 1988.

Before Mark left for Jersey Jerry Shannos told him to ring the Lifeguard Tower when they got to Jersey and one of the boys would pick them up. However, their connecting flight arrived after the lifeguards had finished on the beach for the day and no one was at the tower. As Mark and John Rowlatt stood there wondering what to do a very nice-looking girl called Popsy came over to them and, perhaps hearing their Aussie accents, told them that she knew where the boys were – they were playing cricket on the beach at St Brelade's and having a BBQ with beers. The obliging Popsy took them to meet the other lifeguards.

Mark says, 'After the cricket match and a BBQ the guys decided to go to the rugby club. I had never been there of course but after a few more beers I was feeling pretty jet lagged so I decided to walk back to St Helier then I had to walk from there back to St Aubin's to the Doghouse. It took me quite a while.' No surprise there – it was at least five miles!

The rookies shared a room in the Doghouse on the bottom floor facing the courtyard at the back of the house because, Mark says, 'some guys from the previous year preferred the street side, maybe because they could get in and out through the window'.

Mark describes his first years in Jersey as very interesting because everything was new. Being at heart a team player despite his individual swimming performances, Mark organised several fun competitions down at St Brelade's beach with boys and girls. He and his fellow lifeguards persuaded the fellows who rented out the wind surfers and pedal boats to loan their craft and 'we put a guy and a girl together as a team to make it more interesting. We also made sure that the lifeguards were mixed in a team with the locals to mix it up and ensure that the lifeguards didn't dominate. That happened in beach cricket as well'.

Very keen on fitness, Mark continued his training regime during his time in Jersey. He says, 'I like having goals and I competed in events such as the Castle to Harbour and the Green Island swims. I trained at the Fort Regent pool. We had the Land Rovers parked in the car park across the road from the Doghouse each night and often they would need filling up and me, Graham Skeffington, Richard Rothero and a few others would take the Jeep to do our swim and then fill the Jeep up. Coming home afterwards we would bring the Jeep back to the Doghouse, have breakfast and get to the beach for a 10 a.m. start. Most of the guys did a two-mile run from the Lifeguard Tower and it was a competition to see who could go the fastest. I did it occasionally, but I also did ocean swims on quieter days when it wasn't busy. I would swim from El Tico to the Watersplash or down to the [Le Bray] Slipway and back – it was about three kilometres down and back which would take me about 45 minutes. Sometimes I would swim shorter distances depending on how much time I had off. The water temperature was really cold when we first got to Jersey in May, so cold that your head would ache, and your fingers and toes would tingle. When I worked at the West Park pool I would run home, but I wasn't an avid runner like some of the guys'.

With the States government clamping down, Mark didn't have a permit for work anywhere apart from the beach. He couldn't work as a doorman but, he says, 'I didn't really need the extra money anyway'.

Each year at the end of the season the lifeguards had a gathering called the Last Supper which Mark really enjoyed. It would often be at the Old Court House Hotel or sometimes a restaurant in St Helier. Mark laughs, 'I wasn't as big a drinker as some of the guys. My favourite beer was Grolsch in the flip top bottle. On one occasion we were having shots of Sambuca and I was wondering why no one but me was getting drunk but I found out later that when they bought a shout they were having water and giving me Sambuca, so they stitched me up'.

Mark recalls that a lot of young Scandinavian people came over to Jersey in the summer to attend summer camps to learn English and do beach activities. He remembers that in 1990 a few of the Aussies were asked to attend one of the schools to talk about Australia, so Mark hired a kangaroo suit and his mate got dressed up as an Aboriginal and covered himself with boot polish (political correctness be damned). Mark describes the event as being very funny and the kids loved it.

Ever up for a laugh, the lifeguards did a few treasure hunting pub crawls where they had to obtain certain items, including bras, as part of the fun. Mark says, 'The Swedish girls were always willing to take their bras off for us or take their skirt off and give them to us'.

In the late 1980s and early 1990s Mark did the normal Aussie thing during the break between seasons on the beach – travelled around Europe. After that at the end of each season between 1992 and 1995 he came back home to the Newcastle area to work as a lifeguard in a seasonal job.

Mark says that he respected Paul Berghouse as the boss even though Mark was to suffer a disappointment later in his time in Jersey over a more senior position. He says, 'I would do everything asked of me as a lifeguard. I always tried to do the right thing'. However, in 1995 when a new supervisor position became available that Mark could have done, Paul elected to give it to another lifeguard 'because he thought that I would get a permanent position [as a lifeguard] back home, which I did. I was disappointed because I'd been there seven years'.

In 1996 Mark got a full-time job on the beach back home as a lifeguard with the Lake Macquarie council so that was it for Jersey, although he says he has always been keen to go back. In 2010 Paul Berghouse visited Mark in Australia. Mark asked him about prospects for going back to Jersey, but Paul told him that the States government had tightened up on the work visas and they were normally now only applicable for those under 30. Paul said he could only get exemptions for Darren Knowles and Noddy Reeves because they had been going back for so long.

Mark says sadly, 'So I didn't get to go and that was the last year. I would have liked to have gone back to Jersey for a couple of seasons to make it 10 years – I had plenty of long service leave available but it wasn't to be'.

Just because he was older, winning Australian surf titles didn't stop for Mark. He says, 'When I came back from Jersey I won the Australian Masters open surf race (over 35) in 1998'. He continues to compete although his training regime isn't quite as rigorous as it used to be.

The Jersey experience ignited in Mark an urge to work as a lifeguard in another part of the world, Japan, a place one doesn't normally associate with beach goers. The advantage for Mark was the short season – only six weeks long – so it didn't impact on his summer lifeguard job back home.

Between 2001 and 2008 Mark worked part-time on several beaches in Chikura province just to the south east of Tokyo. The beaches themselves were reasonable but the surrounding area was sparsely populated (unusual for Japan) with only a few seasonal restaurants scattered along the beach front. Mark says, 'During the summer time the water temperature was actually not too bad – 17 to 18 degrees rising into the mid-20s later in the season with the air temperature in the 30s. The water was shallow with warm currents'.

Mark wasn't all that excited about the Japanese approach. He says, 'I didn't always

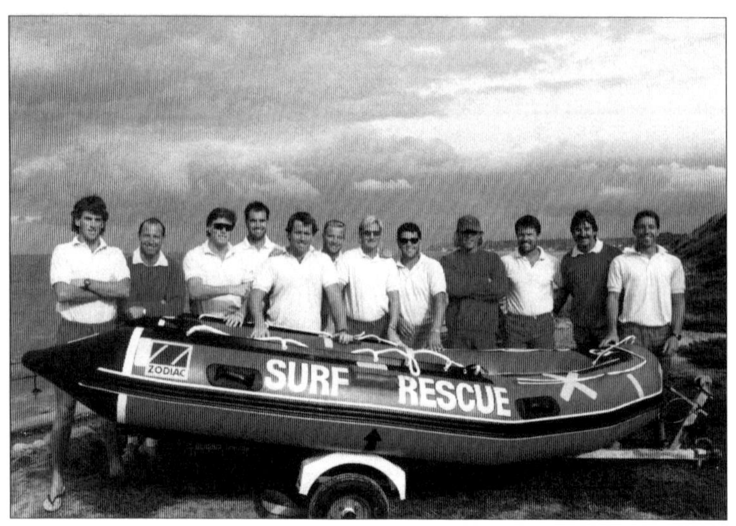

Australian Beach Guard Team 1990
Left to right: Gavin Skeffington, Mark Scully, Steve Hannon, Jim Reeves, Neil Gilroy, John Rowlatt, Richard Rothero, Ben Lewis, Troy Barren, Paul Berghouse, Des Ball, Tim Wilson,
(Photo courtesy of Mark Scully)

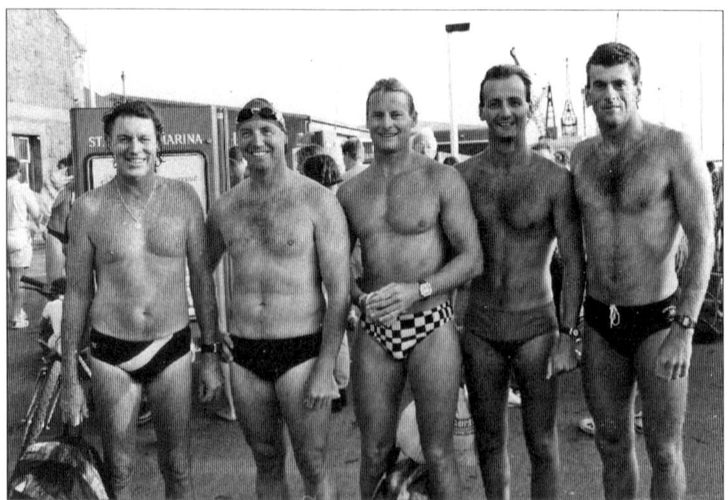

1992 Castle to Harbour Swim
Left to right: Basil Bridal (visiting from South Africa) with Australian lifeguards Mark Scully (four time winner of the event who placed second), Richard Rothero, Ben Marsh and Gavin Skeffington
(Photo courtesy of Mark Scully)

agree with the way that the Japanese lifeguard system worked but I had to go along with it. The season is short because the Japanese don't get a lot of holidays'.

Mark's abilities as a champion swimmer were about to be equalled by the first, and only, woman lifeguard to work on the beach under the Australian run service. Her name was Alison Horsfall.

22 Alison Horsfall – Maid of The Isles

'When she got employed [as a lifeguard] she performed as well as the other guys.'

Paul Berghouse, Senior Lifeguard,
describing Jersey born lifeguard Alison Horsfall

In the summer of 1998 a young Jersey woman named Alison Horsfall became the second Jersey Bean, and the first female ever, to be employed as a lifeguard. Although Alison made history hers wasn't an easy path. A renowned open water swimmer, before she got a job on the beach Alison had to prove herself as being capable of meeting the high professional lifeguard standards demanded by Paul Berghouse.

Alison's swimming credentials were more than impressive. At the age of 21, she had set a new women's record in August 1995 for swimming around the island of Jersey (a distance of 41 miles) in the time of 10 hours, 20 minutes and 15 seconds. Although Alison was assisted by Jersey's tidal patterns (as are all that attempt this swim), forty-one miles is a long way. This feat, which is commemorated on a stone plaque in St Helier, put her well and truly on the swimming map.

Well, not quite, at least not as far as lifeguarding was concerned. When she applied for a lifeguard job Paul Berghouse, the Senior Lifeguard, knocked her back twice, not because she couldn't swim, but because the Jersey lifeguards had moved onto a fully professional footing. And Alison, despite her prowess in the water, didn't qualify. As Paul says, 'Applicants had to have worked professionally on the beach or to provide evidence of a good sound amateur background including five years experience provided they had the necessary qualifications. She only had a basic lifesaving qualification through the Royal Lifesaving Society'.

To Alison's credit this didn't deter her. Determined to qualify, she travelled to Australia in 1996 and did her Australian bronze medallion qualification at Sydney's North Bondi surf club. However, Alison only managed to get one patrol in because she got her surf Bronze Medallion at the end of the season. Additionally, she had no qualifications in IRB crewing, a necessity for a job in Jersey.

The following year (1997) Alison achieved the notable feat of swimming the English Channel from England to France in 17 hours and 24 minutes. She then travelled to New Zealand and worked professionally as a lifeguard on a beach in Auckland which gave her further experience even though it was a flat-water beach.

After that, Paul Berghouse recalls, 'We came under a fair bit of pressure from the Tourism Department at the time to employ her. The problem I had was that everyone employed on the beach had to be at the same level, so I had to be very careful not to lower the standard and create dissent amongst those who had the right qualifications. I knew very well that Alison had swum the Channel and was a very good long-distance swimmer'.

Paul decided to give her a job in 1998. However, Alison couldn't work at St Ouen's because there were no facilities in the Lifeguard Tower for females, so her beach work was confined to St Brelade's. Regardless of this limitation, Paul says, 'When she got employed she performed as well as the other guys'.

Alison went on to work as a lifeguard for five seasons, finishing up in 2003. During that period, she was to go on to complete other significant long-distance swims, including swimming around all four major Channel Islands. In 1998 she did the 28-mile round-Guernsey swim which she completed in nine hours, 53 minutes and 39 seconds. This was followed by the very tough five-mile swim around Sark in 1999 (four hours 25 minutes and eight seconds) and then the six-mile round Alderney swim in 2000 which she completed in four hours and 43 minutes.

In 1999 Alison also completed the 28.5-mile Manhattan Island (New York) Marathon Swim, finishing in 20th place in a time of seven hours, 46 minutes and 35 seconds. Of note, Australian marathon swimmer Susie Maroney finished in eighth place in that event.

After her time as a lifeguard Alison Horsfall married and obtained employment in Jersey as a paramedic. Undoubtedly the skills she learned as a lifeguard held her in good stead in her new profession.

In 2010 the *Jersey Evening Post* dubbed Alison 'The Maid of the Isles' after successfully completing a four-mile swim around Herm, one of the Channel Islands located near Guernsey, in the time of two hours, eight minutes and 56 seconds. She became the first person to complete the circumnavigation of the largest five of the eight Channel Islands.

In the same year she set a record for the fastest female to swim between Jersey and France (18 miles) in eight hours and seven minutes.

Alison continues to swim long distance events and in 2016 she and a male swimmer named Andy Truscott completed a relay swim between a group of small islands and rocks just over nine miles south of Jersey called Les Minquiers, and Jersey.

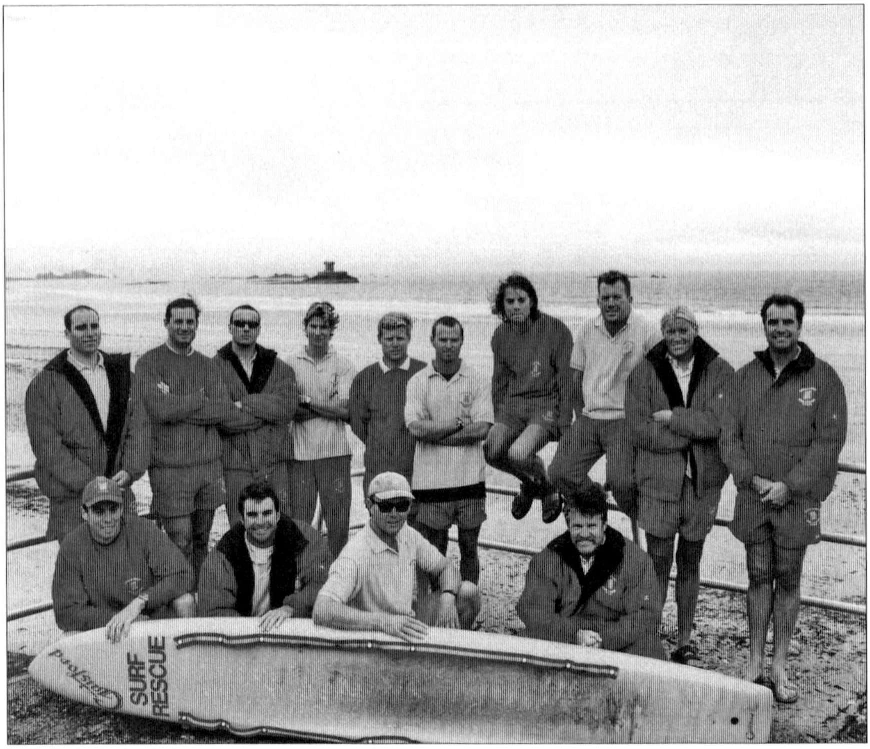

The First Female Lifeguard Alison Horsfall, 1998
Back row: Jamie Sydney, Glen McKissack, Brad Downs, Adam Metcalf, Darren Knowles, Matt Wehr, Nick Woolnough, Paul Hedderman, Alison Horsfall, Jim Reeves
Front row: Ben Deagon, Greg Slater, Gary Richards, Paul Berghouse,

(Photo courtesy of Jim Reeves)

Part 4: The RNLI is Coming

The Beginning of the End

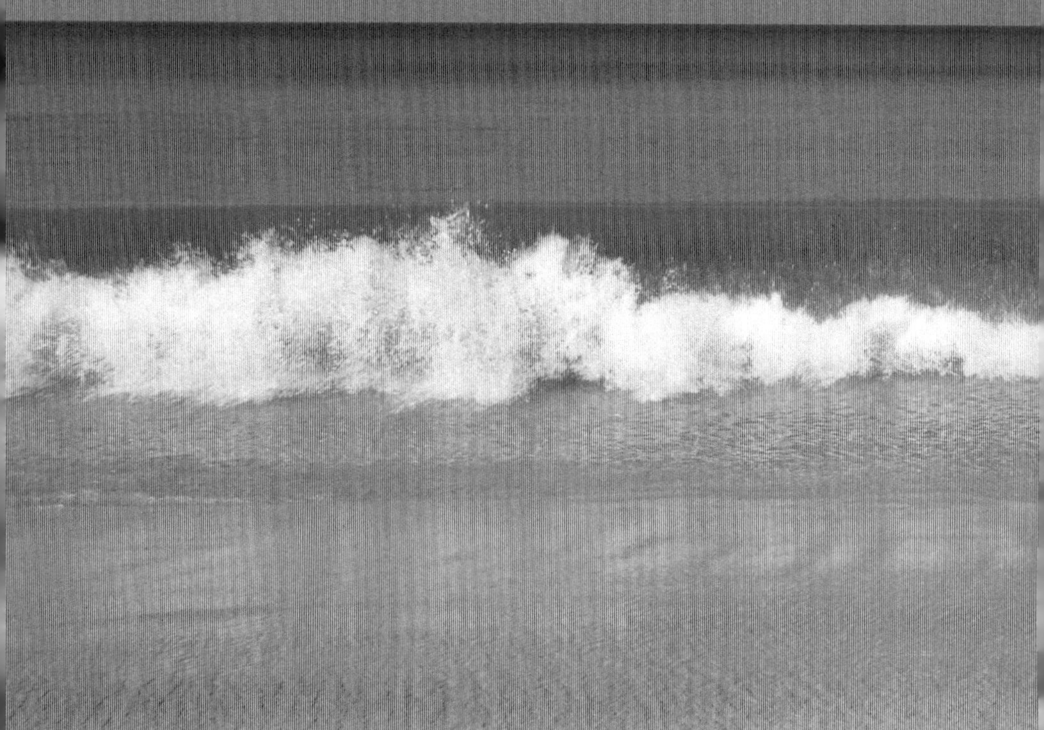

23 The New Millennium

'All of the HR department were females and they told us that when we did our swim test they were going to turn up with the media. They took a team photo and turned it into a poster which went in the middle of the *Jersey Evening Post*. That weekend there were girls coming up to the boys and saying, "Oh, you're my favourite". They knew all the names as well. That opened a few doors.'

Extract from interview with Scott Hammerton,
Australian lifeguard between 2004 and 2009.

The new millennium saw a massive influx of Portuguese, Polish, Czech and Romanian workers to Jersey looking for work because of the free border arrangements under the EU. Says Scott Hammerton, an Aussie from Newcastle who arrived in Jersey in 2004, 'They were really hard workers. Some had two or three jobs, particularly the Polish. They added a lot to the young demographic to Jersey, ages ranging from 18 to 25. The majority of them were girls which wasn't a bad thing as they were very friendly. I had worked alongside dozens of Polish people during my time at the Silver Springs [Hotel] and could speak a few words of Polish and I found it quite important to have mates outside of my lifeguard circle'.

Scott, who had been a lifeguard in Newcastle, had decided to go to Jersey to work after a friend named Tim Wilson, himself an ex-lifeguard, asked him to fill in as a pool lifeguard at the Silver Springs Hotel. The hotel had been built at St Brelade's in the 1970s and, according to Scott, it was a very nice place. Scott recalls with a laugh, 'I had no idea what I was getting into, I just turned up on the plane by myself with my backpack. I was 23 years old. The hotel had tennis courts and gardens with glimpses of St Brelade's bay'.

Reflecting the highly competitive nature of being employed as a Jersey lifeguard, Scott had tried to get a job on the island but had been unsuccessful. Scott says, 'I was pretty young and green, and I think they were looking for more experienced guys'. However, as luck would have it, a position on the beach came up two months after he arrived in Jersey because one of the Aussies decided to take a position in Japan as a lifeguard. As Scott was in Jersey and was qualified he was asked to jump ship and work on the beach. Scott accepted eagerly. 'I gave the Silver Springs two weeks' notice and a friend filled that job. The lifeguard pay was good but not as good as later. I was being paid £180 a week at the Silver Springs and the lifeguard position I remember was paying around £300 a week so I rubbed my hands together in glee'.

Scott lived in the Doghouse on St Mark's Rd on the boundary of St Helier and St Saviour parishes, opposite the Hotel de France. That particular Doghouse was a massive hostel that had apparently been used to accommodate women with children who needed a place to stay. There were about 16 bedrooms over five stories and the lifeguards had the place all to themselves. Scott recalls that the conditions in the St Mark's Road Doghouse were pretty atrocious, lots of mould, very dark, and borderline derelict. But it was in a good location and there was a bed for each of the lifeguards. In any event they didn't spend a lot of time in the Doghouse. It was much easier to go to the pub.

With plenty of space available, the lifeguards spread themselves out, with about three on each floor. The boys organised the Doghouse so that lifeguards of similar ages and with similar interests were on the same floor. The Aussies on Scott's floor would put in money for a kitty and they would cook a few nights a week. There was a car park in the back of the Doghouse which would accommodate about six cars where they parked the lifeguard trucks, plus room for parking for friends. The trucks were meant to go straight from work back to the Doghouse but sometimes they didn't quite do that, particularly when the surf was pumping. The Aussies would do a detour and hope that Paul Berghouse, who lived elsewhere, didn't find out. Occasionally he did and then they would be in the bad books for a few weeks.

Scott says he got on well with Head Lifeguard Paul Berghouse: 'Although he was an older guy he wasn't all that stern, but he was pretty straight with us and you knew what he expected of you. I enjoyed rugby league and rugby and so did Paul, so we had something in common'.

Every day the lifeguards would pick Paul up from his place on the way to work. Paul, says Scott, had a habit of giving the boys a driving lesson on the way to the beach. He was very particular about how he wanted the lifeguards to drive so sometimes whoever was driving would throw their hands up in the air and say, 'you drive' but Scott says he did teach them some good things about driving – after all he was a bus driver in the Jersey off season. Paul had an idiosyncrasy where if the lifeguard was doing something wrong on the drive Paul would take a big sniff and then the boys knew he was stressed. Scott laughs, 'So if you were getting sniffed at on the way to St Ouen's beach you knew you were not impressing him'.

For the Australians, the Essential Services visa issued by the States of Jersey to allow them to work on the beach was a constant source of confusion. Scott recalls, 'You would turn up at Heathrow Airport with this work permit and the Customs guys would say, "This work permit isn't valid", so you'd be put into a quarantine room for a period of time, usually a few hours, while they figured out what to do with you. Once they sorted it out they'd let you go. If you had a return flight ticket it made it easier but if you had a one-way ticket they thought you were trying to enter and live in the country illegally. I believe that immigration in Heathrow would ring Jersey and get them to explain the permit and sort it out that way'.

Like the lifeguards before him, Scott patrolled at St Ouen's, St Brelade's, Plémont and Grève de Lecq. West Park pool was closed during 2004 because of some environmental problems. Scott found Grève de Lecq to be entertaining, not because of the beach but through the antics of the tourists, sixty to seventy percent of whom were older people, mostly Poms, but the occasional German or French day tripper. A lot of tourist buses would pull up at Grève de Lecq and the tourists would buy ice creams. The boys would sit back in the lifeguard truck having a laugh, watching as the seagulls snatched the ice creams, usually before the tourists had even taken a bite. Scott says, 'Those seagull attacks would account for the majority of first aids tallied as the gulls would bite the hand that carried the ice cream and draw blood. Those Grève seagulls were the smartest and most vicious of the gulls in Jersey. Living off a diet of mainly soft cones and ice cream'.

Scott is unequivocal about his feelings for the job. 'I loved the lifeguard work. It was probably the best job I've ever had, actually it was probably the best job in the world for me. Although we were busy at times there was also a lot of down time, so you could train and keep fit. Even though I was pretty young when I first got there I tried to keep fit and I always turned up – I took pride in my work and I was there to do the lifeguarding work like most of the guys and to enjoy myself outside of work, whereas a couple of the other guys were there mostly for partying'.

Scott continues. 'You could go for a run or a board paddle. When the weather wasn't too good we would play Scrabble or cook roast lunches to keep ourselves entertained with an eye on the water. On average there were only about 20 days or so in the summer where the weather was great. When the weather was good it was like all the islanders flocked to the beach. A nice sunny day at St Ouen's with five miles of coastline and the tide out you would get maybe 5,000 people on the beach during the day and that was the same at St Brelade's. About 1,500 or 2,000 at Plémont or Grève de Lecq because they were a bit more inaccessible'.

Crowds also flocked to the shores in between St Aubin's and St Helier and the secluded beaches of Beauport and Portelet on the west coast, although they were unpatrolled. Scott says, 'We had a set of flags at the Le Braye slip [south of El Tico] and a lot of people would gather around El Tico and the Watersplash where the surfboard riders hung out, but that wasn't patrolled. However, it was monitored by the senior lifeguards including Paul Berghouse, Gary Richards, Darren Knowles and

Jimmy Reeves. Their role was to sit up in the tower and monitor the beach using binoculars. They didn't miss much, even something happening a few kilometres up the beach and the team would respond from there. They would run the beach from the tower and we were like soldiers who would go out and do the work'.

In Scott's time in Jersey there were also a lot of people who would attend the beach at Kempt Tower, about two kilometres north of El Tico, where there was good beach access via ramps. Although they only patrolled at St Brelade's beach there was another big beach to the east of it called Ouaisné but there weren't as many facilities on the beachfront as at St Brelade's. There was a couple of deckchair hire places and perhaps a windsurfing class but most of the people came to swim at St Brelade's.

The States of Jersey had a caravan permanently sited at St Brelade's for the lifeguard's use. Those on patrol would tow it onto the beach with the Jeep once the tide was low enough and tow it off again when the tide came in. Scott says, 'It was a massive big caravan – we called it the hot dog stand because the kids who didn't know would turn up expecting to buy a hot dog from the lifeguards. Overnight it resided in the car park of the l'Horizon Hotel. It was convenient to use but occasionally taking it off the beach our surveillance would drop a bit because we were busy trying to rig it up to the Jeep'.

In the mid-2000s two lifeguards were rostered at St Brelade's and four at St Ouen's with five or six at the weekends. Plémont had two and Grève de Lecq had another two. When the season started to wind down Plémont would be cut to one lifeguard although occasionally, Scott recalls, 'we could have used two'. During the period 2004 to 2009 there were 15 to 16 lifeguards, including Paul Berghouse, employed doing 42.5 hours a week with no lunch break. They worked a 10-day fortnight. The roster was fair but, as Scott recalls, 'We didn't find out until each Friday night usually about what our roster was for the next week. Sometimes we got a bit annoyed if we found we had Saturday and Sunday off because we could have planned to be off the island or somewhere for the two-day break. However, Paul was good in the sense that if you asked him to set aside some time off he was happy to do so'.

At the end of each season he was in Jersey Scott would stay on the island until the very last day and then go off surfing at places such as Biarritz in the south of France, or Portugal. Scott had made a few contacts with some of the local guys in Jersey who had accommodation in the Canary Islands and occasionally he would go surfing there for a couple of weeks. Scott found the waves there to be great and, importantly, not crowded. Then he would travel back to work as a lifeguard on the beach in Newcastle. He had a seasonal job at Newcastle's Nobbys beach from 2001 to 2007 and after that he moved to Newcastle beach, where he has remained.

Scott remembers returning to Jersey two weeks before the *Pasha Bulker* storm event in 2007. What is termed an East Coast Low (pressure system) formed off the NSW north coast in June of that year and moved south, deepening steadily. The result was that gale force south-easterly winds accompanied by heavy rain and storms began to lash the coast around Newcastle. Widespread flooding of low-lying areas occurred.

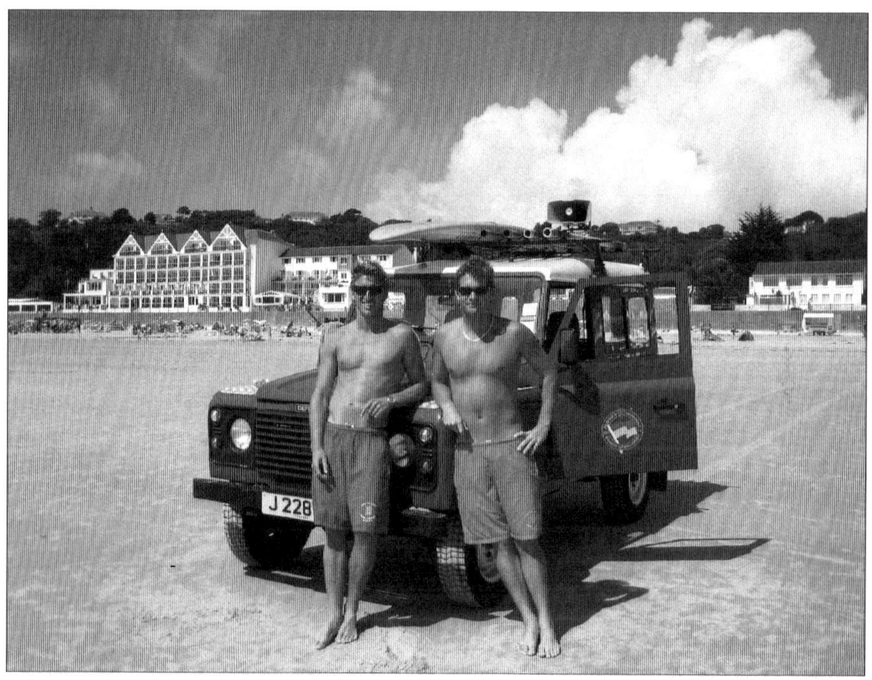

Not Much Changes – St Brelade's 2006
Australian lifeguards Scott Hammerton (L) and Leon Hay on patrol
(Photo courtesy of Mark Hammerton)

There were a large number of big container ships anchored off Newcastle waiting their turn to proceed into port and load cargo, most of which was coal. One of the ships was the 40,000-tonne bulk carrier MV *Pasha Bulker*. Although being warned about the storm, its master ignored advice to proceed further out to sea and the ship began to drag its anchor in the storm. Driven by the wind, the ship went aground on Nobby's beach and the 22 crew members had to be rescued by the Westpac rescue helicopter service. The incident was reported around the world. The ship was stuck on the beach for 25 days before finally being towed off.

In Jersey Scott got a phone call from ex-lifeguard Johnny Rowlett who said, 'Hey mate, there's a ship on your beach'. Scott found it a bit hard to believe so he told Jim Reeves and Drew Blatchford who were fellow Newcastle boys. Seeking more information, they asked Paul Berghouse for permission to search online at the Lifeguard Tower at St Ouen's which was the only place they could access the internet. Paul gave the okay and the boys accessed the story. Scott says with a laugh, 'We were reading the news and Paul said with a sniff, "Be aware guys – that is costing two pence per minute". He was getting stuck into us because we're on the Internet for five minutes! It cost a whole 10 pence!'

Ex-lifeguard Peter Martine, then a member of the Westpac rescue helicopter service, also missed the *Pasha Bulker* incident because he was overseas undertaking helicopter flight simulator training in Stockholm, Sweden. He and the crew were just about to leave Sweden to return home when they saw the coverage on CNN and realised it was Nobby's beach! Peter rang his wife Tina to find out what was going on. During the call Peter could hear a lot of noise in the background, almost drowning Tina out and he asked what it was. She told him it was the sound of the torrential rain hitting the roof. Several of Peter's colleagues were involved in the rescue.

Scott met his wife-to-be Lisa in Jersey in 2005. That story later.

Knowing that a permanent lifeguard position at Newcastle beach was coming up in 2010, Scott decided to pull the plug in Jersey at the end of 2009. Scott says, 'I thought I'd better show a bit more commitment to Newcastle Council [his prospective employer] if I wanted to get it. I knew I was in contention for the position and if I had missed out on the winter before I might have lost some momentum with my name being forgotten. I ended up getting the position otherwise I would probably still be going back to Jersey even with the RNLI running it because I loved the job so much'.

Scott's reading of the tea leaves was that the Jersey lifeguard situation was about to change so he felt it was probably a good time to move on. The RNLI had been regularly coming over to Jersey to do audits of the lifeguard service which were commissioned by the Harbours Department (see later) and to provide recommendations to the States on what they thought would be a better service. Along with the rest of the Australians, Scott took those recommendations with a grain of salt. Scott recalls, 'I remember being at Plémont beach and it was very busy, with a swell coming in and the sun shining, and we were run off our feet. The RNLI auditors turned up and saw how busy we were, and they suggested that we could do with three or four lifeguards on patrol. Their recommendation to the States was that 28 lifeguards would be needed to run the service. We weren't too concerned at the time because we thought that would cost a lot more than what they were paying us. Of course, we didn't know they would introduce a lower award rate for their lifeguards. But as time went on there was a lot of talk amongst the guys that we were on the way out'.

Scott's view of the interplay between the stakeholders is quite insightful. 'As far as Paul [Berghouse] was concerned I think the combined efforts of the Harbour Department and the RNLI left him with little room to move. He had to be seen to be playing along with them otherwise he might have been sacked and then we would have had no chance. Some people feel angry that we lost the service, but I don't think Paul was to blame. In my view it was inevitable that it would eventually happen'.

The HR section of the Harbours Department decided to get more involved in promoting the lifeguard service during the latter part of the 2000s, perhaps, as Scott notes, because it was an all-female section. He says, 'They told us that when we did our swim test [at the beginning of the season] they were going to turn up with the media. They took a team photo and turned it into a poster which went into the middle of the *Jersey Evening Post*. That weekend there were girls coming up to the boys and saying, "Oh, I saw your photo in the paper, you're my favourite". They knew all the names as well. That opened a few doors'.

The boys occasionally tested the patience of the locals. Scott says, 'One morning on the way to Grève de Lecq we did the usual and stopped for our food for the day. A few of the boys were hungover from the night before. I remember walking into a little co-op with the boys in our lifeguard uniforms and one of the boys demanded to see the manager. We were getting concerned about why he would want to see the manager, but he wouldn't tell us. So, the lady came to the checkout asking what was wrong and he said, "I just want a cuddle"'.

Another day the lifeguards, having left a couple of their band at Plémont, were driving down a country lane on the way to Grève de Lecq. Given the area was rural, it wasn't unusual to occasionally have to stop for people on horses. This day there were two women riding horses down the middle of the road, blocking the path of the lifeguard truck. Says Scott with a grin, 'One of the women was very well endowed and she was bouncing along on the horse. She had a smirk on her face and then she turned around and flashed her boobs at us. So, the boys gave her a good cheer'.

The Doghouse on St Mark's Road was believed by some lifeguards to be haunted. Scott recalls that there were stories of Aussies waking in the night with haunting feelings and their skin being covered in goose bumps. At one stage there was scaffolding around the Doghouse while the exterior was being painted. One night at 2 a.m. lifeguard Darren Knowles, whose room was on the fourth floor, woke to the sound of his window being lifted open. Understandably, Darren could not comprehend how this could be happening and was petrified. Then the curtains parted, and he feared the worst when to his astonishment an attractive young woman climbed through the window. She took one look at Darren and quickly realised she had entered the window of the wrong floor and woke the wrong guy. She smartly retreated back down the scaffolding and ran off into the night.

Scott recalls sleep often being broken by the sound of the boys returning from nights out on the town. He says with a laugh, 'Sometimes whole parties would come rolling through those doors in the early hours of the morning. All types of shit went down at these times. If you were quick enough to get up, you could lock your door and border it up so the drunken boys returning wouldn't stumble into your room looking for a party or to raid your fridge for beer. But there were times you would wake with a fire extinguisher being unloaded of its contents onto your bed while you slept or to the sound of a lifeguard's whistle being blown to wake the entire house up. The most common noise to wake to was the sound of bed squeaking from your flat mate getting it on with some girl. It was a crazy house'.

There was always a bit of banter between the lifeguards and the people living and working in Jersey. They knew when the lifeguards turned up summer had begun, and the good times were about to roll. For Scott, the best thing about Jersey (apart from Lisa) was the camaraderie. 'Living with a bunch of blokes, I worked with around 45 different guys over my six seasons, most were great guys. You found out who your closest mates were and some of my best friends now are the guys I lived with over there'.

For Scott, another really good thing was that he worked with guys from all over, from the Gold Coast, Wollongong or Sydney and he would get great ideas from them about best practice in lifeguarding. The outcome was a really good system that the lifeguards operated under. The Aussies tried to pick the best ideas and run with them. That exposure to broader ideas was really beneficial and it made for a more professional service, according to Scott. The same occurred with training exercises. He says, 'Guys from different parts of Australia had different training concepts. I always tried to keep really fit over there (and I still do). We picked the eyes out of the best techniques to try to make a hybrid of training regimes which was really good. A lot of the guys were great swimmers and as I had never really been into swimming laps I learnt a lot from them. Also, things like free diving skills. There was a guy named Scott Mortimer who once beat Kelly Slater in a surfing competition and a guy called Daniel Young whose father was the head of the lifeguard service at the Gold Coast, so there was a lot of knowledge available. Drew Blatchford, Drew Cairncross and Leon Hay for example were Uncle Toby's Ironman competitors. I tried to saddle up alongside the best to pick their brains and become better in the water'.

In Scott's time in Jersey about a half dozen people drowned but they were well away from the lifeguard's jurisdiction. The Aussies did a lot of rescues. A lifesaving club had started in Jersey and the Aussies rescued their whole group one day in 2008 or 2009. It was probably the biggest rescue Scott has ever been involved in.

Scott picks up the story. 'It was just on six o'clock in the evening and we were preparing to pack up for the day. We told them [the group from the lifesaving club] not to go in the surf but their instructor disregarded our advice. The tide was coming in and the swell started to increase. About 10 of them went in the water and the supervisor mustn't have known there was a rip there. We went to check the beach for the last time and saw them in trouble. Four of us had to run down to them, a distance of about 400 metres. By the time we got to where they were there was about a two-metre swell running and really punching onto the sand. There were kids being thrown over the falls in the white water and held under water by these powerful waves, they were really struggling. Four of us responded with rescue tubes as we had to run 400 metres to the shore. Our supervisor reopened the shed which was an old German war bunker and ran down with a rescue board'.

Scott managed to commandeer a body board off a youngster as he ran down the beach and used it as a flotation device. After a head count on the beach the Aussies breathed a sigh of relief when they realised the group were all out of the water. However, a couple of them had to go to hospital having swallowed a lot of water. Scott says, 'If we hadn't been there it would have certainly resulted in a few deaths, it was a frantic couple of minutes. Ironically, we believed at the time that these were the guys that were going to take over our jobs. They may have been good still water swimmers but their experience in the ocean was not up to scratch at that time. Interestingly, it was never mentioned in the media – it seemed to be all hushed up'.

Scott's words were prescient. The time of the RNLI lifeguards was fast approaching.

24 The Rise of the RNLI Lifeguards

'The initial reaction from lifesaving clubs and the international lifesaving community, which is represented by the International Life Saving Federation (ILS), was one of suspicion and in some cases open concern. Such a large, comparatively wealthy organisation such as the RNLI was seen by some to be a threat to their independence and identity.'

Excerpt from a paper entitled 'An Integrated Approach to Beach Lifeguarding and Lifeboating' presented at the 2007 World Conference on Drowning Prevention

In 2007 two men, members of the British Royal National Lifeboat Institute (RNLI), presented a paper at a world conference on drowning prevention. They were Adam Wooler, former Chief Executive of Surf Lifesaving Great Britain and the initiator of the RNLI Lifeguard Service, and Michael Vlasto, Operations Director of the RNLI, That paper, entitled 'An Integrated Approach to Beach Lifeguarding and Lifeboating', provided the background to how the RNLI got into the business of lifeguarding in Britain. It provides fascinating reading.

Founded in 1824 as the National Institution for the Preservation of Life from Shipwreck, the RNLI's objective was, and continues to be, to save lives at sea. It was renamed the RNLI in 1854 and awarded Royal charter in 1860. It is a registered charity, mainly funded by legacies (gifts of money) and donations. The RNLI's lifeboat arm has rescued more than 140,000 people since its inception. The biggest rescue in its history occurred in 1907 when in gale force conditions combined with thick sea fog, the SS *Suevic*, a 12,000-ton liner hit a reef near Lizard Point in Cornwall. Over a 16-hour period all 456 passengers and crew were rescued. This was an incredible effort.

The RNLI lifeboat operations in Britain are substantial, with 237 lifeboat stations and 443 rescue craft in operation in 2016. These include a combination of all-weather and inshore lifeboats with the latter comprising Inflatable Rescue Boats (IRBs) and Rigid Inflatable Boats (RIBs).

As the new millennium approached, surf lifesaving in Britain had come a long way from the early days of Bude in Cornwall and the pioneering efforts of Australian Allan Kennedy which led to the creation of the Surf Lifesaving Great Britain (SLSGB) organisation. Despite this, things weren't exactly rosy, particularly when it came to beach safety during the summer weekdays, given volunteer lifesavers were normally only available to patrol over the weekends. Increased levels of tourism were dictating that British beaches had to be patrolled by qualified and skilled lifeguards. Ironically, this had been happening in Jersey for over 40 years, but in the rest of Britain there were no uniform rules and regulations in place when it came to lifeguard services. National standards were lacking. Local authorities in many instances were not adequately resourcing their lifeguard services. Something had to be done.

It was. SLSGB, along with the Royal Lifesaving Society UK, got together with the RNLI to formulate a plan to create a new lifeguard service under the umbrella of the RNLI. Adam Wooler was seconded to the RNLI as part of this initiative. Local authorities responsible for providing lifesaving services on British beaches were involved in the project and the project team members set about overcoming obstacles, of which there were plenty. For a start there was considerable suspicion about this new initiative, not only from within the ranks of British surf lifesaving clubs but from within the RNLI which for almost two centuries had not deviated from the path of saving lives at sea through its lifeboat service. This service was iconic and had attracted substantial charitable income and built an enormous and very valuable asset base. Would this new initiative put the RNLI's charitable status at risk? How would members of the RNLI's traditional lifeboat service view a new, unproven arm of the RNLI? And would the RNLI's massive fundraising capability swamp that of the surf clubs which were members of SLSGB?

The project team pushed ahead and managed to overcome these obstacles, with the result that in 2001 the RNLI piloted a new lifeguarding service on 43 beaches in England's south-west. Service agreements were entered into with the relevant authorities which saw each authority pay only for the cost of employing the lifeguards, with the RNLI covering the cost of sorely needed new equipment. This was the financial model that was to form the basis of future agreements for lifeguard services in Britain. The service, initially called Beach Rescue, changed its name to Beach Lifeguards and then finally to RNLI Lifeguards.

Over the years since its inception the RNLI has amassed an enormous asset base valued at well over half a billion pounds. In 2001 an independent audit group named Ethical Audit claimed that, between 1993 and 2000, the RNLI raised two hundred million pounds more than it spent on lifeboat services. Ethical Audit asserted that this large amount was unnecessary and that donors would not donate if they knew about the excess. The RNLI retorted by claiming that the money was necessary to help fund new initiatives, including lifeboats and lifeguards.

The money did indeed help. The RNLI lifeguard service kept expanding after its 2001 start. By 2007 some 400 RNLI lifeguards were working on 71 beaches in the UK under a seasonal funding formula where the local authority paid 40%, equating to the lifeguard's salaries, and the RNLI provided the remaining 60% that covered equipment, training, clothing, management and facilities (presumably RNLI owned). Management and administration was provided by an RNLI team of 20 together with a headquarters team of 10. Policies and procedures for the maintenance and technical support for the lifesaving equipment had been developed which reflected that of the lifeboat side of the RNLI equation.

By the end of 2008 the number of UK beaches patrolled by RNLI lifeguards increased to 110 and by the end of 2015 this number had risen to more than 200 beaches, with over 1,300 lifeguards employed.

25 Sowing the Seeds

'Their way was to approach the local UK authority running lifeguard services and provide an offer which included updating the lifesaving equipment while the local authority paid the equivalent of the lifeguard wages to the RNLI for running the service.'

Extract from an interview with Paul Berghouse, Head Lifeguard

In 2003, as a result of an internal government restructure, the Jersey Harbours Department assumed control of the Jersey lifeguard service from the Tourism Department. Paul Berghouse recalls that the Harbourmaster was the acting head of the RNLI lifeboat service in Jersey at the time. He invited some representatives of the RNLI lifeguard service to Jersey where they met with him and Paul. Paul says bluntly, 'Essentially they picked my brains because we [the lifeguards] had the reputation as being the best in Europe. I socialised with them during their visit, just being friendly, there was nothing untoward about it'.

Then one of the Jersey RNLI lifeboat guys Paul knew told him that the Harbourmaster had the idea of the Harbours Department running the lifeguard service for a few years, then passing it over to the RNLI. According to Paul the Harbourmaster couldn't push the RNLI case too much because the Australian-run service was held in very high esteem.

The RNLI came over to Jersey three to four times subsequently, Paul says, to conduct audits aimed at benchmarking their service against the Jersey model. Paul was suspicious but there wasn't much he could do. He says, 'Their way was to approach the local UK authority running lifeguard services and provide an offer which included updating the lifesaving equipment (IRBs, jet skis, rescue boards etc) while the local authority paid the equivalent of the lifeguard wages to the RNLI for running the service'.

Over time most of the authorities in Cornwall, North Devon and elsewhere had signed up with the RNLI, but not Jersey. Paul's understanding was that the RNLI wanted Jersey because they considered it to be the jewel in the crown – the best run service with the highest standards and the highest calibre of lifeguards. Several beaches elsewhere in Britain had some high-quality lifeguards but overall the quality on the British mainland did not reflect the consistently high standard maintained in Jersey. Paul claims that the RNLI fitness standard was (and still is) of a lower level than the lifeguard service provided by the Australians in Jersey. More on that later.

Paul asserts that he spoke to a senior RNLI official in 2009, the last time they did an audit before the takeover in 2011, and he told Paul that in their view there were lots of rich people in Jersey which would mean more donations to the RNLI if they were to run the lifeguard service. This cannot be verified but the reference to rich people was certainly true enough.

The Jersey lifeguard service management arrangements were slightly confusing because of the historical way it had been set up. Under the restructured arrangements the Tourism Department paid for the lifeguard wages out of their budget, but Harbours had operational control of the service. Harbours was a self-funding government entity because it charged for its services, but it had no funds for the lifeguards, so the money was transferred annually from Tourism. Consequently, Tourism was still indirectly linked to the lifeguard service through the funding.

For years Paul had been trying to get the lifeguards onto a graded pay scale based on the Jersey public sector manual workers' pay scale. That had been resisted by Tourism and then subsequently Harbours. The manual workers' pay scale had eight grades with four increments in each grade. At that time the lifeguards were being paid at an equivalent rate to Grade 1 increment 0. Even the government tea ladies were paid at Grade 2 level. This made for a persuasive argument which helped to turn the tide in favour of Paul's case.

In 2006, with the support of Paul's supervisors, he was successful in getting a manual workers' pay scale agreement put in place for the lifeguards. This was no simple task; the case had to be put before a tribunal and to do that required a heck of a lot of documentation such as written job descriptions and the like. The agreement meant the lifeguard's pay level moved to Grade 5. Their pay increased by around 200 quid a week – a massive jump. The agreement also included payment for overtime and a shift allowance. Consequently, the lifeguard's hourly rate rose to around fourteen quid. Of course, the States government also increased the subsidised rent paid by the lifeguards to live in the Doghouse.

Even though this was quite an achievement and one gleefully accepted by the lifeguards, it may have inadvertently led to the RNLI getting its foot in the door in Jersey.

In recognition of the role tourism still played in the lifeguard management arrangements, Paul was required to attend regular monthly meetings along with his supervisor from the Harbours Department, a representative from Tourism and another from the Economic Development Department, the latter department also having a role in promoting Jersey as a visitor destination. The objective of the meetings was for these stakeholders to discuss the operations of the lifeguard service including its performance. Paul recalls that as late as 2007 the officials for the three departments were very supportive of the current lifeguard service arrangements, noting that by then, according to Paul, the RNLI had already put in two separate bids to run the service, both of which were rejected.

26   21st Century Wife's Tale

'When I came to Australia to live I really loved it.'

Extract from interview with Lisa Hammerton,
wife of Australian lifeguard Scott Hammerton.

Lisa Le Sueur was a nineteen-year-old Jersey local when she met Scott Hammerton at El Tico on St Ouen's beach in the summer of 2005. After studying psychology at university on the mainland, Lisa decided that studying how people behave, think and feel wasn't for her and elected to have a year off. Back in Jersey and 'a bit of an entrepreneur in those days', she was working in a beach shack at El Tico, right next to the Lifeguard Tower, selling jewellery that she had imported from Indonesia. As well, Lisa was renting boogie boards to tourists provided by the owners of the El Tico café. Lisa says, 'There was never really a crowd around but a few of my friends used to hang around out the front of the shack for the day'.

Scott Hammerton grins when he recalls meeting Lisa. 'The first time I saw her the lifeguard upstairs [in the tower] was Gary Richards and he sang out to me and said, "Have a look outside, Scotty". As I stepped out of our lifeguard tower I saw Lisa and gave her a wave. It was a quiet day on the beach and I went over and had a chat to her'. Says Scott with a laugh, 'Lisa had been warned by her mother about the lifeguards. The reason for this was that her mother had been irritated by a lifeguard who had insisted she swim between the flags; she didn't want to swim in the flags'. Scott continues, 'When I eventually met Lisa's mum I got along great with her'.

Lisa says, 'Scott was the only bloke to ever look around my jewellery concession store'. Well, he must have liked what he saw, and likewise with Lisa, because they started going out off and on in 2005. Then Scott returned to Newcastle to his lifeguard job at the end of the season.

Lisa takes up the story. 'We began to go out more seriously in 2006 when he came back to the beach [in Jersey]. We started going on short holidays together to places like Cornwall and France during that year. After I met Scott I had heaps to do with the lifeguards. We'd all hang out together with a few of my girlfriends and other mates. On Friday and Saturday night we'd be off to the pubs and clubs, to dinner or a party, all sorts of things'.

Lisa decided to go to Australia, independently of Scott, in September 2006 for a period of about nine months. She says, 'I travelled to Australia on my own and started in Western Australia. I had a friend over there, so I stayed with her. Then I came over to the east coast and stayed with Scott on and off and did some casual work. Then a friend of mine flew over from England and we did the Wicked van thing and did the rest of the east coast'. The 'Wicked van thing' was a campervan hire business targeting young backpackers that started in Brisbane, Australia in 2000 and expanded across Europe, North America, South America and South Africa.

Returning to Jersey in May 2007 Lisa was offered a traineeship for an accountancy firm where she studied an internationally recognised chartered accountancy qualification called an Association of Chartered Certified Accountants (ACCA). The firm paid the fees and the qualification took three years to complete.

Scott came back to Jersey for the 2007 summer and by then their relationship was getting serious. Scott says, 'Lisa's father asked me, "Are you going to move to Jersey?" and I said "No, I like the sun and the waves so we're going to move to Australia". By that stage she had a really good job in Jersey and she was being groomed for big things in the Jersey finance world'. Scott didn't reveal what Lisa's father thought about that.

But the Jersey financial world was about to receive a big jolt. Lisa explains: 'I had just started out as a trainee when the Global Financial Crisis hit'. Although, as will be detailed later, the GFC had a substantial impact in Jersey, Lisa was able to keep her traineeship and she worked for the accountancy firm for just over two years, until September 2009.

During the period 2007 to 2009 Scott was back to Australia to work as a lifeguard every northern winter and Lisa also spent some time in Australia over each Christmas break. Scott started to come back to Jersey a month before the beach season started and they would take a break and go off together for a brief holiday.

Then came Scott's decision at the end of the 2009 Jersey season to put his best foot forward in terms of being employed full time on the beach back in Newcastle. Lisa says, 'When Scott decided to finish off in Jersey I decided to move to Australia with him [in September 2009]. I came straight to Newcastle with Scott on a holiday visa then waited until I got my residency permit, so I could get a job. This worked out really well because during that time I studied. My parents were really good about the decision. They knew that they would miss me, particularly my mum because we are pretty close, but they knew Scott well by then and saw that we were really happy together and they knew I had been out here a lot prior to the move. When they came out to visit they realised how happy I was'.

Lisa has no regrets about her decision. 'When I came to Australia to live I really loved it. I am a really outdoorsy person who loves the sun. When I first got here I would just go and lie on the beach all day. I found that a lot of the shops here are very similar and people talk the same language. I do miss my friends and family on and off, but my family always moved around a fair bit when I was growing up and that made me pretty adaptable. My father was in the British Army and I had gone to boarding school and was used to living away from home. My father met my mother, she is English, in Germany, when she was teaching'.

The chartered accountancy studies continued. Lisa says, 'A lot of the study I did after I got here wasn't available online then and so it was mainly through books. I would go down to Sydney and sit exams. I worked for a local chartered accountant firm in Newcastle for a short period then I got a job with a local utilities company in January 2011 and I have been with them ever since'.

The couple decided to tie the knot. Lisa says, smiling, 'We got married in Newcastle on November 9th, 2013. My parents and my sister and brother came out for the wedding and my best friend who was my bridesmaid plus a couple of friends living in Sydney. [Sons] Bon Jack was born 20 July 2014 and Val Thomas was born on 6th June 2016'.

Lisa Hammerton discloses an amazingly accurate premonition she had as a child. 'Looking back when I was growing up, my sister always reminds me I said that I was going to live in Australia and marry a lifeguard! So, my childhood dream became a reality. I always thought that I would be living in a sunny country. I do still get itchy feet every now and then and feel the need to book a holiday and do a trip somewhere. We will always be travellers because we both enjoy it so much'.

Describing her views on taking the plunge and deciding to live halfway across the world from where she grew up, Lisa says, 'I think it's much easier to move to Australia these days. Communications are much easier – I Skype my parents every week. When we do spend time together it is real quality time. Also, the flight from Australia to Britain is now much more doable. I love going back to England but after two and a half weeks I'm ready to come back to Australia'.

27 Matters Economic

The spectre of the RNLI wasn't the only dark cloud on the horizon for the Australian lifeguards in the mid to late 2000s. The Jersey economy was about to be significantly affected by the Global Financial Crisis and the introduction of a new taxation regime called 0/10. Both had roles to play in the eventual demise of the lifeguard system set up and run by Australians.

Experts around the world have had their say about the causes of the GFC and how it impacted on the economies of countries far removed from its origins in the sub-prime mortgage market in the USA. Britain and Western Europe were no exception as financial institutions dabbled in what is known as securitisation, the bundling of mortgage debt into bonds and other financial instruments and on-selling them to willing investors. To reduce risk, the mortgage debt was moved off the books of the financial institutions, the banks and building societies, into entities specially set up in offshore financial centres such as Jersey. In Britain, two such banks, HBOS and Northern Rock, were players in this game.

HBOS (Halifax Bank of Scotland, created through a merger of the Halifax Building Society and the Bank of Scotland) was Britain's largest mortgage lender. In 2002 HBOS established an entity called Grampian Funding and registered it in Jersey. Grampian was in the business of arbitrage, which means earning money by borrowing funds from banks on the short-term money market and purchasing (housing) asset backed bonds which paid higher interest rates than the short-term borrowings. Within a few years Grampian became the world's largest player in this lucrative market. They bought only highly rated (AAA) mortgage bonds which generated hundreds of millions of pounds in profit for HBOS.

Northern Rock, formerly the Northern Rock Building Society, adopted an aggressive approach to gaining market share in the UK mortgage business and in the early 2000s established itself as Britain's fastest growing mortgage bank. Northern Rock used a similar business model to that used by HBOS; its Jersey based securitisation vehicle was called Granite. However, there was one important difference: Northern Rock obtained funds to grow its mortgage business from the short-term money market rather than from deposits by bank clients.

By mid-2007 Northern Rock had become Britain's fifth largest mortgage lender. It was growing like topsy, but bank deposits accounted for less than 25% of its assets at a time when its main competitors had a 50:50 ratio of deposits to loans. Northern Rock's short term (three months or less) liquidity gap (the difference between its assets and its liabilities) was an astounding £25 billion. But it was on the merry-go-round and it couldn't get off. Even so, its principals were unfazed – liquidity via the short-term money market at that time was like a very large tap which was running at full open.

Then in August 2007 the GFC hit with the impact of a hurricane and financial institutions worldwide took the brunt of the damage. Banks worldwide suddenly became very defensive and began to curtail what is termed interbank lending which is necessary to smooth out fluctuations in bank liquidity (the amount of cash and other assets available to meet short term obligations). This lack of liquidity led to a credit squeeze in the banking system and banks and related institutions, including HBOS and Northern Rock, found themselves in big trouble in the latter part of 2007.

In the case of Northern Rock, the credit squeeze very quickly created a crisis where the bank couldn't continue to meet its short-term loan obligations. In desperation it turned to the Bank of England for help to bail it out. This was provided in September, but the resulting publicity saw a run on the bank. Over three days some £11 million was withdrawn by anxious depositors. Northern Rock was nationalised by the British government in February 2008. The Jersey-based Granite, as a separate legal entity, was not part of this deal but its effectiveness was severely diminished as the supply of mortgages from Northern Rock was cut off.

The credit squeeze also heavily impacted on Grampian, and by association, HBOS. In August 2007 the latter was forced to extend credit to Grampian which, until then, had flown under the radar of most people (except the financial sector). The public learned that Grampian had been valued at £18 billion, almost 60% of the capitalisation of HBOS. As a result, Grampian was absorbed back into HBOS. Over the next eighteen months the fortunes of HBOS declined as it lurched from crisis to crisis. In January 2009 it was taken over by Lloyds Banking Group.

The GFC didn't exempt other Jersey-based financial institutions from its impact. Many made job cuts as the credit squeeze hit. The HSBC advised it was going to axe around 90 jobs in Jersey. Tellingly, in the debt securitisation sector the demand for bundling loans suffered a big fall, impacting on other sectors such as lawyers who were faced with less work. Unemployment grew.

Another impact of the credit squeeze was that people suddenly found it much harder to borrow money as bank loans dried up. New investment was impacted: housing and construction declined, business expansion suffered, and taxation revenues fell.

Like others in Britain, the ordinary people of Jersey were affected by the GFC because it created uncertainty about what the future would hold. Would they have jobs? Could they pay their household bills and mortgages? Financial uncertainty leads to a disinclination to spend and retail sales fell as people elected to hold on to their money rather than spend it.

It wasn't just the banks and the legal sector in Jersey that was impacted. Accounting and insurance firms were also in the firing line. Lisa Le Sueur, who was later to marry Australian lifeguard Scott Hammerton, had just started a traineeship with a Jersey firm of Chartered Accountants when the GFC hit in the middle of 2007. The firm's client base consisted of a lot of offshore clients who were very high net worth individuals, some of which were well known personalities. She recalls that people in the firm began working long hours to justify their jobs in the hope that they wouldn't be laid off. A lot of people in the finance industry were leaving their jobs. Lisa was lucky: her bosses told the staff that they wouldn't lay off anyone even though business was suffering because of the GFC.

If the GFC wasn't enough of a challenge for Jersey, the announcement of the introduction of a new corporate tax regime just before the credit squeeze compounded the problem. This new tax scheme, labelled '0/10', was to be introduced from 1 January 2009 and would see the tax rate for non-finance corporations set at zero, with a 10% rate for financial services firms.

The 0/10 scheme was originally mooted in the early 2000s in response to increasing competition in the financial services sector from other so-called tax havens in Singapore, Guernsey and the Isle of Man. In 2003 this sector had contributed just over £1 billion to the Jersey economy. About 70% of Jersey's corporate tax revenues and around 50% of individual tax revenues had come from the finance industry, so unsurprisingly the States government was keen to retain, and grow, the presence of this sector on the island.

There was another reason why this new tax scheme was introduced. In the late 1990s EU officials decreed that Jersey and other jurisdictions had to comply with a new code of financial conduct. The new rules were not going to be applied for a decade (the latter part of the 2000s) but they were aimed at eliminating the discrimination between the way that local and non-local (but registered in Jersey) companies were taxed, with the former taxed at 20% and the latter at zero if they paid a £600 fee.

The downside of the new tax regime was that the States government was going to suffer a loss of tax revenue, estimated to be of the value of some £80 to £100 million per annum. To offset these projected losses, a Goods and Services Tax (GST) of 3% (later raised to 5%) was introduced, and the government adopted a strategy to eliminate waste and increase efficiency in the delivery of public services.

One outcome of these economic problems was that the lifeguard service employing seasonal workers from overseas who were the recipient of a large pay increase became a prime target for an efficiency review.

Jim Reeves also had a tax problem, a debt, although he didn't know that he had it. He had married in Jersey in 2000 to a local policewoman whom he had first met in 1995. Finally, a woman had got him! She moved to Australia with Jim when he returned home after the end of the season in 2000.

However, things didn't work out and they were divorced in 2006. By that stage he was back on the beach in Jersey (she remained in Australia) for what was to be his final stint. When Jim got divorced he found out that his wife had not paid her tax bill before she left so, Jersey being Jersey, it fell to the husband to pay the tax – £7,000 – not exactly a small amount.

Says Jim, 'When I went back to Jersey in 2006 my tax rate was 15% but when they realised I had a tax debt it went up to 25%. Before 2005 or thereabouts the tax payable was assessed annually. After that it became pay as you earn arrangement, but you had to clear your debt before you went on to the new system. In the last year I was in Jersey (2010) I was paying 35% tax which cleared the debt'.

Speaking from personal experience, Jim notes that the introduction of the GST on goods and services meant things became more expensive and therefore other holiday destinations became more popular. However, he says, 'Wages went up considerably but so did the cost of living. That didn't stop us from frequenting the pub as much as ever'.

Notwithstanding the lifeguard's free and easy approach to life, the threat was growing to that lifestyle as the island's economic conditions tightened. But before that threat materialised, an incident at one of the beaches was to create headlines in the local paper.

28 Pizza Hut

Plémont Bay, on the north-west coast of Jersey, is very popular spot for beachgoers in the summer when the tide is low. The beach is surrounded by rocky headlands which guard the bay, and beach access is at the eastern end of the bay via a long set of steps set into a rugged cliff. The white sand beach stretches to the west of the steps for several hundred metres before meeting the cliff face.

The surf breaks close into shore at low tide, which means that surf board riders, boogie boarders or body surfers do not have to venture into deeper water in search of a wave. At one end of the beach is a waterfall which flows when there has been rain and behind the waterfall is a small cave, with other caves dotting the cliff faces surrounding the beach. There are also plenty of rock pools for kids and adults to splash around in. At high tide the sand is covered, with the water lapping against rocky outcrops and making the beach less attractive to visit. When the surf is up danger lurks at high tide.

At the top of the steps on the eastern end is a kiosk popular with the beachgoers. Perched above the flat concrete roof of the kiosk is a small wooden hut with a shallow pitched roof that is used as a lookout by the Jersey lifeguards patrolling the beach. The windows of the hut offer a great view over the beach, handy for spotting any beachgoers in trouble in the water. The hut was erected by the States government in the early 1980s although the Australian lifeguards started patrols at Plémont in the early 1970s.

Access to Plémont beach is not so easy because of its rather secluded location. A narrow road some 350 metres long leads down to the kiosk and a very small car park. The road, called Route de Plémont, has a sharp 180-degree bend near the top which leads to a large unsealed car park built to cater for the overflow of vehicles that can happen on busy days. At that time vehicles line the grass verges of the narrow Route de Plémont, making it difficult for anything larger than a car to drive down the road. A footpath winds its way down the hill from the car park for those who wish to park at the top and walk down.

Over the years Plémont has seen many rescues by lifeguards. However, in August 2008 an incident occurred involving a lifeguard that had nothing to do with the surf. This became known famously among the lifeguards as the Pizza Hut incident. For the sake of preserving the dignity of those involved, the identity of the lifeguards on duty that day must remain undisclosed.

On that fateful day at the height of the summer, two lifeguards were patrolling at Plémont beach. The weather was good, and the crowd was sizeable, the surf conditions a little boisterous, keeping the boys busy. However, one of the two Aussies managed to grab time to organise a quick meal. He left his fellow lifeguard on the beach and hurried up the steps to the lifeguard hut where he began to cook a frozen pizza he had brought with him to eat.

The lifeguard hut was sparsely furnished: a stretcher bed for use by those recovering from being rescued, a first aid kit, a water dispenser, a fire extinguisher, several old chairs, and an old stove that had been there for over twenty years. The stove was the sort that had an oven with a couple of hotplates on top. In the hut as well were several old surfboards used by the lifeguards after hours if the surf was good, and an old 'boom box', a transistorised portable music device with a cassette player and an AM/FM radio. The boom box sat, perhaps unwisely, on top of the stove, probably because that's where the power sockets were. Also stored there was an Oxy Viva medical oxygen resuscitator and a defibrillator, although they were normally taken down to the beach during patrol hours.

In a hurry to get the pizza heated up, the lifeguard put it into the oven and turned one of the dials, thinking he had turned on the oven. But, unbeknown to him, he had accidentally turned on one of the hot plates. His attention was then drawn to a call by the other lifeguard, asking for assistance on the beach. He left the hut and ran down the 200 or so steps to the sand.

The Aussie was helping on the water's edge when he heard a shout from behind and above him. He turned and noticed the kiosk owner screaming out for help. It was then he saw smoke billowing out of the windows of the lifeguard hut. He freaked out, realising something had gone wrong with the cooking. He raced up the long set of steps, knocking people out of the way in his haste to get to the fire.

When he got up to the top of the steps the kiosk owner screamed, 'What have you done?' He said, 'It's the pizza', thinking that somehow it had caught on fire inside the oven. Looking for a means to fight the fire, the lifeguard remembered with a sinking feeling that the fire extinguisher was inside the hut which was now well on fire. Thinking quickly, he grabbed a fire extinguisher from the kiosk and bravely, and perhaps rashly, entered the hut to try and put the fire out. There was smoke and flames everywhere and he quickly became covered in black smoke and soot, although, thank goodness, he didn't receive any burns.

As he worked to quench the flames he could see that the fire and the smoke had damaged the first aid gear and the stretcher had partially melted from the heat. He was joined by the other lifeguard who had run up to the hut to help. In the meantime, some quick-thinking person had organised the evacuation of the kiosk, and about 75 people were assembled in the small car park outside watching the drama unfold.

Somehow in the excitement the fire brigade was summonsed, although they had to respond from the island's western fire station north of St Brelade's, about five kilometres' distance as the crow flies. Along the narrow Jersey roads, the fire truck sped, siren screaming.

By the time the fire truck got to the top of the hill above Plémont the two lifeguards had put the fire out and were standing in front of the hut surveying the damage. Smoke was still trickling out of the burnt remains and the stench of burnt material was wafting over them. They could see that the surfboards were buckled, the water dispenser and the stove had melted, and the interior of the hut was a mess. Above them, the firefighters found that they couldn't get the fire truck down Route de Plémont because of the insufficient gap between the cars, mainly tourist's rental vehicles, parked on the sides of the road.

Seeing and hearing the fire truck arrive, the lifeguard who had inadvertently started the fire decided to run up to them to liaise with the firefighters and to tell them that the fire was out. What happened next is the stuff of comedy. The firies, seeing the lifeguard running up the hill covered in soot and smoke and observing smoke still drifting out of the lifeguard hut, perhaps acted a trifle overzealously.

Assuming the hut was still on fire they decided it was essential to get the truck down to the scene of the fire. So, engaging gear, the driver of the fire truck started down the narrow road, barging cars out of the way, creating carnage. That is probably what did the most damage in the whole incident!

The lifeguard managed to reach the fire truck and tell the firies the fire was out. However, he was in such a state that they had to administer oxygen to him. He was freaking out, in shock, a little bit smoke affected and convinced that he was going to get the sack for starting the fire.

Quite a while later, after the lifeguard recovered and things settled down, he reluctantly decided he had better ring Head Lifeguard Paul Berghouse to tell him what had happened. But as Paul received the call he had another problem he was dealing with, namely the death of a tourist by drowning near St Brelade's.

Scott Hammerton had been on duty that day at St Brelade's. It had been a beautiful sunny day and very busy on the beach. The swell was low, but a big tide was starting to flow in quickly. At 6 p.m. the lifeguards finished for the day and took the lifeguard caravan up off the beach and unhitched it at its usual spot in a carpark. They did a last survey of the beach to check everyone was okay, then made an announcement on the loudspeaker that the lifeguard service was finished for the day. Although there were still people in the water and on the beach, this wasn't unusual, so they departed.

The lifeguards were driving home when they saw the fire brigade going the other way. The fire brigade had the role of providing the after hours' response for rescues using an IRB they had for this purpose. Scott says, 'We got on the two-way [radio] to Paul [Berghouse] figuring that something was not right because there were a lot of Emergency Services flashing lights going towards St Brelade's. He got back to us and advised us that someone had drowned. We were already back at St Helier at the Doghouse by this time but a few of the guys responded and tried to resuscitate the guy but he was dead. He was a 24-year-old Romanian'. Scott recalls, 'There had been a big international soccer game on that day and some tourists who were full of booze jumped at the Bayside Slip near St Brelade's and one of them ended up drowning'.

Then Paul got the phone call from Plémont. As Scott recalls, 'Paul said on the two-way radio, "Apparently one of the boys has burnt the hut down and I'm going to throw myself off a cliff". We could tell he was not happy, but we were all sniggering to ourselves'.

The next day the *Jersey Evening Post* had a humorous story on the fire under the heading 'Pizza Hut'.

The lifeguard didn't get sacked. But the States government left the hut unrepaired for the rest of the season, about six weeks. If it was raining at Plémont the lifeguards had to put wetsuits on and stand around in the rain.

Scott Hammerton recalls, 'If it was raining too heavily we tried to go inside the hut but there was charcoal and shit everywhere. A lot of the time if the beach wasn't busy with bad weather or the high tide we just ended up working out of the kiosk in our lifeguards' uniforms looking out the window at the beach. Otherwise we would be down on the water's edge patrolling'.

Perhaps the saddest thing about the hut fire was that it destroyed a significant piece of lifeguard history, not something stored there, but graffiti written on the walls over the years. As Scott Hammerton relates, there were 'lots of poems, plus tallies of how many conquests some of the guys had made over the season. Some of the poems were very funny'. All gone, up in smoke.

Several years later Dave Blake, a rugby playing Jersey 'Bean' who was a close friend of the lifeguards in the 1970s, was visiting Australia to catch up with some of the Aussies including Jerry Shannos, Brian 'Jughead' Jones and Jim 'Noddy' Reeves. Dave visited Manly beach just before travelling to Newcastle and he approached two lifeguards to ask them for advice about where to go for a long swim. After some derisory comments the older of the two established that Dave was a good swimmer and that he came from Jersey. The lifeguard told Dave that he was working in Devon in England at the time Jerry Shannos was the Head Beach guard in Jersey. He asked Dave if he knew him. Dave replied, 'I'm going to stay with him'.

Both lifeguards then became much friendlier and told Dave where to swim. As he was about the go into the water, the younger lifeguard piped up sheepishly that he was the one who caused the fire in the lifeguard hut at Plémont. It is a small world!

In any event the lifeguard hut was repaired in time for the next season, but it is very unlikely that anyone cooked anything in there again. However, that next season was to be their last.

29   Enter the RNLI

'As good as the RNLI is I don't believe they are going to be able to match the experience the Australian lifeguards bring to the job.'

Paul Le Clair, a Deputy in the States Assembly, in a statement to the BBC News after the announcement that the RNLI was to take over the provision of lifeguard services in Jersey.

In response to the emerging pressure on States government revenues, in the 2008-09 time period there was a directive from the States Assembly to cut costs by about ten percent across all government departments. A decision was taken to look at outsourcing as much as possible to save money. The lifeguard service became a target because none of the lifeguards apart from Paul lived permanently in Jersey, Paul being a resident but not a citizen. This would arguably mean little political fallout for the government if the service was outsourced. Paul was told the lifeguards were chosen as a test case which if successful would allow other services to follow.

But bureaucracies move slowly, and it took at least a year before the mechanisms of government were to focus on the Australian lifeguards. In the meantime, Jim Reeves was becoming more concerned about the threat posed by the RNLI. He says, 'Paul's approach was to keep the lifeguard service in the background, out of the public eye. However, the RNLI were the exact opposite – they were like Surf Lifesaving Australia, they were out there promoting themselves'.

Seeking to sway public opinion, Jim suggested to Paul that introducing a program for the Australian lifeguards to educate Jersey schoolchildren in surf safety might be a winner. As a lifeguard back home working for Lake Macquarie council south of Newcastle Jim had been involved in a similar arrangement which had proven very successful and had generated good publicity. However, says Jim, Paul 'wasn't interested'.

Finally, some government action. The June 2010 States of Jersey Parliamentary Hansard reported a discourse between several politicians concerning the lifeguard services. An amount of £75,000 was suggested as being able to be saved from lifeguard services, £50,000 from the beach lifeguards and £25,000 from pool lifeguards employed by the Department of Education, Sport and Culture. The latter referred to the removal of (non-Australian) lifeguards from Havre des Pas swimming pool.

However, a public outcry and a backlash from several government members put a stop to the pool being unpatrolled. Unfortunately, the Australian lifeguard service continued to be under review.

It was supremely ironic that, in June 2010, 30 or so ex-lifeguards along with their wives travelled to Jersey to hold a reunion at a time when the future of the service was under threat. The *Jersey Evening Post* reported, 'With the perfect surf and golden sands of St Ouen as their backdrop, 30 of those former Australian lifeguards were reunited where it all began. The place buzzed with memories and stories of summers spent "working hard and playing harder", as one former beach guard put it. And Islanders who had known the men during their time on the Island turned out to welcome them back'.

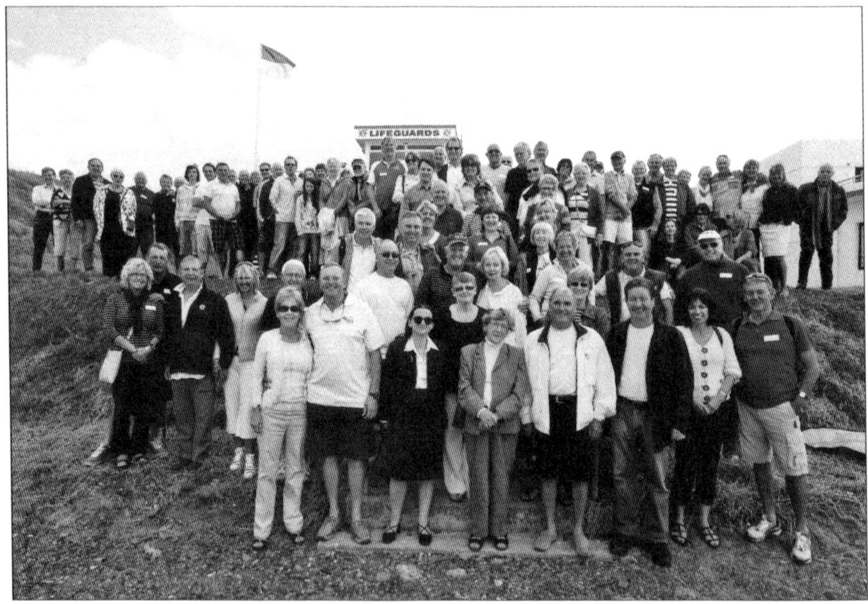

Jersey Beachguards' Reunion 2010
Australian beach guards and partners visit Jersey to celebrate 50 years of Australian Surf Lifesaving in Jersey at El Tico, St Ouen's, June 2010

(Photo courtesy of the Jersey Evening Post*)*

As enjoyable as the reunion was, darker days were ahead.

Later in 2010 the RNLI offered once again to take over the service. Paul Berghouse was invited to a meeting in October or November of that year, run by the Economic Development Department. An official asked whether Paul would be interested in working for the States to run the lifeguard service on behalf of the RNLI. Paul, aware that the RNLI pay scales were less than enjoyed by the Jersey lifeguards, declined, remaining loyal to his team. Paul noted that the offer was not put in writing, so he started to smell a rat.

On 30 December 2010 the *Jersey Evening Post* ran an article entitled 'Cuts Threat to Lifeguard Service'. The article quoted Senator Alan Maclean, the Minister for Economic Development, as saying that there were several options on the table to save money. These included withdrawing the lifeguards from some beaches, in particular Plémont (presumably by cutting back on lifeguard numbers) or reducing the number of days a year they were on duty (perhaps the same number of lifeguards but a shorter season). Senator Maclean admitted that the savings were likely to come to a significant extent from the salaries paid to the Australian lifeguards. He also stated that his department had held talks with the RNLI about the provision of the lifeguard service.

The newspaper article stated, 'It is understood that employing the RNLI lifeguards would end Jersey's 50-year association with Australian lifeguards, as the charity would pay less than the States currently do and would not be able to afford the highly experienced Australians'.

News of the possible change to the lifeguard service was met with dismay by two local people, one a former volunteer surf lifesaver and the other an unlikely ally. On 31 December 2010 the *Jersey Evening Post* included an interview with Barry Jenkins, a member of the Jersey Lifeguard Club in the 1960s. Barry was incensed about the possibility of the cuts and asserted that lives would be put at risk and Jersey's reputation as a popular holiday destination would suffer. Referring to the lifeguard service, he said, 'It is not a business. You just cannot cut emergency services like this'.

The New Year arrived, and another meeting occurred in early January 2011 between Paul, his supervisor and the same official who offered Paul the job managing the RNLI lifeguard service. Paul was again offered the job, but again refused. Representatives from the RNLI met with officials from the States government during the second week of January 2011, which according to Senator Maclean 'went very well'.

In early January 2011 senior past and present officials of the Jersey Surfboard Club wrote a letter of concern picked up by the *Jersey Evening Post* about the possible changes to the lifeguard service. The signatories of the letter said: 'The possible demise of the Australian lifeguard service has, in our view, not been fully thought through and we are against the proposals'.

At the same time in Australia professional lifeguard Gary Richards, who had spent ten years in Jersey as a lifeguard, wrote a letter of condemnation and lodged it on the *Jersey Evening Post*'s website. Subsequently interviewed by phone in Newcastle by the *JEP*'s Richard Heath, Gary stated: 'If the RNLI say they can provide the service for less, then they will have to reduce wages. At the moment Jersey gets some of the best and most experienced lifeguards in Australia, and the Island has a reputation of having the best lifeguard service in the whole of Europe. But if wages were reduced, these experienced guys would simply not go to Jersey'.

Public opposition to the government's plans was growing. The *Jersey Evening Post* on 18 January 2011 reported that a petition against the mooted changes to the lifeguard service had been launched by Andrew Hosegood, the owner of the El Tico Beach Cantina and Nick Durbano, a former chairman of the Jersey Surfboard Club and owner of the Laneez Surf Centre at St Ouen's. The petition was to gather around 1,000 signatures.

Questions continued to be asked in parliament. On 18 January 2011 Senator Maclean was asked whether a decision had been made about 'our much-valued lifeguard service' and whether the Minister would guarantee that the level of individual experience offered by any new provider would be the same as currently provided.

In his response the Minister reiterated that the lifeguard service was under review and that the government was undertaking discussions with organisations including the RNLI. He confirmed that, whatever the review outcome, an equivalent level of service would be maintained. Of note, Senator Maclean went on to extol the prowess of the RNLI lifeguard service in order to rebut adverse comment in some sections of the media about the RNLI. The writing was on the wall.

Then the hammer came down. Paul Berghouse left Jersey for a holiday in Australia towards the end of January 2011. Soon after he arrived in Australia he received a call from the *Jersey Evening Post* asking for a comment on an announcement by the government that the RNLI was to take over the lifeguard service, with a claimed saving of £100,000 a year. Paul was extremely disappointed but not at all surprised. The States of Jersey on January 26th had provided the RNLI with a Letter of Intent, although the news was not made public until the second week of February.

The Australian-run lifeguard service was finished; dead and buried. This time public opinion did not sway the decision makers.

The decision to allow the RNLI Lifeguard Service to take over in Jersey was met with concern locally, nationally and internationally. Paul Le Clair, a Deputy in the States Assembly, told the BBC News he was not convinced about the change. He was quoted as saying, 'As good as the RNLI is I don't believe they are going to be able to match the experience the Australian lifeguards bring to the job'. Le Clair added, 'Unfortunately, in my view this has been done to save money'.

According to the *Jersey Evening Post*, Deputy Le Clair approached Senator Maclean to ask why States members had not been allowed to vote on the move. Senator Maclean reminded the Deputy that the decision to generally reduce funding to the lifeguard service was taken in 2010. 'Our proposal to reduce the cost of the lifeguard service to the public purse was included in last year's Budget which the States debated. There was no amendment to this proposal and our 2011 Budget proposals were approved by the States.'

In response to criticism about the quality of the RNLI lifeguard service, Senator Alan Maclean told the BBC News, 'Twelve lifeguards were coming over from Australia including four who had worked in Jersey before'. And he claimed the package offered to lifeguards was similar to the Australian run service. 'The hourly rate is slightly lower but in fact there are other parts of the package which make it overall quite attractive and certainly of a similar level to in the past.'

However, despite these assurances from Senator Maclean, the RNLI did not appear at that stage to have a rock-solid arrangement in place to run the service. On return to Jersey after his Australian holiday Paul says he was approached by the States to help out for eight to ten weeks in getting the RNLI service up and running. He declined. Jim Reeves was also approached but he declined as well. Obviously, the RNLI was after an experienced senior person to bed in the new arrangements, but the charity wasn't going to get the desired expertise from the Australians who had run the former service.

30 The 2011 RNLI Agreement

'The Beach Operator [the States of Jersey] acknowledges that the RNLI is not receiving full cost recovery or a commercial profit margin in return for the provision of the Services. Consequently, the Beach Operator has agreed that the RNLI's liability under this Agreement shall be limited to that provided under this Clause 17.'

Extract from clause 17 of the 2011 agreement between the States of Jersey and the RNLI that limited the extent of liability to the value of the agreement, namely £150,000.

The RNLI lifeguard service started in Jersey on 28 May 2011, just under 54 years after the first Australian beach guards commenced the provision of lifeguard services in Jersey. However, for some reason the formal agreement to provide the services wasn't signed before that date (the effective date). The agreement was not signed by Michael Vlasto, the RNLI Operations Director, until 3 June 2011 and by Senator Maclean on behalf of the States of Jersey on 13 June 2011.

The practice of signing an agreement, a contract by another name, after the effective date is called Backdating and it can have pitfalls, although it would appear that the delay in signing had no impact on service delivery. It is quite probable the gap between the effective date and the signature dates occurred because of bureaucratic delays, given the States government signatory Senator Maclean resided in Jersey and the RNLI signatory Michael Vlasto was located in Poole in Dorset.

Interestingly the RNLI contract manager was also located in Poole, which is probably why the agreement stipulated that there would be twice-yearly face-to-face meetings, at the start of the season and then at the end of the season, between the parties' authorised representatives. The RNLI did not nominate any person residing in Jersey as an authorised representative.

The initial period of the agreement was until 31 December 2015. The cost to the States of Jersey (the Contribution) was £150,000 per annum with an annual adjustment to reflect any increase in the Retail Price Index (RPI) and any changes (additions or deletions) to the Patrol List (number of lifeguards). At the twice-yearly meetings a review would be held on whether any changes to the value of the Contribution were necessary.

The Patrol List in the 2011 Agreement did not specify the number of lifeguards to be provided by the RNLI, although it did stipulate that 'a main seasonal lifeguard service' would be provided at St Ouen's, St Brelade's, Plémont and Grève de Lecq. Presumably that meant a permanent lifeguard presence during the summer. The absence of a figure for lifeguard numbers may have been because the RNLI was still recruiting for the Jersey lifeguard service at the time the Agreement commenced.

In any event, as Senator Maclean had advised the BBC News on February 14th, twelve lifeguards were initially employed for the 2011 season, but that number subsequently increased to 15. The period of lifeguard activity was to be 18 weeks during the main season, from 28 May to 2 October 2011, with the peak period being defined as between 2 July to 4 September. Five part-time lifeguards were to be additionally employed during the peak period. Two of the 15 were supervisor lifeguards (but not authorised RNLI representatives) employed to oversee the other lifeguards, generate rosters and provide paperwork to the States of Jersey as stipulated in the Agreement. This has been verified by Chris Emery, an Australian lifeguard who worked for the RNLI in Jersey during 2011 and 2012.

Under the agreement the States of Jersey handed over to the RNLI three second hand vehicles (a Ford Ranger, a crew-cab Honda CR-V, and a Honda TRX350 quad bike), two jet skis, two rescue sleds and seven rescue boards. Any future equipment needs would be met by the RNLI.

Of note, clause 17.1 of the agreement which covers limitation of liability, stated:

> 'The Beach Operator [the States of Jersey] acknowledges that the RNLI is not receiving full cost recovery or a commercial profit margin in return for the provision of the Services. Consequently, the Beach Operator has agreed that the RNLI's liability under this Agreement shall be limited to that provided under this Clause 17. The Beach Operator acknowledges that the RNLI has offered to negotiate higher limits of liability in return for payment by the Beach Operator to the RNLI of an increased Contribution and the Beach Operator has chosen not to pursue this offer. The Beach Operator should obtain its own insurances in respect of this Agreement.'

The agreement restricted liability to the amount of the Contribution (£150,000). This reduced both the risk to the RNLI of being sued by the States government over breach of the Agreement and the cost to the RNLI of insurance premiums that would cover such risk. However, the Agreement did stipulate that the RNLI lifeguards would be covered for public liability and employer's liability to the value of £20 million.

Leaving the nuts and bolts of the Agreement aside, some analysis is warranted of the cost of both the Australian lifeguard and the RNLI services, as well as the resultant savings and benefits claimed in introducing the new service.

Firstly, the cost of the Australian service. Senator Maclean advised on 30

December 2010 in the *Jersey Evening Post* that the annual cost of the current service since 2007 had been £250,000 and that most of this amount was for wages. Since 2004 the number of Australian lifeguards working in Jersey had averaged around 15, one of which was the head lifeguard on a slightly higher wage. Based on hourly rates supplied by several Australians who had been in receipt of the higher wages, that would put the wages bill at somewhere between £160,000 and £170,000 per annum.

When calculating the total cost of a service it is usual to include not only wages, but other costs associated with service delivery. These would typically include overheads associated with employing the lifeguards (payroll and records administration for example), the cost of the equipment (the cost of the vehicles amortised over their life, uniforms, communications equipment, first aid equipment, rescue boards, jet skis and the like), plus the full economic cost of their subsidised rental accommodation less what the lifeguards paid. The quality of the latter varied considerably, but regardless of the standard they each paid £80 per week. With 14 lifeguards living in the Doghouse (Paul Berghouse didn't) the annual lifeguard rental payment to the government was about £20,000.

What is not known is whether the Australian lifeguard rental payment of £20,000 was taken into account in the £250,000 annual cost. However, regardless of this the annual cost of overheads for the Australian provided lifeguard service on Senator Maclean's figure would have been somewhere between £80,000 and £90,000, around 35% of the total cost of the lifeguard service.

Now to the RNLI lifeguard cost which was stipulated in the Agreement as £150,000, plus adjustments depending on the number of additional lifeguards employed. At the start of the 2011 season, 10 full-time lifeguards, two supervisors, and five part-time lifeguards were to be employed.

Chris Emcry says his hourly rate in 2011 as a Grade 1 lifeguard (the lowest level in the RNLI stable) in Jersey was £10.90, about £3 an hour lower than that paid by the States government to the Australians. By RNLI standards this was generous – the charity acknowledged that the cost of living in Jersey was higher than in many other places in Britain. The going rate for a Grade 1 lifeguard elsewhere (including Cornwall) was only a shade over £8 per hour. Chris also says that the Jersey supervisory lifeguards were being paid a slightly higher rate, £12 an hour.

Based on those figures, the wages bill from this number would have been just under £110,000, so the other £40,000 must have been for uniforms and other overheads. The overhead cost ratio of 36% was similar to that of the Australian lifeguard service.

Of note, the contribution of £150,000 rose by £20,000 during the season. This increase was derived from a statement by Senator Maclean in parliament on

18 November 2011 when he described the outsourcing of the lifeguard service to the RNLI: 'It saved £80,000 per annum in running costs.' So, the £100,000 savings became £80,000. Where did the £20,000 in savings go?

Assuming the original £150,000 contribution didn't include the additional three full-time lifeguards who did not start employment at the beginning of the 2011 season, the wages bill for these three at Grade 1 rates would have been around £20,000. This may have been the reason for the reduction in savings.

There is one other factor to consider in the claimed savings. The Australian lifeguards were provided with subsidised accommodation through the Jersey Housing Department and were paying about £80 a week, an annualised figure of around £20,000. However, the RNLI lifeguards who weren't local (Chris Emery says that all but two lifeguards in 2011 were Australians) lived in States government provided housing and paid no rent at all in 2011 and 2012.

Free rent was a significant drawcard for Chris and other Australian lifeguards as it went some way to compensate for the lower wages paid by the RNLI. Was firstly the £20,000 in rent paid by the Australians and secondly the rent-free accommodation provided to the Australians employed by the RNLI taken into account when calculating the claimed savings? Certainly, the bonus of free rent for the non-local lifeguards was not mentioned in the RNLI Agreement, nor was it common knowledge.

Senator Maclean also stated in parliament on 18 November 2011 that, with the introduction of the RNLI lifeguards, the standard of service had improved, most capital costs had been removed, and four locals had been employed by the RNLI as lifeguards. The latter two assertions are undoubtedly true and in fact as time went on more locals were employed which was good for the local economy.

Senator Maclean's statement about improvements in the standard of the lifeguard service is worthy of further examination. In 2010, as in previous years, the lifeguard service in Jersey was widely regarded as being very good indeed. In fact, Senator Maclean himself in January 2011 described it as 'highly valued'. The implication is that the standard in 2011 became even better than highly valued. Was this assertion correct?

The RNLI service in 2011 included four Australian lifeguards that had been employed on the beach in 2010. However, Paul Berghouse asserts he wouldn't have employed those four the following year. According to Paul they were satisfactory on the beach but their conduct outside work wasn't up to scratch. Paul's assertions could be dismissed as merely sour grapes except for the fact that the RNLI subsequently sacked three of those four Australians for gross misconduct within six weeks of the new service starting. This was confirmed by Chris Emery who was working in Jersey with them. Another (non-Australian) lifeguard was subsequently sacked for drunk driving that year.

What about the standards required of the RNLI lifeguards? Chris Emery states: 'The RNLI standards were much lower than I was used to as a lifeguard in Australia'. He was referring not only to the physical requirements but also the qualifications in resuscitation, first aid and beach management. Now Chris was no slouch as a lifeguard. Even though he was only 19 years of age he had been working as a lifeguard for four seasons in Perth and once he left Jersey he was employed as a supervisor lifeguard back in Perth.

These examples don't back up the claim that the standard had improved, at least in 2011.

On 16 March 2015 the States of Jersey entered into a renewed agreement with the RNLI for the provision of lifeguard services for the period up to 31 December 2019. Obviously, the services provided by the RNLI between 2011 and 2015 had met the expectations of the States of Jersey.

The Consideration in the new agreement was for the sum of £213,998 per season, an increase of almost £64,000 over the initial 2011 agreement. What was the States of Jersey getting for its money?

Well, for a start new equipment and facilities were provided by the RNLI, which meant they were delivering on what was promised back in 2011. Secondly, patrols were to be conducted at St Brelade's Bay on the southwest corner of the island, three locations at St Ouen's (the Watersplash, Main Beach (El Tico) and Le Braye slipway), on the west coast, and the northern coast beaches of Plémont Bay and Grève de Lecq. Thirdly, the duration of the season had been extended. There was a two-week period from 28 March to cover the Easter holidays, then the main season commenced on 2 May and went through to 27 September, with a week at the end of October for school half term.

This would have required around 25 lifeguards, 11 of them senior, to meet the obligation. That number has been verified by anecdotal information provided by Paul Berghouse.

So, the result has been new equipment and facilities, and a more than doubling of the number of lifeguards to that on patrol in 2010 under the old regime, patrolling six spots in Jersey for a slightly extended season at a cost of £213,998. Arguably, the bottom line is that no lives have been lost on patrolled beaches during the RNLI's time in charge.

Enough of the facts and figures. Two former lifeguards, one a Jersey Bean and the other an Australian, have provided their opinions on the changed arrangements.

Gordon Callendar, the first Jersey local lifeguard under the Australian regime, says: 'I have followed the RNLI saga a little bit. To me the locals were curious about what would happen. The first year the RNLI took over we noticed that there were some unusual things happening such as the flags being in the wrong place. Also, the mixture of youth and experience didn't seem right, but I understand things have improved since. The locals certainly had a huge affection for the Australian lifeguard service. They were known in a good way for doing a good job. One of the local politicians asked me my opinion of the change because he knew I had worked on the beach. It was clear to me that he was keen to keep the existing service going but obviously he didn't succeed'.

Scott Hammerton says: 'I went back to Jersey in either 2013 or 2014 and visited the lifeguard tower at St Ouen's to say hello to the guys there. I had left three surfboards behind when I left in 2009 and I was hoping that I could get them back. I didn't know it was going to be my last year in 2009 so I left a lot of gear behind. I met the RNLI lifeguards' supervisor, a guy called Will Glen. He was in his mid-20s and he had come out to Australia earlier and had worked at the Gold Coast and established his career as a lifeguard then. When I met with Will I discussed with him the concept of doing a reciprocal swap of lifeguards between Jersey and Australia. He thought it was a great idea, but the problem was the essential service visa that was applicable in our day was no longer valid and anyone that went there needed patriality to qualify. I checked all the beaches and talked to a lot of the lifeguards there. They were mostly very young and green and interestingly some didn't seem to appreciate the lifestyle they were experiencing'.

Scott continues: 'I asked them, "Do you like your job, boys?" and some replied, "Well, it's pretty boring". I said, "You don't realise how good this job is". It seemed to be just a job for them whereas for me and my mates it was a novelty to be in a foreign country working on beautiful beaches. Still, I thought to myself the service is in good hands with Will running it. He is a local boy and I remember him as a youngster in Jersey from when I was there. I knew he was good in the water and a good surfer and he seemed to be taking the service in the right direction, so I thought at least it is not being run by someone who doesn't care. I was impressed with the way Will was running the service and I would have gone back and worked under him for sure even though I would have had to take a massive pay cut'.

Will Glen worked as a supervisor for the RNLI lifeguards until 2017 when he joined the Jersey Fire Service.

31 The Last Word

'The locals certainly had a huge affection for the Australian lifeguard service.'

Gordon Callendar, Jersey Bean and former lifeguard.

So, there we have it. The era of the Australian run lifeguard service in Jersey was over after a continuous run of over 50 years from go to whoa. Amongst the ranks of the 280 odd surf lifesavers who worked in Jersey were the standouts: international athletes, champion rugby league players, swimmers who won national titles in the surf or who swam amazingly long distances, or big wave surf board riders. Then there were the ordinary blokes who loved the beach and were up for adventure, and the women who married some of them and were brave enough to make their homes in Australia. And, of course, the two locals who proved themselves to be proficient and worthy of being called a Jersey lifeguard.

Their stories are the stuff of legend, whether they have been told in these pages or are just too risqué to put into print. The lifeguards put in long hours on the beaches of Jersey, effecting countless rescues of people in distress, living in substandard accommodation, drinking countless alcoholic beverages, wooing countless women and making many friends. They trained hard, partied even harder and drank like fishes (most of them). Up until the late 1970s, for many, rugby played a strong role in their off-season lives. They turned up to work day in and day out, in good weather and bad. They were poorly paid until the mid-2000s and until the latter part of the 1980s most worked second jobs at night to make ends meet. They lived in the various Doghouses, some a better standard than others, but enjoyed them all.

Those lifeguards may have been at the bottom of the Jersey food chain, along with the other itinerant seasonal workers, but they played a vital role in making Jersey an attractive and safe place to visit and live. Substantial economic change occurred in Jersey during their time, in economics and tourism, and although some of this change impacted on them they got on with what they were trained to do – save lives. They came from the beaches of Sydney, Newcastle, Perth, and a host of other Australian towns and cities, from the beaches around Durban in South Africa, a few from England, at least one from New Zealand, and from Jersey itself. They loved what they did, and many came back season after season.

Most importantly, they were held in high regard by the locals, the Jersey Beans and the holidaymakers adored them. Public opinion got them their jobs back after they were unfairly sacked in 1960 and public opinion almost did the same in 2011 when they lost the final battle. Their ultimate demise was no reflection on the quality of the service they provided; rightly or wrongly, economics got in the way.

Gordon Callendar, the first Jersey Bean lifeguard, sums up the way the islanders felt. 'The locals certainly had a huge affection for the Australian lifeguard service. They were known in a good way for doing a good job.'

Gordon also expresses his concerns about how Jersey has changed over his lifetime. 'These days in Jersey there is considerably less tourism and it is much more expensive to live. Jersey has repositioned itself as a short breaks destination. The number of hotel beds has plummeted, but the place still has a great lifestyle compared to the rest of the UK. The tax haven status doesn't apply to workers. The advantage of being a tax haven means that we pay less tax than the rest of the UK, but we also get less services. For example, health care in Jersey – you have to pay to visit the GP whereas it is free in the rest of Britain. Also, with university education you can't get grants or loans. The tax haven status applies to a very small minority only. The government is now actively trying to encourage the very rich to come to Jersey to live because they believe they are good for the economy. Whether they want to spend their money in Jersey is a different question. Property in Jersey is as expensive as living in London which makes it difficult for most people on normal salaries.'

Was the Australian managed lifeguard service better than the RNLI service? It may well have been, but the fact is that, under the RNLI control, no lives have been lost in Jersey's beaches. Surely that is the bottom line.

Dean Koontz in his novel *Dead and Alive* aptly summed it up: 'What has been is no more. Change has come'.

Epilogue

In the latter part of 2014 a group of four former beach guards/lifeguards got together in Newcastle, Australia, to plan a second reunion in 2015. The four were Jim 'Noddy' Reeves, Brian 'Jughead' Jones, Mark Scully and Guy Littler. They felt another reunion was needed. Although the first one was a resounding success with 30 plus former beach guards, predominantly from the period 1960 through 1980, plus partners, the cost and time away was a barrier to the attendance of many. Most made the 2010 event part of a longer European holiday and as such it appealed to those who had retired and/or had grown up children. That reunion had been brilliantly organised by Mike Gray and Tony Taylor, who had done four years on the beach in the late 1960s and early 1970s.

The 2015 event was aimed at providing a more affordable assembly and particularly to allow the younger lifeguards, perhaps with small children, the opportunity to attend. It was also five years since the first reunion in Jersey which, although the participants weren't to know, was to mark the end of the Australian managed lifeguard service. The month of May was chosen as it coincided with the time that the boys would arrive in Jersey and after the Australian lifesaving season, both from a competition and work point of view, as many the younger cohort worked as professional lifeguards.

Getting together as complete a list as possible of former beach guard/lifeguards to issue invitations was a big challenge. Mike Gray had put together a mailing list in 2010, which was comprehensive from the 1960s perspective. In the 1970s, with Jerry Shannos as the head beach guard, recruitment came largely from Newcastle, so that helped. For the later years, Noddy, Jughead and Mark Scully between them had covered most of that period. The group, by scrutinising old team photos, managed to construct a Jersey roll and then set about creating a database. After a lot of hard work, particularly by Mark Scully who trawled through Facebook, LinkedIn and other social media platforms, the database finished up containing the details, some very scant, of about 285 people who worked on the beach in Jersey between 1958 and 2010 – see following pages. At least 26 are deceased. The first part of the database contained 182 contacts by name, address and/or email. Another 35 were found on Facebook. Unfortunately, for about 42 of the names, their whereabouts is still unknown.

Because of those efforts, 105 people (over half of those for whom contact details were found) converged on Newcastle to attend the 2015 event. Some travelled long distances, from places such as Fiji, Perth, Adelaide, Buniyong in Victoria, Brisbane, the Gold Coast, the Sunshine Coast, the NSW South Coast. A large contingent came from Sydney, Wollongong and Newcastle. From the reports of the event, a good weekend was had by all and many stories told, most of them true, many of which couldn't be recounted in this book!

Although many of the attendees met each other for the first time at the 2015 reunion, they were all bonded by their common experiences in working as a beach guard/lifeguard in Jersey. They went back to where they came from, content in the knowledge that they belonged to a club, a special club, of people who saved lives over a period exceeding half a century on an island which for most of them was far away from home. What a magnificent achievement, those Other Jersey Boys (and Girl)!

List of lifeguards and years served

Michael Abbott*	1961		Peter Compton	1975-1976
Jason Acott	2008-2010		Ryan Cook	2000
Gavin Akers	1997		David Craig	1969
Tim Allen	1985-1987		Paul Cramsie	1979
Colin Ambrosoli	1964-1965		Simon Crumblin	2007
Bill Anderton	1971		Warwick Crumblin	1974
Adam Andrew	1989 & 1993			
John Andrew	1965-1968		Larn Darragh	2001
Robert Armstrong*	1962-1963		Leigh Davies	1981
			Murray Davies	1989
Roger Bagot	1968		Neville Davies	1972
Kerry Baker	1966		Mark Davis	2002
Zane Baker	2004-2008		Bruce Deagan	1998-2000
Des Ball	1972, 1978, 1990		Kevin Devine*	1966
Kevin Banks	1981		Bruce Douglas*	1961
Alex Barrell	1993		Brad Downs	1996 -2001
Dave Barrell	1964-1965		Paul Duffy	1970
Troy Barren	1990		Charlie Dunmore	2001
Robert Barry	1982		Saul Duran	2009
Neil Beachley	1958			
Stuart Bear	1975-1976		Les Edmonds	1967
Noel Bennett	1963-1965		Robert Elford	1974
Mark Berghouse	1977-1978		Jason Elliot	2001
Paul Berghouse	1977-2010		Ross Erickson	1985
Phil Bernasconi	1965		Len Ethell	1972
Don Black*	1968		Russell Evans	1977-1979
Drew Blatchford	2006-2007 & 2009			
Michael Body	2008-2009		Simon Farrer	1997
Nick Boers	2003		Chris Fawkner	1966-1967
John Booth	1958		Ken Fawkner*	1961-1964
Colin Braun	2002		Greg Fettell	1980, 1982
Bruce Bridal	1979-1984		Ian Fitzpatrick	1972-1975, 1982,
Steven Bridges	1980 & 1984			1984
Wayne Bridges	1976-1980		Kim Flower	1973-1976
Graham Brimage	1977-1978		Stephen Ford	2001-2002
Danny Brosnan	1966-1968		Brian Foster	2000-2004
Heath Brown	2004-2007		David Franklin	2010
Bill Burke*	1962		Noel Frogatt	1967
Dennis Burrage	1969			
Bernard Byrnes	1983		Kyle Garrett	2010
			Doug Genders	1972
Drew Cairncross	2004-2005		Neil Gilroy	1990-1992
Gordon Callendar	1986-1989		Matt Gray	2005
Barry Cardiff	1966		Mike Gray	1961-1963
Tony Cassidy	1970-1971		Ray Green	1983-1986, 1988,
				1995-1997
Chanan Clark	2010		Nathan Greig	2005
Kailan Collins	2000-2004			
Matthew Colquhoun	1995		Darryl Hadfield	1983 & 1985-1987
			Daniel Hagan	2008-2010

Michael Hall	1958
Scott Hammerton	2004-2009
Colin Hammond*	1973
Pat Hanley*	1970
Steve Hannon	1990-1992
Patrick Harrington	1970
Bob Harris	1960 & 1962-1963
Phil Harris	1974
Jason Harvey	2008
Matt Hastie	2010
Leon Hay	2003-2006
Matt Haymes	1985
Paul Hedderman	1997-2000
Maclay Heriot	2008
John Herron	1980-1981 & 1993-1994
Brian Hill	1962
Geoff Hodgson	1964-1965
John Hogan	2003-2006 & 2008
Bob Holloway	1973
Jack Holloway	2010
Ken Holloway	1973-1974
Tony Holt	1968
Brian Holway	1971 & 1973
Alison Horsfall	1998-2001
Rex Horsley	1987-1988
Charlie Hull	1965-1966
Peter Ind*	1969
Luke Ingwersen	2002 & 2006
Andrew Jackson	1991-1992
Dwayne Jefferson	2003
Brian Jones	1971-1973 & 1976
Michael E Jones	1984
Michael J. Jones	1975
Peter Jones	1987-1988
Michael Jordan	2010
Tim Joyce	1978-1979
Dave Kennedy	2003-2004
Roger Kennedy*	1961-1963
Andrew Kent	2009
Darren Knowles	1995-2010
Peter Kusmanoff*	1970
Howard Langford*	1965
Bill Lavarack*	1975-1983
Ian Lee	1994-1995
Alan Lerpiniere	1992-1994
Benjamin Lewis	1990
John Lewis	1991 & 1993-1994
Murray Lewis	1995-1996

Martin Linz	1982
Guy Littler	1978-1979
Chris Lougher	2009
Geoffrey Lowe	1969
Michael Malady	1984
Brad Malyon	2002
Ronald Marriott	1967-1969
Ben Marsh	1989 & 1991-1993
Peter Martine	1986-1989
Sean McBean	2008-2010
Nathan McCoy	1995
Bill McDonald	1979-1981
Glen McKissack	1998-1989
Ben McRae	2003-2004
Peter McRae	2005-2006
Tim Merrifield	1969
Adam Metcalf	1998-2002
Keith Miller	1982
Dennis Milne	1968
Scott Moritimer	2003-2007
Bob Morris	1963-1964
Danny Morris	1983
Bruce Morton	1965-1966
Ron Morton	1963-1964
Trevor Morton	1971-1972
George Murchie	1969
Adam Murphy	1994 1971-1972
Geoffrey Myer*	1963-1964
Rex Neve	1975
Martyn Newby	2001-2003 & 2005
Dave O'Brien	1961-1962
Chris O'Conner*	1963(WP), 1964-1966 John
O'Grady	1993-1997
Greg Owens	1999-2000
Duncan Page	1960
Mick Parnell	1967 & 1969
John Paton*	1963-1964
Brad Patterson	1995-1996
Wayne Paul	1985
Ian Peacock	1965
AlexPenklis	1971
Steve Porter	1973-1977
Greg Price	1977
Mark Rabjohns	1984
Reg Rainey	1966-1967
John Rankin	1972
Chris Redler	1987

Martin Rees	1993	Wayne Stewart	1983
James Reeves	1976 & 85-96 & 98-00	Peter Surgenor*	1971-1973
	& 06-10	Ben Surrest	2002
Jim Reynolds	1971	Terry Swan	1971-1972
Stephen Rich	1976	Mick Sylvester*	1981-1989
Gary Richards	1997-2005		
David Rider	1974	David Tagg	2007-2009
Kirk Rides	1994	Tony Taylor	1968-1969 &
John Roberts	1964(WP) 1965 &		1971-1972
	1968-1970	Tim Thompson	1996
Mike Rodger	1961	Peter Townend	1968-1969
Wayne Rolph	1981	Alan Tunnicliff	2006-2007
Brad Rope	2007 & 2010	Bill Turton	1959-1960
David Roper	1967		
Richard Rothero	1987-1994	Ralf Van De Scheur	1981
John Rowlatt	1988-1992		
Ross Ryan	1976-1977	Peter Walkaden*	1970
		Alan Walker	1976
Peter Sailer	1974	Paul Wallace*	1971-1973
Roman Salamon	1985-1986 Charles	Jon Webber	1995-1996
Salzman*	1960	Matt Wehr	1997-1998 &
George Sawras	1974 - 1975		2000-2001
Luke Scales	2006	Bruce Westwood	1966 & 1969-1970
Robert Scammell	1980	Alan Wheeler	1975
Mark Scully	1988-1995	Blake White	2007-2009
Hugh Secomb	1977-1978	Allan Willet	1974
Jerry Shannos	1968-1988	Barry Williams	1970
Rob Shaw	1979-1987	Lawrie Williams	1982
Eddie Shields*	1969	Peter Williams	1964 -1965
Ron Siddons*	1963	Jim Wilson*	1958-1959 &1961
Jamie Sidney	1998	Scott Wilson	1977-1979
Tony Sinclair	2003-2006	Tim Wilson	1990
Gavin Skeffington	1986 & 1988-1992	Graham Wise	1970
Andrew Skene	1997	Peter Withers	1980
Glenn Slater	1999	Graeme Wolfenden	1975 - 1976
Gregg Slater	1997-2001	Pelum Wooderson	1973
Rick Small	1991-1992	Ken Woods	1960
Daniel Smith	2000	Brad Woodward	2010
Jason Smith	1996	Nick Woolnough	1997-1999 &
Jason Smith (No.2)	2005-2007		2001-2004
Peter Smith*	1967		
Shane Smith	1994-1996	John Yabsley*	1960
John Spicer	1984	Barry Young*	1968
Grant Spradbrow	1967	Daniel Young	2007-2010
Brian Sprain*	1967	Mark Young	2002-2003
Bruce Stanger	1977	Paul Young	1983

Notes:

* Deceased at time of writing

(WP) West Park Tidal Pool prior to it being part of the beach guard service.

Acknowledgements

The following is a list of all those who kindly allowed me to interview them in my research for *The Other Jersey Boys*

Hilary Andrew
John Andrew
Col Ambrosoli
Neil Beachley
Paul Berghouse
Steven Bridges
Wayne Bridges
Danny Brosnan
Gordon Burgis
Dai Burton
Gordon Callendar
Barry Cardiff

Vee Cardiff
Chris Emery
Mike Gray
Brian Jones
Carol Jones
Scott Hammerton
Lisa Hammerton
Tony Hurford
Barry Jenkins
Ida Lavarack
Guy Littler
Peter Martine

Ron Morton
Duncan Page
Steven Porter
Vicki Porter
Jim Reeves
Gary Richards
Enrica Roberts
John Roberts
Mark Scully
Jerry Shannos
Ken Woods

The following publications have been consulted in writing this book:

An Illustrated History of the Occupation of Jersey by German Forces 1940-1945, published by Sanctuary Inns Limited, 1 Somerset Place, St Helier Jersey, 1995

Jaggard, Ed: *From Bondi to Bude: Allan Kennedy and the exportation of Australian surf lifesaving to Britain in the 1950s,* , Edith Cowan University publication, 2011

Jersey Lifeguard Club History, unknown author

Jersey's Population – A History, Mark Boleat, Societe Jersiaise, 2015

The Changing Economic Face of Jersey, Société Jersiaise, 1984

O'Connor, Chris: Summary of 1963 Beach Guard Service and Recommendations Arising Therefrom, 1966

Wooler, A. and Vlasto, M.: 'An Integrated Approach to Beach Lifeguarding and Lifeboating' – paper presented at the 2007 World Conference on Drowning Prevention

Agreement for the Provision of RNLI Lifeguard Services, signed on 3 June 2011 by M. Vlasto on behalf of the RNLI and on 13 June 2011 by Senator A.J.H MacLean on behalf of the States of Jersey Government

Agreement for the Provision of RNLI Lifeguard Services, signed on 11 March 2015 by Paul Broissier on behalf of the RNLI and on 16 March 2015 by Steve Pallett on behalf of the States of Jersey Government

I also wish to cite the following for their help with source material and references:

BBC; *The Economist; The Guardian;* islandwiki; Jersey Archive; *Jersey Evening Post;* Jersey Heritage; Lifesaving Society; Royal National Lifeboat Institution; *Sydney Morning Herald;* Wikipedia

Index of Names